THE BEST OF **WOODWORKER'S JOURNAL**

Woodworking
Techniques

Ingenious Solutions & Time-Saving Secrets

Woodworking Techniques

Ingenious Solutions & Time-Saving Secrets

from the editors of *Woodworker's Journal*

Fox
Chapel Publishing

1970 Broad Street • East Petersburg, PA 17520
www.FoxChapelPublishing.com

Compilation Copyright © 2008 by Fox Chapel Publishing Company, Inc.

Text and Illustration Copyright © 2008 by *Woodworker's Journal. Woodworker's Journal* is a publication of Rockler Press.

Woodworking Techniques: Ingenious Solutions and Time-Saving Secrets is a compilation first published in 2008 by Fox Chapel Publishing Company, Inc. The patterns contained herein are copyrighted by *Woodworker's Journal*.

Our friends at Rockler Woodworking and Hardware supplied us with most of the hardware used in this book. Visit *rockler.com*. For subscription information to *Woodworker's Journal* magazine, call toll-free 800-765-4119 or visit *www.woodworkersjournal.com*.

Woodworker's Journal
Founder & CEO: Ann Rockler Jackson
Publisher: Larry N. Stoiaken
Editor-in-Chief: Rob Johnstone
Art Director: Jeff Jacobson
Senior Editor: Joanna Werch Takes
Field Editor: Chris Marshall
Illustrators: Jeff Jacobson, John Kelliher

ISBN 978-1-56523-362-1

Publisher's Cataloging-in-Publication Data

Woodworking techniques : ingenious solutions & time-saving secrets
/ from the editors of Woodworker's journal. -- East Petersburg, PA :
Fox Chapel Publishing, c2008.

p. ; cm.
(The best of Woodworker's journal)
ISBN: 978-1-56523-362-1

1. Woodwork--Handbooks, manuals, etc. 2. Turning--
Handbooks, manuals, etc. 3.Woodwork--Technique. 4. Woodwork-
-Equipment and supplies. I.Woodworker's journal. II. Series: Best
of Woodworker's journal.

TT180 .W66 2008
684/.08--dc22   0804

To learn more about the other great books from Fox Chapel Publishing, or to find a retailer near you, call toll-free 800-457-9112 or visit us at *www.FoxChapelPublishing.com*.

Printed in China
10 9 8 7 6 5 4 3 2 1

Note to Authors: We are always looking for talented authors to write new books in our area of woodworking, design, and related crafts. Please send a brief letter describing your idea to Acquisition Editor, Fox Chapel Publishing, 1970 Broad Street, East Petersburg, PA 17520.

Introduction

Woodworkers often put a lot of attention on finding or making the right jig for the job. It is an honest and useful approach to working accurately and efficiently in your workshop. But it is only half of the answer. The other half, as the 40 articles in this book make clear, is learning the appropriate technique for solving the shop problem at hand.

So, what is a woodworking technique? The simple answer is it's a method of working, sometimes a traditional method handed down from woodworkers of the past, though equally often a contemporary one devised to suit today's huge assortment of tools, machines, and materials. The more accurate answer is any technique or method really has two components: know-what and know-how. Know-what is having information, learning what to do, which tools and materials to use, what order to perform the steps. You can get know-what from books and magazines. Know-how is another matter altogether. Books like this one can get you started, and so can a good teacher standing beside you, but know-how really means skill. To acquire skill there is no substitute for trying it for yourself, then practicing until your hands and your body get it right. When you've got it, you'll know it: the workpiece comes out the way you wanted — you no longer have to sweat it. You will experience an almost indescribable feeling of joyous mastery when you realize you have acquired a new skill. Your hands know what to do, and your heart leaps with the knowledge.

The projects in this book cover the whole of woodworking to bring you useful new pieces of know-what and know-how. We'll start with maintaining your workshop and tools, leading into Bill Hylton's masterful router tricks: know-what and know-how at its very best.

Next, you will find several articles on the fundamental problem of transforming the gnarly lumber you have into the flat, smooth and square boards you want. Every woodworking project begins with choosing and preparing your material, so it pays big dividends when the sequence and the skills become second nature to you.

We move on to making joints, the techniques you need to know to hold your woodworking projects together. There's a million joints out there, but as Ian Kirby explains, it all boils down to just three: the butt joint for making wood wider, the dovetail joint for making a box out of wide pieces of wood, and the mortise-and-tenon for making frame joints out of sticks of wood. Everything else is an embellishment on those basic techniques. Ian goes on to share the secrets of the frame-and-panel door, which is at the heart of traditional woodworking.

After learning joints and other furniture-building techniques such as clamping, carving, and bending, this volume concludes with a terrific series of finishing articles. That's a subject with as much know-what as know-how in it, but for great results you really do need both, and fortunately, you've got Woodworker's Journal finishing expert Michael Dresdner at your elbow. Like the other authors who have contributed to this book, Dresdner not only knows what to do and how to do it, he also knows how to share his skills with you. Moreover, that is what makes woodworking the most fun of all, the sharing of ideas and techniques, which, in an earlier time, would have been considered trade secrets and mysteries. We are very lucky to live in an era when information at this high level is freely shared and available to all.

Larry N. Stoiaken, Publisher

Acknowledgments

Woodworker's Journal recently celebrated its 30th anniversary— a benchmark few magazines ever reach. I would like to acknowledge both the 300,000 woodworkers who make up our readership and Rockler Woodworking and Hardware (*rockler.com*), which provided most of the hardware, wood, and other products used to build the projects in this book.

Our publishing partner, Fox Chapel, did a terrific job re-presenting our material, and I am especially grateful to Alan Giagnocavo, Paul Hambke, John Kelsey, and Troy Thorne for their commitment to our content.

Larry N. Stoiaken, Publisher

Contents

Essential Shop Maintenance Guide

No one will deny that it's more fun to use the shop and tools than it is to clean and maintain everything, but you really can't have one without the other. Here's a helpful maintenance guide that would make your high school shop teacher happy.

by Sandor Nagyszalanczy

A clean, well-organized shop with sharp bits and blades and well-tuned power tools and machines is not only a more efficient and pleasant place to work, but a safer one as well: Sawdust and chips that are allowed to accumulate pose both a health and fire safety hazard.

Furthermore, machines that go out of adjustment or fall into disrepair are not only frustrating to use, but can also cause miscuts and accidents.

Among the various woodshops I've visited over the years, the best ones are always run by woodworkers serious

about taking care of their tools. Rather than just fixing tools and machines when they break, they service and adjust them at regular intervals to keep them running at peak performance. Even if you're not a follower of the "stitch in time saves nine" adage, doing a little cleanup and

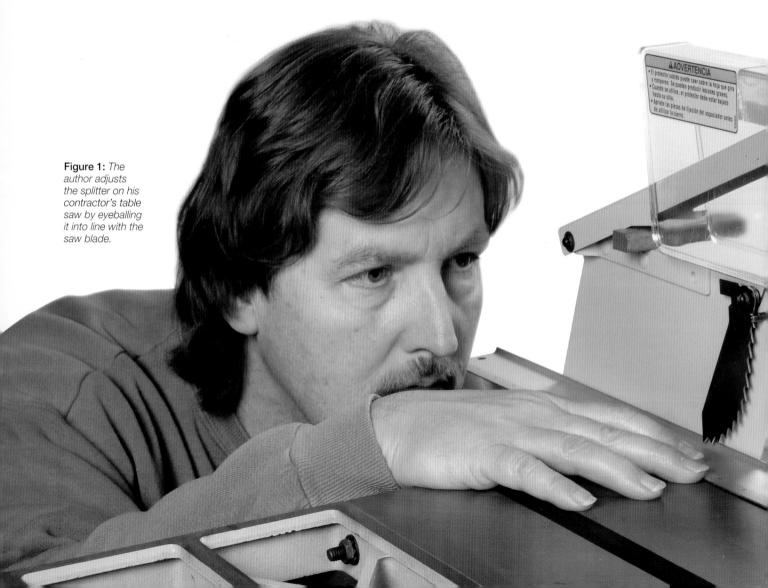

Figure 1: *The author adjusts the splitter on his contractor's table saw by eyeballing it into line with the saw blade.*

tool maintenance on a regular basis will save you time, trouble, and money in the long run (tools kept in good tune require less in the way of expensive repairs and usually last much longer).

On the other hand, properly maintaining your shop can be a confusing matter: What should you do and when and how often should you do it? To provide a leg up on the what-and-when issues, here's an overview and a calendar of daily, weekly, monthly and bi-annual maintenance duties (see page 2) required in a typical small shop.

This includes important fire safety clean-up tasks (example: vacuuming fine dust from light fixtures and electrical junction boxes) and the upkeep of spray booths, air compressors and dust collection systems.

The rest of this article addresses the question of how to maintain specific tools and provides in-depth information on proper cleaning, lubrication, inspection, adjustment and replacement of worn parts. Because the exact procedure for certain adjustments depends on the specific make and model of the machine, only general information is given here; consult your tool's manual or contact the manufacturer for more detailed instructions.

General Machine Maintenance

One theory of machine maintenance is to just let things go until they break; then fix them. But this is not only expensive, it is inconvenient—you just know your router won't poop out until just days before the winter holidays, when you're frantic to finish making gifts. Unless your shop is powered by a water wheel

or steam engine, all your tools operate with electric motors, pulleys, belts and gears that need periodic attention. The following section offers a comprehensive list of standard cleaning and lubricating procedures, tune-ups and adjustments, and even small repairs that you can do yourself to keep your machines in top working order. Of course, all described procedures should only be attempted with sharp blades and cutters removed and the tool or machine disconnected from electrical power. Safety first, folks.

Cleaning Equipment

One of the easiest ways to prolong the life of all your equipment is simply to keep it clean. Accumulating sawdust and chips get in the way of using machines and can upset accuracy and usability. Sawdust build-up on mechanical components, like a table saw's trunnion or a compound-miter saw's turntable, can throw off the accuracy of adjustments and make setting sluggish or impossible. Sawdust

Shop Maintenance Calendar

Every Day (of use):
- Empty shop garbage cans and any open dust bins.
- Clean out rag storage cans; spread rags soaked with oil finish out to dry.
- Lubricate air-powered tools (nail guns, random-orbit sanders, etc.) and/or refill reservoirs on automatic oilers.

Every Week:
- Clean sawdust from shop's floors and benches.
- Drain moisture from compressor's air storage tank, pipes and manifold and filter/moisture trap(s).
- Shake dust collector's filter bags to remove excess dust cake (more often if necessary).
- Empty sawdust from dust collector bags or bins (more often if necessary).
- Empty shop vacuum and clean filter (more often if necessary).

Every Month:
- Vacuum fine dust from tops of light fixtures and out of electrical outlets, switches and junction boxes.
- Vacuum prefilters on air filtration devices.
- Clean out sanding tables, machines not connected to dust collection.
- Clean off built-up finish on spray guns, spray booth walls, etc.

- Check the condition of the air filter and the oil level in your compressor's pump (latter not required for oil-less models).
- Test and reset ground-fault interrupt (GFI) outlets and circuits.

Twice a Year:
- Inspect condition of machines and portable power tools; service as needed (see sections above).
- Check fire extinguishers; recharge or replace as necessary.
- Change oil in air compressor pump (oil-less compressors exempt).
- Treat stationary tool tops, metal tools, clamps, etc. with rust preventative.
- Check compressed air system (tank, hoses, fittings) for leaks.
- Check condition of filter bags or cartridges on dust collectors, air cleaners and shop vacuums; replace as necessary.
- Inspect central dust collection system's ductwork and flexible hoses for air leaks or clogs.
- Check first aid kit for completeness; refresh supplies as necessary.
- Check condition of glues and finishes; properly discard products that have spoiled or are past their expiration dates.
- Check shop for leaks or moisture that may ruin tools and stored lumber and supplies.

that clogs cooling vents on motors can cause tools to overheat. And fine dust (which tends to accumulate in electrical switch and junction boxes) can actually ignite from a tiny spark and cause a devastating shop fire!

Vacuuming a machine or portable power tool with a high-velocity shop vacuum is usually better than blowing dust out with compressed air, which can propel debris farther inside a motor or mechanical assembly. That goes for shop floors and benches too; blowing launches fine dust into the air, where it is respirable, only to settle again on every surface. If you must use compressed

air, keep the pressure below 50 pounds. Loosen oily gunk with a bristle brush before vacuuming, or pry it from narrow slots and cavities with a flat stick or narrow screwdriver. Use a crevice tool to vacuum hard-to-reach spots and remove fine dust from electrical components, Figure 4.

In addition to the machines themselves, you should also clean all your saw blades, router bits, shaper cutters, and so forth, to keep them in top cutting condition. Remove pitch and resin build-up by scrubbing them with a nylon-bristled brush and a cleaning product. Some woodworkers use oven cleaner for this chore, while others prefer to use a specialized blade/bit cleaner, such as "Oxi Solve" or "Pitch Rx."

Lubricating Machines
If your shop is graced with vintage cast-iron machinery, you're already aware of the lubrication needs of older machines fitted with Babbitt bearings or bronze bushings which required occasional lubrication. Most of these machines are fitted with oil cups or reservoirs: fill them with SAE 10 or 20 non-detergent machine oil (NOT auto motor oil). On machines with grease nipples, use a grease gun to inject a lithium-soda type bearing grease (never substitute oil!). Make sure to clean gummy deposits and sawdust from oil cups and nipples before lubricating them. To keep your drill press quill operating smoothly, occasionally apply a few drops of SAE 40 machine oil into the center of the quill's pulley. If your thickness planer has a gear-driven power feeder, top up its gearbox with a heavier-viscosity gear oil between SAE 90 and SAE 140.

Most modern machines have arbors and power transmission shafts fitted with permanently sealed ball bearings that don't require any additional lubrication—oiling them only attracts dust and creates a gummy mess. But that doesn't mean that other

Figure 2: *Vacuuming a belt sander with a high-velocity shop vacuum removes fine dust build-up from the motor and running parts, helping them to run better and last longer.*

Figure 3: *Spraying a machine's working parts with a dry lubricant such as Boeshield T-9 helps the parts turn, slide and run more smoothly, and it won't attract dust as a liquid grease or oil would. To prevent rust and aid parts sliding, the machine's cast-iron tabletop is sprayed with Bostik TopCote.*

parts of your machines don't require attention. Mechanisms that raise and lower the arbor on a table saw or shaper, raise and lower the table on a planer or jointer, and tilt the table on a band saw, as well as other mechanical adjusting components, all need occasional cleaning and lubrication to work at their best. Because woodshop machines are constantly pelted by sawdust, never use wet lubricants on these parts, such as greases, oils and non-drying sprays. Dust will stick to these compounds, and this is a sure way to create a sticky mess that will eventually gum up the works. Instead, coat trunnions, gears, dovetailed ways and screw threads with a dry lubricant, like powdered graphite, or with a spray lubricant that dries to the touch, such as Boeshield T-9, Figure 2. Drying spray lubricants are also good for machine tabletops, miter gauge slots and other surfaces, as they not only prevent rust from forming, but reduce friction to help tools and workpieces glide smoothly along.

Checking Bearings and Arbors

Permanently sealed ball bearings can last for decades, especially in machines that only receive occasional use. But any bearing can go bad over time and produce an audible death rattle in the form of a clicking, thumping or whining noise emitted when the tool is running. If you hear such noises, it's possible that the bearings need replacement—a job that's beyond the scope of this story. Check your owner's manual for replacement instructions and a parts list, or contact your local service center.

Vibration and poor performance in a machine may indicate bad bearings or a bent arbor, shaft, warped flange or other drive component. You can check components for these problems by reading the amount of excess play (known as "runout") with a dial indicator, as shown in Figure 3. This precision tool basically uses a clock-like gauge to show the in-and-out movement of a short rod protruding from the case. If you can't borrow a dial indicator from a well-equipped friend, they're fairly inexpensive to buy from many woodworking supply catalogs. The dial indicator is fastened to an adjustable arm mounted on a magnetic base that's easy to temporarily secure to a cast iron or steel tabletop or surface. Position the end of the indicator's rod in firm contact with the arbor, shaft or flange you are checking. Zero the indicator's dial (rotate it until the needle shows a zero reading, then lock the dial down), then manually rotate the arbor/shaft and watch the needle. It shouldn't show a movement of more than a few thousandths of an inch. If it does, it indicates excess runout (the part isn't running straight and true). The component is therefore suspect and requires further inspection by an experienced machinery repair person. If arbors and shafts show no runout, yet there is still machine vibration, another cause might be warped blades or bent bits. You can also check the trueness of these with a dial indicator.

Servicing V-belts and Pulleys

Transmission of power from the motor to a stationary machine's blade, bit, knives, belt or disc is handled by rubber

Figure 4: *Checking for excess play or "runout" that can cause vibration and poor performance in a table saw is easy with a dial indicator. The tool's magnetic base holds it firmly in place as the indicator's plunger reads the concentricity of the arbor.*

Figure 5: *After checking for correct pulley alignment on a table saw with a straightedge, the author repositions the drive pulley on the motor by first loosening a setscrew, then sliding the pulley.*

V-belts and metal pulleys (benchtop machines fitted with universal motors use short-toothed drive belts or are direct drive). Drive belts need to be occasionally checked and adjusted to keep machine performance in top form. First, inspect all belts, and replace any that show excessive or uneven wear and/or cracking. Make sure to choose a replacement belt that is not only the same length as the original, but is also the same size. The majority of the smaller woodshop machines use B-series belts, but there are exceptions. It's best to take the tool with you to your power tool dealer for comparison. If an original belt is unavailable or difficult to obtain, you can replace it with a segmented "Power Twist Link" belt. For proper operation, machines with multiple V-belt drives require that both or all three belts be replaced at the same time with a matched set of belts; contact your tool dealer or machine manufacturer for replacements.

Adjust belt tension as necessary (some tools use spring pressure or the weight of the motor for tensioning),

setting tension according to the tool's manual. If instructions aren't available, set the tension just tight enough so that the belt doesn't buck or oscillate rapidly when running at full speed.

Check pulleys and sheaves for excess wear. This is usually only an issue on often-used tools fitted with inexpensive cast zinc pulleys, which can and do wear out over time and cause excess vibration and uneven belt wear. Use a straightedge to make sure that pulleys are in good alignment, Figure 5. Reposition pulleys by loosening their setscrews and sliding them along their shafts. While you're at it, tighten all pulley setscrews, and replace any missing ones.

Removing and Preventing Rust

It's an unfortunate fact that rust never sleeps, and it continues to grow and degrade the condition of our metal tools even when we're not using them. Surface rust on cast-iron tool tops makes it difficult for wood parts to slide smoothly across them, which is a safety concern as well as an annoyance.

And heavy rust on mechanical components—trunnions, screw threads, etc.—makes tool settings and adjustments difficult or impossible to perform. It takes less time to prevent rust than to deal with it once it's formed, so take time often to coat all non-painted or anodized ferrous metal parts with a rust-preventative (if you live near the ocean, also coat bare aluminum parts, which salt air can corrode). Spray-on rust preventatives, such as Boeshield "T-9" or Bostik "TopCote," are easy to apply and form a dry film, which won't rub off onto raw wood parts. Avoid all sprays and coatings that contain silicone, which can create serious finish contamination problems.

To clean up rusty machines, remove light rust with a plastic abrasive pad (e.g., ScotchBrite), a wire brush or a wire wheel chucked in a drill, Figure 6. Heavier rust may require a chemical cleaner, such as Naval Jelly or Bullfrog Rust Remover. The fastest way to remove really heavy rust deposits is to scrape them off with a single-edge razor blade, fitted to a safety handle.

Figure 7: *If the motor housing on your power tool has visible caps, unscrew them to check the condition of the motor brushes. Replace both brushes if one or both are worn down to ¼" or shorter.*

Figure 6: *Depending on how rusty your machines gets, try a ScotchBrite pad, a wire brush chucked in a drill, or chemical cleaners. Scraping with a razor blade on really heavy rust works well.*

Inspecting Electrical Components

Although a machine's power cord and plug, on/off switch or magnetic starter aren't particularly prone to wear (the exception may be benchtop tools that are plugged and unplugged more often) any problems here can lead to serious safety hazards. Therefore, check electrical cords for fraying and plugs for cracks and exposed or broken wires and replace or repair them at the first sign of trouble. To keep electrical switches working properly and prevent fires, vacuum out junction boxes that are accessible. Replace switches that work intermittently, or spray them with contact cleaner.

Induction motors, found on most stationary machines, don't require much in the way of servicing (aside from being kept clean). Universal motors found on nearly all portable power tools, however, have brushes that should be checked and replaced occasionally, Figure 7. With every 50 hours of use, check them, if accessible, by removing the caps on the sides of the motor housing. If the carbon portion of either brush is less than ¼" in length, replace both

brushes, even if only one is worn out. (Replacing just one brush will produce uneven wear.) If brushes aren't user removable, or you're unsure of replacing them yourself, have the work done at an authorized tool service center.

Aligning Fences, Miter Gauges and Safety Equipment

Most stationary machines have a basic fence that must be aligned correctly for smooth—and safe—operation. A large try square (or accurate framing square) is handy for checking a fence for square on a jointer, radial-arm saw, compound-miter saw or other type of crosscut saw, Figure 8. (An exception is the table saw, where a rule is used to check and set a rip fence parallel to the saw blade.) A try square

Figure 8: *The author uses a carpenter's framing square to check and set this 12" compound miter saw's fence square with the blade. A quick test cut afterwards confirms the adjustment.*

is also good for setting square on miter gauges used with table saws, band saws, stationary sanders, and so forth. Adjust and lock the stop screw for each angle setting (45°, 22½°, etc.) using a miter square, combination square and/or a protractor. Always take a trial cut after setting a fence or miter gauge and check the workpiece to confirm your adjustments.

The guards attached to and/or built into your power tools are there to protect you. But they can't do their job properly if they're damaged, misaligned or mis-adjusted. Look over plastic blade and bit guards for obvious cracks or broken or missing mounting hardware. Lubricate articulating guards (such as over-arm table saw guards or cutoff saw guards), which must lift or retract smoothly during use; a sticking guard could snag on the work and cause a miscut or an accident. Some guards, like a splitter-type table saw blade guard, require careful alignment to work properly; the splitter must line up perfectly with the blade kerf, or the guard can bind on the work, Figure 1. Check to make sure the splitter and blade are in alignment with a straightedge: With its edge held against the blade, it should clear the splitter slightly. Realign the splitter as necessary, following the directions in the machine's manual.

Here are some tool-specific maintenance tasks to follow:

Table Saws
Clean and dry-lubricate the saw's trunnions and blade height adjustment mechanism. If adjustable, set the throat plate flat with the table. Check the saw's bevel tilt at 90° and 45° and readjust the stops. Check to make sure the miter slots are parallel to the saw blade, and realign the saw table if necessary. Check to make sure the rip fence is parallel to the blade and set the miter gauge stops. Check and align the blade guard and splitter.

Crosscut Saws
Alignment differs by type and style. Radial-arm saws will require the most attention and fuss, as the head and arm must be aligned and set in a specific order to assure parallelism of the blade to the travel of the arm (consult your tool's manual). Newer compound- and sliding-compound miter saws are usually much easier to adjust. Take a few test cuts to check for square cuts and regularly used miter and bevel angles. Re-adjust the stops as necessary. You should also confirm the accuracy of the saw's detents (click stops), which may or may not be adjustable. If a detent is off and you can't readjust it, mark it clearly on the saw, so you'll know you must set that

angle manually in the future. Also check the squareness of the fence to the table with a try square. Clean the arm(s) on sliding-compound miter saws and radial-arm saws and dry-lubricate them.

Band Saws
Check the saw's rubber tires and, if they are encrusted, clean them with a brush or by lightly scraping them. Replace them if they are cracked or torn. If the saw blade is difficult to track, check the alignment of the flywheels to ensure they are coplanar (both—or all three—discs are in the same flat plane) using a straightedge and shimming the wheels in or out on their axles as necessary. Check both upper and lower sets of blade guide blocks for wear, Figure 10, and re-dress

Figure 9: *The author's tools are aging gracefully because of his active maintenance program.*

by sanding or filing them or replace them if they're worn out. Adjust the guide blocks to make light contact with the blade, and set the rear thrust bearing just shy of touching the back edge of the blade. Set the table stop so the saw table is square to the blade, and finish up by setting the miter gauge stops.

Jointers

Check the machine's belts and pulleys. Clean and lubricate the tables and their ways. Confirm that the infeed and outfeed tables are straight and parallel, Figure 11. Check the fence for square and 45 degrees and readjust the stops as needed. Check the knives for sharpness and confirm that they're all set to the same cutting circle, using a dial indicator or knife-setting gauge. Make sure the knife-locking screws are all tight. Set the outfeed table flush to the cutting circle.

Thickness Planers

On small portable planers, check knives for nicks and sharpness. Also check to make sure knives are parallel to the bed and all set to the same cutting circle. Clean rubber infeed and/or outfeed rollers with mineral spirits. Check and align the infeed and outfeed tables. Also, check the accuracy of the depth gauge and depth stops. On larger stationary planers, adjust the pressure of the infeed and outfeed rollers, chip breaker and pressure bar. Check and adjust the height of bed rollers. Check and adjust the power feed drive belt or chain; drain and refill the gear case if your planer has one.

Drill Presses

Lubricate the quill assembly and check and adjust quill retraction spring tension if necessary. Check squareness of the table relative to the chuck and reset stops, if fitted. Check the chuck for concentricity with a dial indicator. Clean, lubricate and adjust the table raising and lowering mechanism.

Stationary Sanders

Clean discs and belts with a rubber cleaning stick; remove and replace the abrasives if they're heavily worn. On belt sanders, examine the drive and idler rollers and carefully scrape off sawdust and debris. Check the alignment of support tables for square; set miter gauges and stops as necessary.

Router Table

Check flatness of the router insert, and adjust its height flush with the tabletop. Clean and lubricate the router lifter mechanism, if fitted. Check the squareness of the router fence relative to the table. Use a straightedge to confirm that the tabletop is flat in all dimensions, and add shims beneath it to eliminate any sagging.

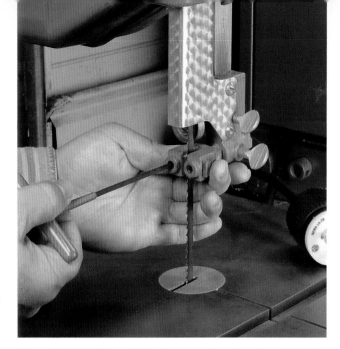

Figure 10: *Adjust the guide blocks on your band saw to make light contact with the blade, and set the rear thrust bearing just shy of touching the back edge of the blade.*

Routers

Thoroughly vacuum air vents on the motor housing. Examine collets for damage, and clean them with a wire brush as necessary. Clean and dry-lubricate the height adjustment assembly. Discard and replace any router bits with bent shafts and replace or resharpen bits with chipped or dull cutting edges. Lubricate pilot bearings with special high-speed bearing lubricant.

Cordless Tools

Check battery packs for cracks or damage. If the tool's charger has the feature, run all batteries through a "conditioning cycle." Clean electrical contacts on both batteries and tools with a spray contact cleaner (rubbing with a clean pencil eraser also works).

Figure 11: *Confirm that the infeed and outfeed tables on your jointer are straight and parallel with a true straightedge. You can use a feeler gauge (the corner of a credit card works well, too) to check the gap between the straightedge and infeed table. If the gap varies along the table, you'll need to adjust or shim the ways to restore parallel.*

Thin, Smooth, and Strong

As my luthiery instructor explained, "The perfect cutting edge would be infinitely thin, infinitely smooth and infinitely strong — anything else is a compromise of one sort or another." With that as gospel, every cutting edge we use must be an appropriately designed compromise. When you sharpen a knife, a gouge or a chisel, your goal will be to create the smoothest, thinnest edge that will remain strong enough to perform its task. This isn't as tricky as it may sound, since most tools have the manufacturer's best guess for the optimum cutting edge already ground and polished.

by Rob Johnstone

Provided you keep the factory bevel when you sharpen your tools, in most circumstances you'll end up with serviceable cutting edges. But as soon as you start changing bevels and regrinding willy-nilly, that's when you'll run into trouble. This sort of significant grinding should be reserved for dire situations — badly nicked or seriously deformed edges.

Thinness: Grinding

Grinding and honing are the two basic steps in sharpening any knife-edged tool. Grinding removes a significant amount of metal and sets you up for honing success. It is also the step where danger lurks. Improper grinding will generate excessive heat and change the metal's temper — the official term for the strength component of our perfect cutting edge. Using a lubricated grinding wheel run at a slow speed and removing the minimum amount of material are keys to keeping your tool's temper ... and yours, too. The wheel also must be the correct coarseness — just coarse enough to cut metal without compromising your ability to control the process.

The first important detail in any single-beveled edge is that the back of the blade must be perfectly flat. Another general principle for those of us who don't do a lot of grinding is to avoid changing the angle of the existing bevel. The bevel of an edge is the compromise of a steel tool relative to our goal of infinite thinness. Most cutting bevels will be within the 25° to 35° range. Unless your expertise exceeds that of the manufacturer, make every effort to keep the existing bevel of the tool — even when you need to remove a good deal of metal (as when eliminating a large nick). This is true if it is a regular chisel, double-beveled knife or a curved gouge. Also, with the aid of an appropriate guide or jig, do your best not to grind out of square or change the shape of the curved or shaped edge you are grinding.

Dull and damaged cutting edges are dangerous and unnecessary. Follow these guidelines and step-by-step instructions to create sharp, clean cutting edges.

Step 1: *Flatten the back and remove milling marks on a lapping plate. Use emery paper mounted to a flat surface and a figure-eight stroke.*

Step 2: *Next, use a bench-top grinder to create a proper, hollow-ground cutting bevel. Grind with a light hand!*

Step 3: *Move through a series of ever finer-grained stones to polish the bevel and back to mirror smoothness.*

Smoothness: Honing

Honing starts where grinding ends. After you have successfully ground the edge to the proper angle (thinness), while retaining the temper (strength), you must hone the edge to a mirror finish (infinitely smooth). Compared to the grinding operation, honing can be a pleasurable, somewhat meditative experience … which is good, as it is a process not to be hurried. Begin with a coarser stone (a diamond "stone" is a good choice) to remove the grinding marks and establish the honing bevel. When the primary bevel is smooth, many sharpeners add five to ten degrees of bevel to the very tip of the ground edge. This "microbevel" makes the actual cutting edge a little stronger and smoother.

Move from coarse to ever finer-grained stones, making the same number of strokes on both faces of the tool. Don't skip a grit level as you hone. Missing a degree of coarseness will not save you time, and will negatively affect your edge. The smoother you hone, the sharper your tool. You may even choose to continue past the point where you can use stones effectively. If so, you'll need a polishing wheel or a leather strop.

Tools with curved or shaped edges are sharpened in the exact same way as flat-edged tools. Their shapes just present more complicated challenges. Slip stones and shaped grinding accessories provide solutions for grinding and honing curved edges effectively.

Infinitely thin, smooth and strong cutting edges are beyond what we woodworkers are able to produce, but by following these basic guidelines, you will have tools of exceptional sharpness. And that's the gospel truth.

Surrounded by Stones

Diamond Stones: *fast cutting, low build-up.*

Ceramic: *efficient and clean.*

Ceramic, oilstone, diamond and natural stone, waterstone, india, washita, Arkansas … stones to the left, stones to the right, which do you choose? Finding the proper stones to hone your blades can be a daunting task.

Ask seven woodworkers which sharpening stones they prefer and you'll get seven different answers. And that's exactly the point. Used properly and regularly, all the popular choices will do the job of keeping your edges sharp.

Rob Johnstone's personal preference runs in the direction of diamond and hard Arkansas stones; he likes to get done in a hurry. The slip stones that keep his gouges keen are also from a variety of materials. The stone's composition isn't nearly as important as how you use it. Using proper lubricants (water for waterstones and whet stones, oil for oilstones), storing your stones properly and using them regularly is far more important.

Select stones and sharpening systems to suit your budget. If you're just getting started, try the stones a woodworking friend uses and see how they work for you.

Oilstones: *the workhorses for honing.*

Waterstones *from Asia have helped to spark renewed interest in sharpening.*

Cabinet, Contractor's or Hybrid Saws?

Discerning the differences between the three categories of table saw is not so simple. Figuring out which is right for you might even lead you into a contemplative confluence of a very personal sort. Be at peace; our yogi of tool geekdom will lead you down the path of power tool enlightenment.

By Rob Johnstone

What's in a name? As the bard observed, "… a rose by any other name would smell as sweet." So a name's meaning is not as immutable as it first appears. This is especially true of technology. With time, as a product evolves, so too do the names we use. In the computer world, the question used to be "Do you use an IBM or an Apple?" Now, the same question is framed, "Are you a Windows® or Mac person?" That same sort of shift seems to be at work in the sphere of table saws. For many years, the three main categories of table saws used in our home-shops (and small professional

Delta 10" Hybrid Saw with Biesmeyer fence (Model 36-717)

RIDGID TS3650

shops), were benchtop, contractor's and cabinet saws.

Historically, these names were simply descriptive in nature: The benchtop was used on a bench; contractor's saws were developed for job site work; and the more robust saws, coveted by those making cabinets, had a metal cabinet that enclosed the motor, trunnions and eventually, gears to raise, lower and tilt the saw blade. Unimaginative, but effective. In the late 1970s, home woodworking began to increase in popularity. The demand for appropriate power tools for the hobbyist market generated products to serve this group. From that point on, the commonly used names for table saw types were used to identify a commodity of tool, in contrast to being a simple descriptor. This natural evolution drove a further event — these increasingly popular saws were fine-tuned to fit the needs of the home woodworker. Additional features and characteristics were added to these saw categories in a sort of mix and match manner. For example, increased horsepower motors and fancy fences that were once only found on cabinet saws became common on contractor's saws. Open stands that were a defining characteristic of contractor's saws became available on benchtop models. This commingling of features blurred the traditionally clear-cut boundaries defined by each saw's name.

Then, in the late 1990s, DeWalt introduced a table saw that they appropriately called a hybrid, which threw a monkey wrench into the mix and essentially made the old naming convention nearly meaningless. Product naming continues to limp along, driven mostly by marketing concerns, with today's contractor's saw being the least meaningful (at least name-wise) of the lot.

Setting the Field

Leaving behind the more limited grouping of benchtop table saws and understanding how these three somewhat ambiguous categories of saws are constructed is the key to determining which of them best suits your needs.

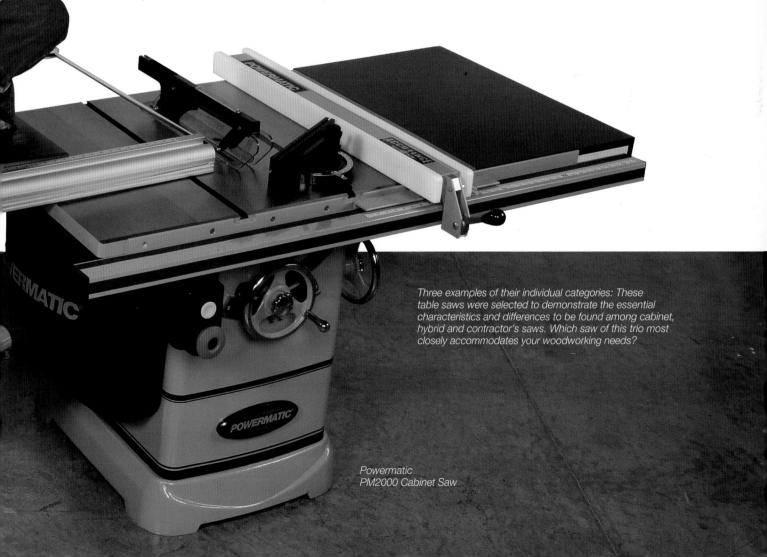

Three examples of their individual categories: These table saws were selected to demonstrate the essential characteristics and differences to be found among cabinet, hybrid and contractor's saws. Which saw of this trio most closely accommodates your woodworking needs?

*Powermatic
PM2000 Cabinet Saw*

Cabinet Saw: Precise, powerful and pricey

The classic cabinet saw is the quintessential woodworking power tool to my way of thinking. I want a Delta Unisaw or a Powermatic 66 in my shop in the same way I want a mint, early-model Thunderbird or a full-sized 4 x 4 pickup truck with the off-road package.

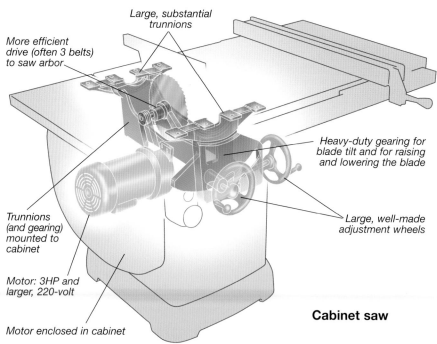

Large, substantial trunnions

More efficient drive (often 3 belts) to saw arbor

Heavy-duty gearing for blade tilt and for raising and lowering the blade

Trunnions (and gearing) mounted to cabinet

Large, well-made adjustment wheels

Motor: 3HP and larger, 220-volt

Motor enclosed in cabinet

Cabinet saw

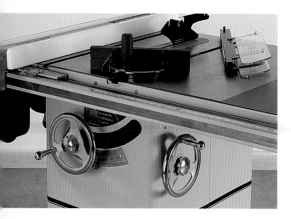

Every feature of this cabinet saw is certifiably heavy-duty. Made for professional shops, these saws are increasingly popular with home woodworkers.

If I look at it rationally, I know that there is little that the cabinet saw can do that I cannot do sufficiently well on one of the less substantial table saws. But in tough tasks that challenge smaller saws, the cabinet saw breezes through without even breaking a sweat.

Power and durability are the key factors that cabinet saws deliver over and above the other table saws under discussion here. In every detail, with the possible exception of the fence systems, cabinet saws are bigger, stronger and, in general, better built.

These saws are designed for professionals but are well-loved by all woodworkers. Cabinet saws have more cast iron and steel, bigger pulleys, gears and more robust bearings. They have more powerful motors (requiring 220-volt circuits for 3HP and larger motors), often with three belts driving the arbor. Their weight is considerable. They are, in general, machined to more exacting standards. All this costs more

money to produce — it's as simple as that. But the additional heft and substance mean that they will also last almost forever. When I started serious woodworking in the 1970s, I used a Unisaw that was built in the 1940s … and it never missed a beat.

Prices for these big-boys range from just under $1,000 (Grizzly's G1023S) to well over $2,100 (Powermatic's PM2000). Within each category of saw, you get what you pay for.

Motors that range from 3HP to 5HP (and larger) are common on cabinet saws. These saws are designed to run all day, every day.

Cabinet Saw Lowdown

More saw than the average woodworker needs, but not more that they can make use of. Here are some common cabinet saw features:
- Fences and miter gauges that are of good quality
- Large, flat, cast-iron tables
- Low vibration due to solid construction
- Exceptional durability
- Powerful motors (won't run on 120-volt common household current)
- Price range: $1,000 to $2,100 plus — some much more

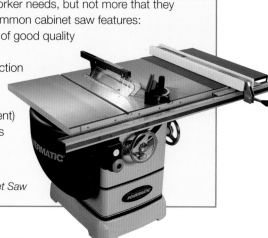

Powermatic PM2000 Cabinet Saw

Hybrid Saw: Bending rules, blending benefits

Hybrid saws are simply a great idea: Take elements of cabinet saws and contractor's saws, by far the two dominant home-shop table saws, and blend them into the perfect home-shop compromise. But alas, no compromise is perfect. While hybrid saws have cabinets, they are not as robustly built as their pro-shop cousins. Their motors all run on 120-volt household current, which makes them much more convenient for the average home woodworker but limits the horsepower. (Although claims of 2HP motors are

The hybrid cabinet is a great help in controlling sawdust. It also contains the motor, which makes it quieter than a contractor's saw.

not uncommon, unless a special 30-amp circuit is provided, the saws will not deliver that much oomph.) The cabinet does help control sawdust and mask a bit of noise as well. Both the DeWalt hybrid and JET Supersaw offer versions with sliding tables, a very sophisticated feature borrowed from top-drawer cabinet saws. The trunnions and gearing of most hybrids are more substantial than contractor's saws, but

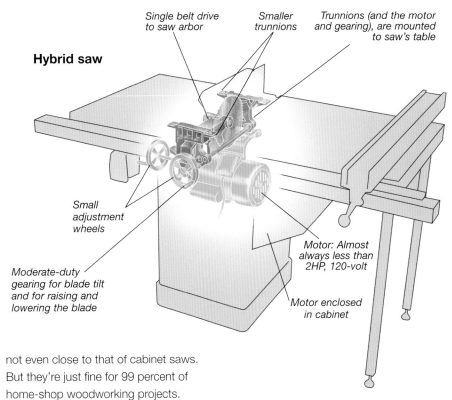

Hybrid saw

Single belt drive to saw arbor

Smaller trunnions

Trunnions (and the motor and gearing), are mounted to saw's table

Small adjustment wheels

Moderate-duty gearing for blade tilt and for raising and lowering the blade

Motor: Almost always less than 2HP, 120-volt

Motor enclosed in cabinet

not even close to that of cabinet saws. But they're just fine for 99 percent of home-shop woodworking projects.

Hybrid saws may well be the future of the home-shop table saw. Their success will likely lead to the death knell of the contractor's saw. Why buy a moderately powered saw with an open base that has its motor hanging out behind it? The major limitations of hybrids is power, and the fact that they will not be as durable as a cabinet saw. Their prices top out at $1,300, but they can be found for as low as $700, depending on the brand.

Like the contractor's saw, the hybrid's motor and gearing are mounted to the tabletop. Trunions and gearing are smaller and less robust than a cabinet saw's.

Hybrid Saw High-points

An ultra-practical power tool for the home-shop woodworker. Moderately priced with great accessories available. Consider these details:

- Fences and miter gauges are of good quality
- Enclosed cabinet for better dust collection and control
- Large tabletops
- 120-volt motors will run on common household current
- Price range: roughly $700 to $1,300 or a little more

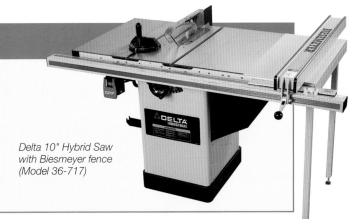

Delta 10" Hybrid Saw with Biesmeyer fence (Model 36-717)

Contractor's Saw:
Traditional home-shop favorite

Contractor's saws are the blue-collar heroes of the home-shop world. Reasonably priced, straightforward in design and operation, few tools fueled the wave of home woodworking half as much as the contractor's saw. Originally designed to be hauled from work site to work site, this open-based saw often had a tabletop of open web-frame cast iron or stamped sheet metal fabrication.

But as these practical saws gained in popularity with the home-shop crowd, solid, cast-iron tops became more common, and upscale accessories arrived on the scene as well. One of the important details that made the contractor's saw so popular was the fact that it ran on 15-amp,

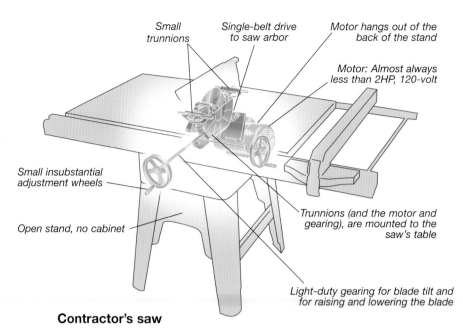

Small trunnions

Single-belt drive to saw arbor

Motor hangs out of the back of the stand

Motor: Almost always less than 2HP, 120-volt

Small insubstantial adjustment wheels

Open stand, no cabinet

Trunnions (and the motor and gearing), are mounted to the saw's table

Light-duty gearing for blade tilt and for raising and lowering the blade

Contractor's saw

An open base is less expensive to manufacture but much messier in the shop. Many folks are concerned about dust collection these days.

120-volt power. This eliminated the cost and hassle of adding new wiring to a basement or garage.

Although woefully under-powered by cabinet saw standards, outfitted with a superior-quality saw blade and an after-market fence, a contractor's saw is the practical Ford Fairlane station wagon, as compared to the cabinet saw's F-350 4x4 pickup truck.

One reason that contractor's saws remain inexpensive is the fact that you virtually have to assemble them from scratch. With prices ranging from around $500 to more than $1,000, this type of saw is the least

expensive of these three types of saws. But I think the days of contractor's saws are numbered. Contractors no longer use them — upscale benchtop saws are ruling their world. With hybrid saws' prices looking similar to many contractor's saws, the intrinsic drawbacks of an open base, smaller trunions and the motor hanging out of the back of the saw will be enough of a drawback to move folks to the hybrids, or whatever their progeny will be.

So ... which model is best for you? That depends, but the flowchart on page 15 may help you decide!

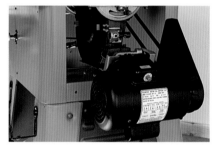

With the motor hanging off the back and small trunnions and gearing, the end of the contractor's saw may be drawing near.

Contractor's Saw Straight Talk

Perhaps the most popular home-shop woodworking saw ever made. This old standby is still the go-to tool in thousands of shops:

- Fences and miter gauges of good quality are available
- Open stand for limited dust collection and control
- Small- to moderate-sized tabletops
- 120-volt motors will run on common household current
- Price range: $500 to $1,000 plus

RIDGID's TS3650

Which Table Saw Type is Best for You?

Deciding which saw works best for you is a process that's affected by many and varied factors, both too broad and too specific to be covered comprehensively in an article like this. However, I've constructed the flowchart above as a good starting point. It incorporates common criteria that many folks find to be important considerations when purchasing a saw. The chart may clue you in to criteria that you may not have yet considered. It will definitely get you started down the right purchasing path. Every tool purchase is a compromise of sorts: Available funds versus quality, space versus features, desire versus reality.

In the end, I always like to pass along the advice that my father gave me years ago: "Buy the best you can afford and you'll only cry once."

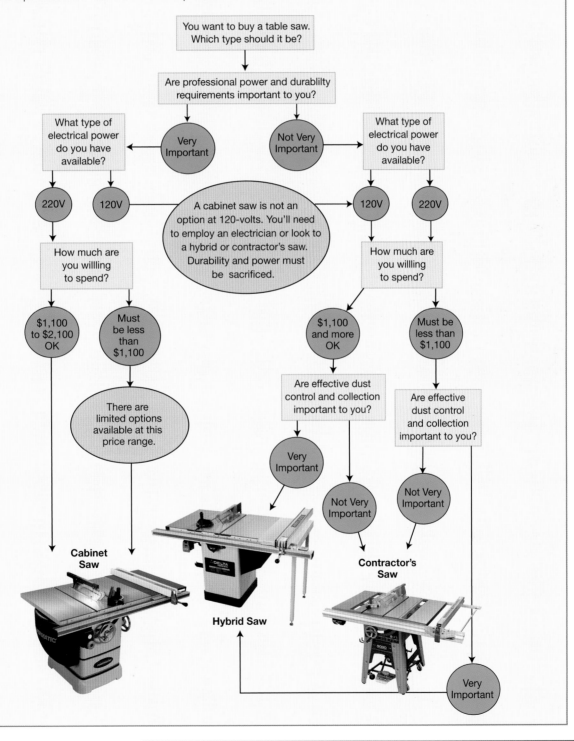

You want to buy a table saw. Which type should it be?

Are professional power and durablilty requirements important to you?

What type of electrical power do you have available?

Very Important

Not Very Important

What type of electrical power do you have available?

220V — 120V

A cabinet saw is not an option at 120-volts. You'll need to employ an electrician or look to a hybrid or contractor's saw. Durability and power must be sacrificed.

120V — 220V

How much are you willing to spend?

$1,100 to $2,100 OK

Must be less than $1,100

There are limited options available at this price range.

How much are you willing to spend?

$1,100 and more OK

Must be less than $1,100

Are effective dust control and collection important to you?

Very Important

Not Very Important

Are effective dust control and collection important to you?

Not Very Important

Cabinet Saw

Hybrid Saw

Contractor's Saw

Very Important

Six Super Router Tricks

There's no question that a router is woodworking's most versatile power tool. All the new routers, bits and accessories that flood the market every year make it clear. But if you only pull out a router for knocking off edges, you're missing out on a bunch of other great things it can do. A router is perfect for cutting dadoes, duplicating parts, cutting circles and more. It will joint edges on par with the best jointer out there and can even surface boards your planer can't touch. All it takes is the right technique and a few simple jigs. Here are six of my favorite, tried-and-true techniques you just plain have to try for yourself. You'll love these, trust me!

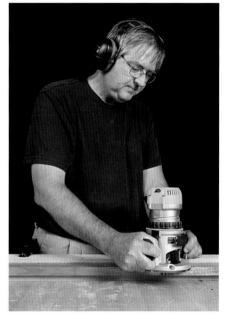

By Bill Hylton

1: Milling Custom-width Dadoes

The dado joint is excellent for casework: simple, strong and easy to cut (especially with a router).

The chip in the glue, so to speak, is properly matching a dado's width to the stock thickness it's intended to fit. Plywood is notoriously variable in thickness, and solid wood continually expands and contracts. But each straight bit cuts a set groove width. So you rout with what you've got and hope you get a snug fit.

Here's a simple-to-make jig that resolves the problem. It has two fences to trap the router: One is fixed and the other is adjustable. The bit can only cut in the gap between the fences. If the fences are just far enough apart to accommodate the router base with no side-to-side play, then the cut matches the bit diameter perfectly. Introduce some additional space between the fences, and you get a controlled cut

Dado Jig Exploded View

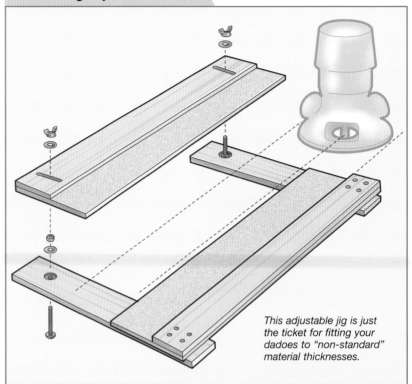

This adjustable jig is just the ticket for fitting your dadoes to "non-standard" material thicknesses.

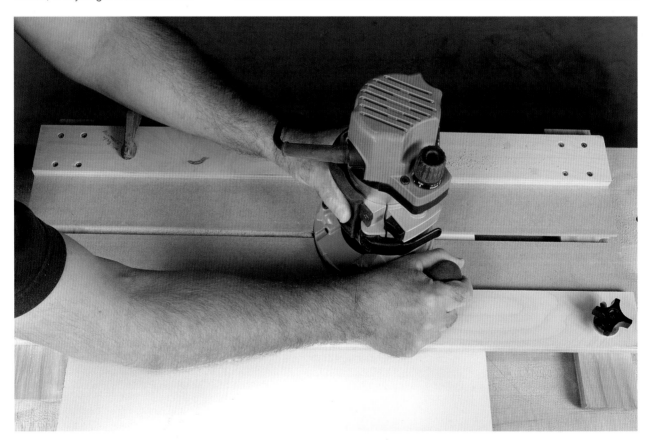

Set the router on the jig with the bit in the gap and clear of the work. Pull the router along one fence, then push it back along the other to mill the dado. The fences keep the router from wandering off course so it cuts the dado to the exact width you require. It doesn't get much easier.

The critical step to building the jig is trimming the fence bases with the router and bit you'll always use with the assembled jig.

Slip a couple of scraps as thick as the dado you want to cut between the fences. Squeeze the fences tight, then tighten the knobs on the adjustable fence. You'll get a perfect, snug fit.

that's wider than the bit. This allows you to adjust the jig for any dado width you want to cut.

While you can set the gap, and thus the dado width, by measuring, it's easiest to use scraps as gauges. Set scraps of the working material between the fence bases. Slide the movable fence so the scraps are pinched tight, and lock down

the fence knobs. Yank out the scraps, and the jig is ready to be positioned on the work. Simply line up and clamp the fence base right on the layout line.

When you cut, the router can't veer off course, regardless of feed direction, because it's trapped. Just run the router along one fence and back along the other to cut the dado.

Construction of the jig is pretty easy, and it should be evident from the Exploded Drawing on page 18. The key step is trimming the fence bases (see photo, above left). Guide the one router and bit you've chosen to use exclusively for this jig along each fence to trim both base sections to their exact final sizes.

As you guide the router along one fence, the cut is immediately adjacent to that fence's base. The cut is completed to the full desired width on the return pass.

Regardless of stock thickness, you can produce perfectly fitted dadoes. Here are dadoes fitted to ⅞" solid wood, ¾" plywood, ⅝" solid wood and ½" plywood, all cut with a ⅜" straight bit.

2: Routing Perfect Edge Joints Every Time

The router is a terrific tool for jointing the edges of boards for an edge-to-edge glue-up. All you need is a 1½ to 2 HP router, a fairly large-diameter straight bit and several long pieces of plywood.

To start, place one of the plywood pieces on the workbench and lay the first of the boards to be jointed on top of it. The plywood elevates the work so the router bit doesn't cut the benchtop. Position a fence carefully atop this board. Here's how: Subtract the radius of the bit from the radius of the router base. From the remainder, subtract ⅟₁₆", which is all you want to joint off the board edge. Place the fence that distance from the board's edge.

Clamp all three pieces — plywood spacer, workpiece and fence — to the bench with large clamps.

Rout the edge. If the first pass doesn't completely smooth the edge, shift the fence a nudge and make another pass.

Now set a second plywood piece on the benchtop, with a second workpiece on top of it. The gap between the second workpiece and the just-routed edge of the first one should be about ⅟₁₆" less than the bit diameter. Clamp this workpiece to the bench. Guide the router along the fence, moving it in the opposite direction of the initial cut to trim the second workpiece.

Check the joint by unclamping the second workpiece and butting it against the first. (Never move the first workpiece or the fence until you are all done and the joint passes muster.) If the first pass doesn't smooth the whole edge, shift the workpiece and rout the edge again.

The result is a tight glue joint without using a jointer. Simple and very sweet.

Here's a simple setup that converts your router and straight bit into a "jointer." With a couple pieces of plywood and two straightedges, you can create a tight glue joint in jiffy.

Determine where to clamp the straightedge by measuring from its edge to a reference line drawn on the workpiece.

Bring the mating board into position, and adjust the gap, with a rule, to ⅟₁₆" less than the bit's diameter. This is the amount the bit will remove from the second board.

Guide the router along the fence, in the correct left-to-right direction, to mill it clean, square and straight.

These router-jointed edges are as square, smooth and chip-free as you could make on a jointer. As you can see, the glued joint is virtually invisible.

3: Surfacing Stock with a Router and Sled Jig

Surfacing a board or panel's face, like jointing its edges, is commonly regarded as a job for a jointer. But it's a job a router can accomplish, and there are times when the router might be a better choice than the jointer. Make no mistake here; you'd be nuts to habitually prepare lumber using the router. You can't beat the jointer/planer/table saw ensemble to dress roughsawn boards.

But every once in a while, there's a special project where router surfacing is appropriate. Maybe you have a gnarly grained board that's beautiful but difficult to face-joint or plane without tearout. Perhaps you've glued up a thick, heavy, wide solid-wood countertop or benchtop and need to flatten and smooth its uneven, glue-blotched surface.

Here're the basics of how to surface with a router:

Make two expendable "tracks" about ¾" higher and 6" to 8" longer than the stock. Plant a track on either side of the work; the tops of the tracks must be in the same plane if the finished surface is to be flat. Clamp or fasten them securely so nothing shifts out of alignment.

Make a sled and mount the router in the middle. The sled must be flat, true and rigid. Fasten the router to the sled,

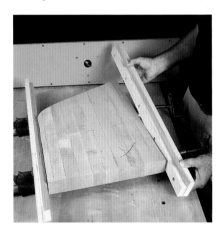

Make up a pair of support tracks and fasten or clamp them on either side of the blank. Attach a narrower ledge to the inner face of each track to provide clearance so you can mill to the blank's edges without hitting the tracks.

Router surfacing will require a sled that's more than twice as long as the workpiece is wide so there's plenty of overhang on the tracks. Milling the surface involves moving the router and sled back and forth along the tracks, methodically widening the surfaced area.

set it on the tracks and adjust a large-diameter bottom-cleaning bit to remove no more than ⅛" to 3⁄16" from the high spots. Spot-check the bit depth.

Then rout. Whether you work side to side or end to end, be an automaton. Sweep on one axis, milling a path as wide as the cutter. Click over a notch and sweep again, widening the path. Repeat the same process all the way across.

Make as many passes over the entire surface as necessary to flatten and smooth the board. Scraping and sanding will then remove any remaining swirl marks.

Though a straight bit works, a bottom-cleaning or planer bit cuts a wider swath and often produces a smoother surface.

Router Surfacing Jig Exploded View

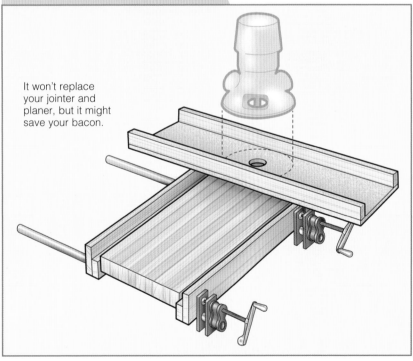

It won't replace your jointer and planer, but it might save your bacon.

4: Routing Curves the Easy Way with a Trammel

"Going in circles" often is a way of saying you're wasting time. In woodworking, cutting circles or arcs is sometimes done in time-consuming ways. So a practical technique for cutting good, clean circles (or arcs) is invaluable.

To cut circles or arcs with the router, use a trammel. Your router may have one among its accessories. If you don't have one, it's easy to cut out an oversized plywood baseplate, mounting the router on one end and driving a screw for a pivot point to set the circle's center. You can make fancier, adjustable versions as well.

Cutting circles is the natural turf of the plunge router. The plunger makes it easy to get the bit into the work and then deepen the cut after each lap. If you are routing completely through the stock, set the plunge depth to the stock thickness plus no more than 1/16".

Setting the cutting radius is where you account for the diameter of the bit.

Measure from the bit and mark the pivot point. Drill a hole at the spot for a pivot nail or screw. The bit is outside the radius if you want a disk, inside it if you want a hole.

If you are cutting a disk, exclude the bit from the radius; for hole cutouts, include the bit in the radius. Typically, you measure from the bit out, either adjusting the pivot point or marking on the trammel where the pivot must be.

Next, you need to secure the workpiece and, at the same time, protect the surface beneath it. Attach the work to some expendable material,

Power up, plunge the bit, and swing the router counterclockwise around the trammel's pivot. (The shop-made trammel shown above left is adjustable.) Plunge a little deeper with the next and additional passes until the bit cuts all the way through. You can use a plywood scrap to make a trammel that pivots on a screw (right) to cut large arcs or circles.

such as 1/4" plywood, and clamp the backup to the workbench.

You're all set. Switch on the router, plunge the bit into the work, and swing the machine around the pivot. Cut your way through in several deepening passes.

5: Duplicating a Workpiece with Templates

A template provides a quick and easy way to produce multiples of parts with contours, like a leg with a kink in it, a curved rail for a chair or a cutout apron for a table or shelf. A template can also be used to make identical joinery cuts.

Template routing can be a smart approach even when you only have one or two tricky parts to make. The materials best suited for templates — MDF, hardboard and thin plywood — are inexpensive and easily worked. If you botch a cheap template when you make it, it's still better than trashing a $20 board.

This simplest form of template-guided routing is done with either a flush-trimming bit or a pattern bit. Both have pilot bearings that are exactly the same size as the bit's cutting diameter. The bearing rides along the template, and the bit cuts the workpiece to match.

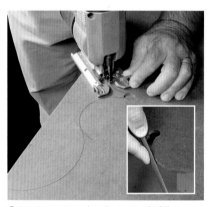

Cut out your template just proud of the layout line, then smooth and refine the sawn edges with files and sandpaper, fairing any transitions.

Make the template exactly the shape you want, using files or sandpaper to smooth the edges carefully. Even little imperfections will telegraph directly into the work.

Draw the template shape on the work and cut it about 1/16" oversize. Mount the template on the blank with

double-sided carpet tape, hot-melt glue or clamps. This way the router only has to shave off a sliver of material to bring the workpiece to final size. Works like a charm.

Now, check out the router table on the next page, and you'll have added six easy techniques that should help turn your router into the wonder tool it's meant to be.

Identical parts, produced with remarkable ease, demonstrate the benefit of templates. All you need is a piloted flush-trim or pattern bit.

6: How to Set Up a Super Simple Router Table

One of the most productive things you can do with a router is mount it, inverted, under a table. This turns it into a precision stationary tool. You'll be able to rout small or oddly proportioned workpieces, cut joinery and even raise panels safely. Router tables also instill confidence if you're a newbie, because you don't have to hold the router.

Building a router table is really no big deal. A quick trip to the local home center and a couple of hours in the shop is all it takes to build a basic table for whatever router you own. I call this design the "Po' Boy." When you shop, buy a quarter-sheet of ¾" plywood (be extravagant and get birch plywood!) and a handful of 2½" drywall screws. Also, buy longer screws to replace the ones that attach the baseplate to your router. All the supplies won't cost you more than about 15 bucks.

Cut the plywood into a 12" by 16" top, two 6" by 14" sides and an 11" by 16" back. You'll have more than half the plywood left, so you'll be able to make a suitable fence. Screw the sides to the edges of the back. You want the back to hang below the sides so you can clamp it securely in a bench vise. Set the top in place and screw it to the base. Now mount your router base to the top using the baseplate as a pattern for drilling mounting-screw holes. To make the bit opening, chuck a big straight bit in the router and plunge the bit through the top.

Bingo! You've got a router table. With the plywood you have left, you can make a low fence — just a straightedge, perhaps with a notch for the bit — and a tall L-shaped model with dust pickup. Secure either fence style to the tabletop with clamps.

Bill's Po' Boy Router Table Exploded View

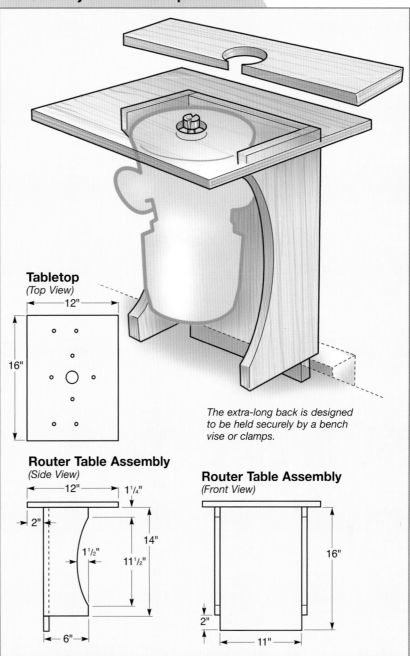

The extra-long back is designed to be held securely by a bench vise or clamps.

Tabletop *(Top View)*
12"
16"

Router Table Assembly *(Side View)*
12"   1¼"
2"
14"
1½"
11½"
6"

Router Table Assembly *(Front View)*
16"
2"
11"

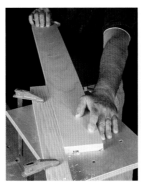  

A router table will cut dadoes and grooves (left), shape edge profiles (center) and even raise panels for cabinet doors with a vertical panel-raising bit. All it takes is a little plywood, a couple of hours' time and Bill's "Po' Boy" plan.

Twist Drill Bits

Whether you're using a drill press, corded power drill, cordless battery-powered drill or hand drill to bore holes, there's a good chance that it has a twist drill bit chucked up in it right now. Twist drill bits are, by far, the most common accessory used by do-it-yourselfers and woodworkers for all manner of drilling tasks — mounting hinges, putting up shelves, hanging light fixtures, or assembling cabinets.

by Sandor Nagyszalanczy

Unlike Forstners, augers and spade bits limited to drilling wood, versatile twist bits will quickly bore clean, precise holes in a wide range of materials, including plastics, nonferrous metals (aluminum, brass, copper, etc.), iron and steel, as well as hardwoods, softwoods, plywood and composite materials, like Masonite® and particleboard. Twist bits are also affordable and come in a wide range of diameters, from hair-thick to 1" diameter and even larger. As in most machine tools and accessories, the last few years have seen a torrent of new twist drill styles and types, some designed for general use, some for specialized boring tasks.

Hardware stores and woodworking and machinist's supply catalogs now feature so many different kinds of twist drill sets that buying bits can be awfully confusing. Are high-speed steel bits best, or should you spend the extra cash and spring for a set of cobalt or titanium-nitride-coated bits? Are split-point bits better than standard points, or are stepped-point bits a better choice?

This story will familiarize you with the many aspects of twist drills, including bit

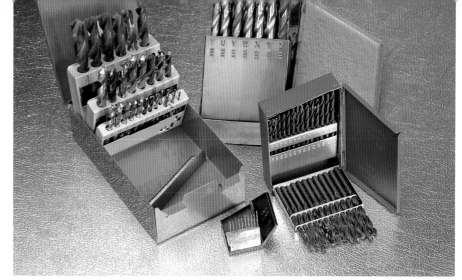

Figure 1: *Twist bits come in many sizes, including fractional, metric, lettered and more. The chart below provides a sampling of the variety of twist bits available.*

sizes, materials and coatings, and point styles. We'll also explore some twist bits designed for specific tasks, such as accurately mounting hardware or drilling pilot holes for tapered cabinet screws. We'll even look at some new twist bits that claim improved performance when used with cordless drills.

Bit Sizes and Sets

Unlike those cute elastic-cuffed slippers they give you at swank resorts, when it comes to drill bits, one size definitely doesn't fit all. Twist bits come in many

sizes, including fractional, metric, lettered, numbered and more (Figure 1). It's far more economical to buy in sets, rather than individually. The exception to this is when you need, say, a single odd-size bit or extra large or extra small bit for a specific job. The question is, which sets do you really need?

For everyday shop drilling tasks, you'll definitely want to purchase a basic set of fractional-sized twist drills. Sets come in several different size ranges, as shown in the chart below. A big 29-piece set will prepare you for the majority of wood

Twist Drill Bit Sets

Fractional	7 pc. set: ⅛" to ½" Dia. in ¹⁄₁₆". increments. 13 pc. set: ⅛" to ½" Dia. in ¹⁄₃₂" increments. 13 pc. set: ¹⁄₁₆" to ¼" in ¹⁄₆₄" increments. 25 pc. set: ⅛" to ½" in ¹⁄₆₄" increments. 29 pc. set: ¹⁄₁₆" to ½" in ¹⁄₆₄" increments.	General hole drilling tasks: setting screws, mounting hardware, running wiring, fitting dowels & pegs, etc.
Metric	19 pc. set: 1mm to 10mm in .5mm increments 25 pc. set: 1mm to 13mm in .5mm increments	Drilling holes for European hardware and fasteners.
Left-hand	15 pc. set: ¹⁄₁₆" to ½" in ¹⁄₃₂" increments 29 pc. set: ¹⁄₁₆" to ½" in ¹⁄₁₆" increments	Drilling into broken screws and fasteners when removing them.
Lettered	A (.234") to Z (.413")	Precision holes for metalworking or for tapping ⁵⁄₁₆" to ½" threads.
Large-number wire gauge	#1 (.228") to #60 (.040")	Precision holes in metalworking or tapping ¼" or smaller threads.
Small-number wire gauge	#61 (.039") to #80 (.0135")	Small holes for jewelry, model making or tapping very small threads.

Figure 2: *The author keeps a 29-piece fractional twist drill set at the ready by his drill press. The large selection can handle almost any woodworking challenge.*

Although a good quality set of bits can be pricey, it's a very practical purchase — in my own shop, I keep a 29-piece set on my drill press table (Figure 2), and a smaller 13-piece set with my cordless drills. The big set has all the bit sizes you're likely to need for practically any drilling job. For example, when boring holes for dowels, it's not uncommon for a ¼" dowel to require a $^{15}/_{64}$"- or $^{17}/_{64}$"-diameter hole. You'll also need specific fractional-sized drill bits when making pilot holes for production-type screws with non-tapered shanks. For best results, you need to size the bit to suit not only the screw size, but also the type of wood — hard or soft (see chart on the next page).

Fractional drills may be the most commonly used kinds of bits, but they're far from the only type available. The chart on page 27 shows several of the other kinds of twist drill sets you can buy from machinist's supply catalog companies. If you work with European hardware, or need to tap holes in metal or plastic for metric sized bolts, it's essential to have a set of metric sized drill bits (1mm to 10mm or 13mm) on hand. Left-hand bits spin in the opposite direction of standard bits, and are designed specifically for boring into ruined fasteners, when removing them. If

Figure 4: *Cobalt drill bits (the dull gold bit above) are heat-treated and generally last longer than regular HSS bits (shown below the cobalt bit).*

shop drilling tasks. Fractional-sized twist drills are also available up to 1½" or more in diameter, but these are expensive and primarily designed for metalworking. Better quality sets come in handy metal index boxes that keep all the bits organized and prevent them from getting lost or knocking about.

you work extensively with metal or plastics and routinely tap holes for fractional sized machine screws or bolts under ¼" in size, you'll welcome a set of large-numbered bits (#1 - #60 wire gauge), as shown in Figure 3. A lettered set of bits (A to Z sizes) is perfect for machine work and thread tapping holes for bolts between $^{5}/_{16}$" and ½" in size. And a petite index of small-size numbered drills (#61 to #80 wire gauge) is perfect for model making, jewelry work, and other Lilliputian-sized jobs.

Bit Materials and Coatings

Just like fine kitchen knives, pool cues or dreadnought guitars, not all twist bits are made the same. The cheapest bits, made from questionable grades of carbon steel, won't stay sharp as long and won't perform as well as bits made of better quality metals, such as high-speed or cobalt steel. Another way that twist drill bit manufacturers improve the performance of twist drill bits is to treat them with oxides or coat them with titanium nitride.

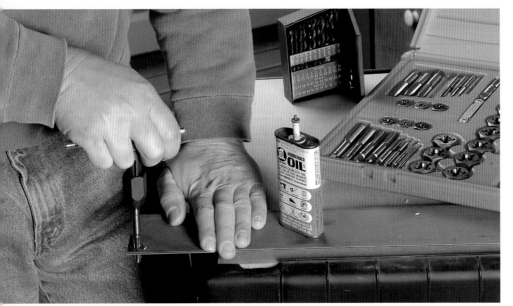

Figure 3: *To make easy work of tapping holes (¼" or smaller) in either metal or plastic, a set of large-numbered wire gauge bits is just the ticket.*

High-tech Coatings

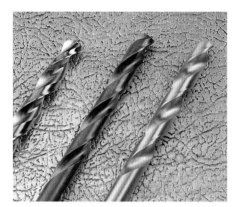

Figure 5: *Ferrous oxide (left), black oxide (center) and titanium nitride (right) are all coatings for HSS steel bits. The coatings reduce heat buildup and help resist rust.*

High-speed Steel

Twist drill bits manufactured from high speed steel (usually marked "HSS") are a good choice for general shop drilling tasks. High-speed steel bits stay sharp up to 10 times longer than carbon steel bits. Better yet, HSS can withstand the high temperatures created when drilling thick metal without overheating, which can draw the bit's temper and ruin it (a rainbow of colors at the tip indicates overheating). Uncoated HSS bits are a bit more expensive than carbon steel bits, but definitely worth the price difference if you plan to use your twist drills for more than just boring wood and plastic.

Cobalt Steel

Twist bits made from heat-resistant cobalt steel can last many times longer than regular high-speed steel bits, especially in demanding applications where heat buildup is a problem, as when drilling hardened steel. Cobalt bits are a dull gold color (see the gold bit in Figure 4) because of a special heat treating process where the bits are baked in an oven which hardens them to between 65.5 to 67 on the Rockwell C hardness scale. Unlike

coated bits (keep reading…), you can sharpen solid cobalt twist bits without reducing their performance. Cobalt twist drills are considerably more expensive than HSS bits, but tend to be more brittle and less flexible. Therefore, they're best reserved for difficult metal-boring tasks.

Oxide Finishes

Giving a twist bit a black oxide or ferrous oxide finish gives a regular HSS bit additional tempering and stress relief, thus reducing friction and enhancing performance. Heat treating also increases a bit's surface hardness, which not only increases the bit life, but allows it to run at higher RPM and at faster feed rates with less heat buildup. A black oxide or light gold-colored ferrous oxide finish (see Figure 5) also inhibits the formation of rust, which makes these bits popular with carpenters who work with wet lumber. The advantages and nominal extra cost of oxide-finished twist bits make them more desirable than plain HSS bits for general woodshop drilling tasks.

Titanium Nitride Coatings

Titanium nitride ("TiN" for short) coated bits have a distinctive rich gold color (see the right-hand bit in the photo at left), which is said to dissipate heat and help bits last up to seven times longer than uncoated HSS bits. The TiN coating increases the hardness of the surface of bits (up to a whopping 82 on the Rockwell C scale!) and adds self-lubricating properties. This makes TiN bits terrific for drilling both ferrous and nonferrous metals, as well as nonmetallic abrasive materials, such as Wonderboard. Unfortunately, TiN bits can't be resharpened without destroying the micro-thin coating on the point (it's likely that by the time the bit needs resharpening, the coating has already been worn away). Like cobalt steel bits, TiN-coated bits are best reserved for tough metal-drilling tasks, since the coating does little to enhance drilling performance in wood and nonmetallic materials.

Pilot Hole Diameters *(straight shanked screws)*

Screw Size	Pilot holes for hardwoods	Pilot holes for softwoods	Hole for countersinking screw heads
#4	5/64"	1/16"	1/4"
#6	7/64"	3/32"	3/8"
#8	1/8"	7/64"	3/8"
#10	9/64"	1/8"	1/2"
#12	5/32"	9/64"	1/2"

Figure 6: *Standard pointed bits (left) are ground at 118°, while split-point (right) have faces ground at 135°. The author considers the split-point bits a better all-around choice.*

Figure 7: *Point styles are one of the variable features to choose from when considering which twist bit is right for a specific task.*

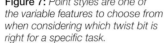

Different Points

Point Styles

A basic twist drill works by using a pair of cutting edges (called lips) to shave a thin layer of material off the bottom of the hole as the bit spins. The design of these lips, as well as the shape of the entire point, significantly affects the way a twist drill performs. Commonly available twist bits feature several different point styles, some made for general use, others for handling a limited range of materials and applications.

Standard and Split-point

The degree of a drill point's angularity determines how easy or difficult the bit is to start, as well as how aggressively the bit bites into the material being drilled. Standard bits with a 118 degree point (sometimes called "mechanic's bits") are good for general-purpose drilling jobs and offer satisfactory results in a wide variety of materials. These bits also center very well in existing holes, allowing you to enlarge them easily, say when the hole you've just drilled for a screw or dowel is just a skosh too small. However, in order to prevent a bit from "skating" (wandering or skipping around) when drilling metal or other hard materials, you must create a dimple using a center punch. To prevent skating with larger bits — say ⁵⁄₁₆" and up — it's best to drill holes in two stages, starting with a smaller hole, then enlarging it to full size.

Today, more and more do-it-yourselfers and woodworkers prefer the split-point design of 135 degree bits (see right-hand bit in Figure 6). This special grind offsets the cutting edges from one another, enabling them to cut aggressively while significantly reducing the tendency to skate and wander. It also allows drilling the hardest materials without center punching or predrilling a centering hole. In my opinion, 135 degree split-point bits are a better choice than 118 degree bits for all-around shop drilling tasks for holes ½" and smaller. Whether you choose 118- or 135-degree bits, you'll get the best performance by keeping all your bits sharp; see the sidebar on page 31.

Figure 8: *To get a nice, clean, large hole, use a two-step process. First, drill a small pilot hole. Next, use a stepped-point bit to bore the desired hole diameter, using the pilot hole to keep the bit centered as you drill.*

Stepped-point

Sold as "Pilot Point®" bits by DeWalt (and once sold as "Bullet" bits by Black & Decker), stepped-point bits have a tip that looks like a very short twist drill that's about half the diameter of the bit's shank. (See center bit photo above) This point not only prevents the bit from skating around when starting a hole, but makes it easier to center a bit on a pencil mark or center-punched dimple. A stepped point also helps keep the bit from veering off-center when drilling thick materials and causes a bit less damage on the underside of the stock when drilling completely through the material. Stepped-point bits are great for drilling large holes in two steps (see Figure 8), with the first hole drilled the same diameter as the size of the larger bit's tip. However, they aren't a good choice to enlarge an existing hole slightly, since the bit won't align readily. Their complex tip geometry means that sharpening isn't an option; once the point is damaged or dull, the bit must be replaced. To make their bits last longer, DeWalt finishes their Pilot Point® bits with ferrous oxide.

Brad Point Bits

If quickly drilling perfect, tearout-free holes in wood is your goal, it's hard to beat the clean drilling performance of brad point bits. (Left bit, Figure 7.) A brad

Figure 9: *Brad point bits have advantages for woodworkers, but cannot be used in metalworking or with other hard materials.*

point's sharp central point allows the bit to be positioned with great accuracy and eliminates skating as the hole is started. The bit's raised side spurs score the wood around the circumference of the hole, providing a very smooth cut and reducing chipping on the top surface of the work, as well as reducing splintering where the bit exits the underside of the stock.

On the down side, these bits are strictly for drilling wood, soft plastics, and solid-surface materials such as Corian™. And remember, like stepped-point bits, brad points aren't a good choice for enlarging existing holes, as they won't center properly.

Sometimes referred to as "dowel bits," brad points come in a wide range of sizes, ranging from ⁵⁄₆₄" to 1" in diameter (see Figure 9). Well-stocked woodworking supply houses even offer brad points in ¹⁄₆₄" fractional increments. Brad points come in many different grades, from the cheapest carbon steel bits, to high-speed steel bits (best for general woodshop use) to TiN-coated and carbide-tipped bits suitable for demanding production shop applications (Figure 10). Brad point bits can only be resharpened with a needle file or fine stone, a difficult procedure to execute properly.

Shank Styles

While most of the differences between twist drills have to do with materials and point design, the shank — the part of a bit that fits into the chuck — is another factor worthy of consideration. Most bits have smooth, cylindrical shanks that are the same diameter all the way up. This gives a bit lots of rigidity — a good thing when boring holes in difficult materials. But in some drilling situations, bits with reduced-diameter, flatted or hex-shaped shanks are a better choice.

Reduced-diameter Shanks

Twist bits with a variety of point styles are available with reduced-diameter shanks, where bits between ³⁄₈" and ½" diameter have their shanks stepped down to a ³⁄₈" diameter (or even ¼"). Referred to as "Silver & Deming" bits (in machinist's supply catalogs), reduced-shank bits are convenient for use in hand and power drills fitted with ³⁄₈" (or ¼") capacity chucks (Figure 11).

Flatted Shanks

Another bit shank style that makes twist drills more "user-friendly" is the flatted shank. Also called "No-Spin" shanks (in DeWalt's terminology), these feature three flats ground on the shanks of bits larger than ³⁄₁₆". The flats provide a drill chuck's

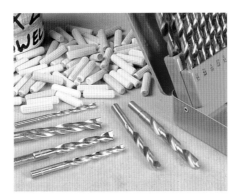

Figure 10: *Sometimes called dowel bits, brad point bits are available in TiN coating and with carbide tips, but their cost in these forms makes them impractical for non-professionals.*

jaws a very firm grip and prevent the bit from spinning in the chuck when the drill stalls, say when you hit a knot in pine. A major complaint of many DIYers, spinning can quickly ruin a bit by galling its shank, making it difficult to chuck properly again. Flatted shanks are especially useful when working with larger bits in a keyless chuck, as such chucks are more difficult to tighten than traditional keyed chucks.

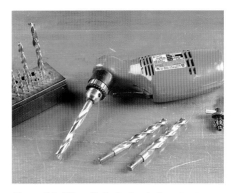

Figure 11: *Bits with their shank diameter "stepped down" allow a drill with a smaller chuck to accept large diameter drill bits.*

Hex-shanks

Yet another handy shank configuration, ¼" hex-shank or "quick-change" bits, have hexagonal shanks designed to work with quick-release magnetic or spring-loaded accessory chucks. These accessory chucks also accept screwdriver bits and drilling accessories, and can make work with a cordless drill very handy: You can drill a pilot hole, then quickly change to a driver bit and set screws in a flash. Hex-shank bits also work in standard drill chucks and aren't subject to bit spin, just like bits with flatted shanks. You can buy hex-shank bits in ready-to-use sets, or you can buy hex-shank adapters that work with all styles of twist bits.

Figure 12: *Tapered bits (with optional countersink collars) must be matched to the correct size cabinet screws. Not for use with straight-shanked screws.*

Figure 13: *Extra long "aircraft bits" can be just the ticket if you find regular bits are too short.*

Special Drill Bits

Special Twist Drills

General-purpose twist drills come in a number of special sized sets (numbered, lettered, etc.), great for jobs like mounting metric fasteners or for making holes for tapping screw threads (see the chart on page 25) But there are times when these bits won't do the trick, and it's time to reach for a specialized type of twist bit.

Tapered Drills

Made primarily for drilling pilot holes for traditional tapered cabinet woodscrews, tapered drills have shanks that go from thick to slender and come to a fairly sharp point. The holes these bits create give the threads of tapered wood screws good "bite" along their entire length. This not only produces strong connections, but decreases the chances of screws stripping out or snapping. (To develop full holding strength, it's important that hole depth matches the depth of the screw's penetration into the work.) Tapered bits are NOT the right choice when drilling pilot holes for straight-shanked production screws (see Pilot Hole Dia. Chart, page 27).

Tapered drills are sized specially for different-sized screws — #4, #8, etc. A typical set (Figure 12) for all the typical

cabinet screws you're apt to use in a small shop would include #6, #8, #10 and #12 tapered bits. Most sets also include removable countersinks that slide onto the shank of each tapered bit, as well as stop collars that allow you to set the exact depth of the countersunk hole.

Extra Long Bits

Most twist drills you buy in sets or individually at hardware stores are "jobber length" drills (e.g. a ¼" bit is about 4" long) which have enough length to do most average boring jobs. But there are certainly occasions when longer bits are called for (Figure 13). Referred to as "aircraft drills" in machinist lingo, extension drills come in several lengths — 6", 12", and even 18"

long — in most common sizes (bellhanger bits, made for carpentry and electrical work, are even longer). Extra long bits are a blessing when you need to bore a hole through very thick material or when you're working in cramped quarters where shorter bits don't provide enough reach.

Quick-drilling Bits

The Vermont American Tool Company's new XTEND and Sidewinder series drill bits are both designed to drill holes more quickly than regular bits (Figure 14). They both feature aggressive starting points and shanks with a fast helix angle (think tighter corkscrew), to rapidly eject material from the hole. According to Vermont American, their XTEND series bit's "Speed Geometry" supposedly uses less battery power when run in a cordless drill, and will bore up to four times more holes per charge than standard twist bits. In my own informal

Figure 14: *XTEND bits (with their fast helix or tighter corkscrew) are designed to get the most efficient use from cordless drills. Compare the Xtend bit helix to the gold cobalt standard twist (inset).*

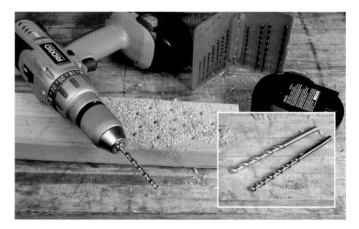

testing, the bits definitely penetrated even hardwoods, like oak and maple, quickly and with less effort than regular twist bits. However, they were a bit grabby when drilling softwood lumber and left holes that were very rough — not much of a concern if you're doing construction projects, but I wouldn't choose them for fine finish work.

Self-centering Bits

For perfectly aligned hinges, latches and other hardware, nothing beats drilling screw holes with a self-centering bit (Figure 15). Also known by the brand

Figure 15: *Self-centering "Vix" bits are one of the most useful drill bits in any cabinet shop.*

name "Vix® bits," self-centering drill bits surround a standard twist drill bit with a retracting, spring-loaded sleeve. The sleeve's tapered end fits snugly into the chamfered mounting screw holes found on most hardware, to guide the bit as the hole is drilled. The bits come in several sizes, each made to work with one or two standard screw sizes (#6, #8, etc.). You can even buy ¼" and 5mm self-centering bits, designed to work with templates used when drilling multiple holes for adjustable shelf support pins.

Stepped Bits

A stepped drill bit is like two bits in one, with a smaller diameter drill at the tip (like a stepped-point bit's tip, only longer), attached to a larger diameter shank. With a stepped bit, you can drill two holes at once: A smaller pilot hole for a screw, and a larger hole for recessing the screw's head below the surface of the work. Stepped drills are also perfect bits for drilling pocket-holes for joining face frames with screws using a special jig (Figure 16). You can also use these bits when drilling freehand with a portable drill; however, care should be taken to keep the bit straight and running true to avoid snapping off its delicate tip.

Figure 16: *Stepped bits are the key to pocket-hole jigs, but are useful in other operations, too.*

To get the best performance out of bits with standard (118°) or split (135°) points, you should sharpen them occasionally, rather than wait for them to get really dull and burn and send up smoke signals with every hole. Unless you're experienced at sharpening drill bits by hand, a motorized drill sharpener is a good investment. These specialized machines reshape and sharpen a bit's cutting edges at the tip. Sophisticated models, such as the "Drill Doctor" shown here, handle both 118° and 135° bits between ³⁄₃₂"- and ½"- (or even ¾"-) diameter, as well as carbide-tipped masonry bits.

Four Steps to Square Stock

Regardless of the project you're building or where you're at with your woodworking skills, it's easy to improve your odds for success by starting with flat, square stock. The size and relationship of all parts depend on flat, square surfaces. But don't be mistaken—even those pre-planed, pre-jointed boards at the home center are often far from flat or straight. Better to think of every piece of lumber as though it's a roughsawn board. If you're a little murky on how to square up stock, here's a crash course.

by Cortland Privateer and Gena Tennyson

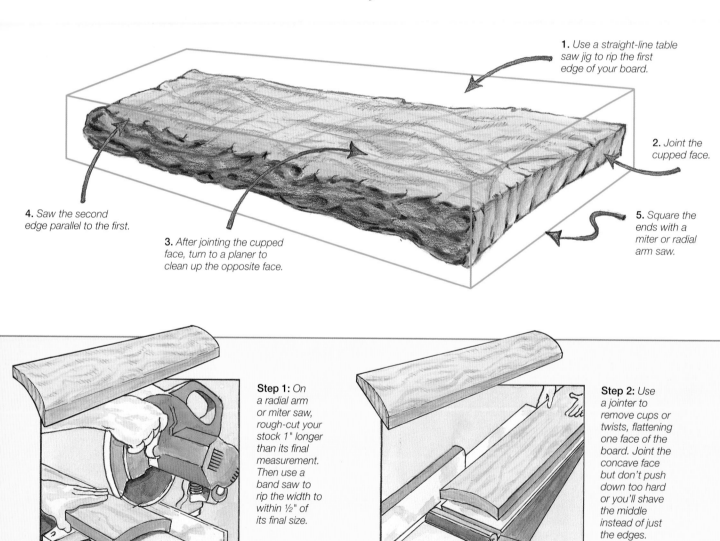

1. *Use a straight-line table saw jig to rip the first edge of your board.*

2. *Joint the cupped face.*

5. *Square the ends with a miter or radial arm saw.*

4. *Saw the second edge parallel to the first.*

3. *After jointing the cupped face, turn to a planer to clean up the opposite face.*

Step 1: *On a radial arm or miter saw, rough-cut your stock 1" longer than its final measurement. Then use a band saw to rip the width to within ½" of its final size.*

Step 2: *Use a jointer to remove cups or twists, flattening one face of the board. Joint the concave face but don't push down too hard or you'll shave the middle instead of just the edges.*

How often have you found yourself forcing pieces of a project together with blows of a mallet? Don't worry, this isn't a message from the gods that you should give up woodworking. Poorly milled lumber is one of the likely culprits for problems like this. Cupped, bowed or twisted stock can wreak havoc on the best laid plans and make assembling a project difficult, if not impossible. Proper rough stock preparation lays a solid foundation for the rest of the machining and assembly process.

Selecting and Acclimating Stock

First off, it's important to select and buy good lumber, so choose a quality hardwood supplier. Try to pick straight boards that are pleasing in color, grain pattern and condition. After you bring the lumber home, let it adjust to your shop for at least a week. This "acclimation" period allows the stock to stabilize to the humidity levels in its new environment, which helps minimize both cupping and bowing.

Determine what boards to use for the individual pieces of your project and mark them accordingly. Make attractive use of grain patterns, while keeping waste to a minimum. Imagine how the grain of different boards will look when glued together, and try to make it flow from one board to the next. Cut adjacent drawers from the same board for continuous grain direction.

Cutting to Rough Size

The first step is to cut boards an inch longer and ½" wider than their final measurements. Don't forget to allow for tenons, or you'll end up with the nicest firewood in town. Use a radial arm or miter saw to crosscut to rough length. When cutting to rough width, it's quieter, cleaner and safer to do it on a band saw rather than a table saw. If you decide to go the latter route, build the jig shown on the next page to make the job easier and safer.

Flattening on the Jointer

The jointer is the tool of choice for flattening cupped or bowed lumber. A planer will flatten a board only for the time it is underneath the cutterhead— a crooked board will quickly return to its former twisted state. Your jointer must be in tune to deliver great results. Make sure the fence is at 90° to the table and that both tables are properly aligned. If the fence is out of square even 1°, the edges of boards will not be perpendicular to their faces, creating a barrel effect instead of square intersections.

To joint a board, place one band sawn edge against the jointer fence. Take thin passes and cut with the grain to reduce tearout. Never take off more than 1⁄16" per pass; use a push block and keep all guards in place. Most important: never hang your fingers over the edge of a board unless you want an emergency room manicure.

To flatten a bowed board on the jointer, orient the concave face down. Don't push down too hard; initially you want to just hit the high spots and not the whole face. Too much pressure just produces a thinner bowed board.

Time for Planing

After flattening one face of a warped board on the jointer, plane the opposite face. If you don't own a planer, you may be able to have a local mill shop plane your stock for a small fee.

Step 3: *With the flat (jointed) face down on the planer table, run the board through to create a parallel surface on the opposite (top) face.*

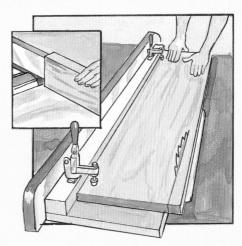

Step 4: *Use the jig shown here or a jointer (see inset) to clean up one band sawn edge of your stock. Then rip the second edge parallel to the first on a table saw.*

This jig lets you rip a straight edge on rough stock. Build it by gluing a guide fence to an 8"-wide platform, then mount toggle clamps on the guide fence. Place your board (with some stock extending past the edge) on the platform and secure it with the toggle clamps. Slide the guide fence along your table saw's fence and slice off the excess lumber.

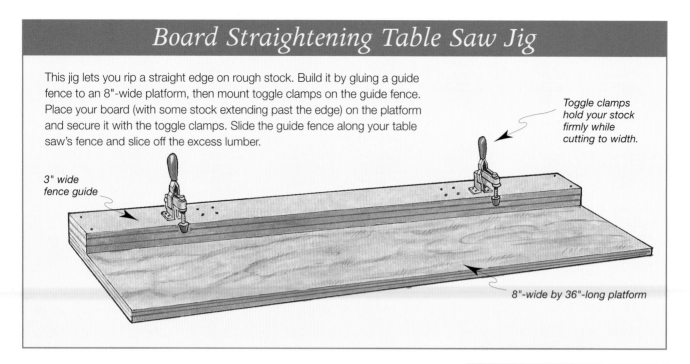

Toggle clamps hold your stock firmly while cutting to width.

3" wide fence guide

8"-wide by 36"-long platform

Plane with the grain as much as possible to avoid tearout, and take thin passes; again, no more than ¹⁄₁₆" at a time. Flip the board after each pass to remove an equal amount of material from both faces. Feed boards with irregular grain as slowly as possible. Don't bring stock to finished thickness in one day: stop planing about ⅛" from final size, then let the wood adjust and equalize overnight. It's a good trick that gives you one more shot at jointing and planing when you actually plan to use the wood. Now you're ready to straighten one edge.

Straightening the Edges

The easiest way to begin squaring your two edges is to move right to the jointer (first making sure the fence is square). Since you've already flattened both faces, either one can be run against the jointer fence. However, if your band sawn edges are too rough, use the jig shown above. Either way, be sure to cut with the grain to avoid chipping, then move on to the table saw to straighten the other edge.

Cutting to Final Dimensions

Before you rip your stock to final width on the table saw, the rip fence must be accurate. Although your trusty table saw fence may be extremely accurate, it's still a good idea to double-check it every now and then by measuring from the rip fence to any saw tooth that inclines toward the fence.

Crosscut stock to final length using a miter or radial arm saw — just take ⅛" off one end to square the pieces, then flip it end for end and trim it to length. You can also crosscut on a table saw, providing you have a sliding table or an accurate miter gauge (an extension fence helps). Begin your project as soon as possible, while the wood is straight and flat.

Congratulations, you've completed the first and perhaps most important step in woodworking. The rest of your work should now produce rewarding, enjoyable and square results—without the help of a 10-pound mallet!

QuickTip

Don't go against the grain

If you're getting areas of tearout or feathering on boards as you run them across the jointer, try reversing the direction of the feed. Sometimes, grain hits the knives at the wrong angle. By switching the front of the board to the back, you offer a different grain angle to the cutters. If the flip doesn't help, try wetting the surface with a damp cloth first, then try jointing again. Use the same logic if you encounter tearout when planing. When nothing helps, set your jointer for a fine pass, and clean up any remaining tearout with a scraper or by sanding.

An Instant Workbench

by Rob Johnstone

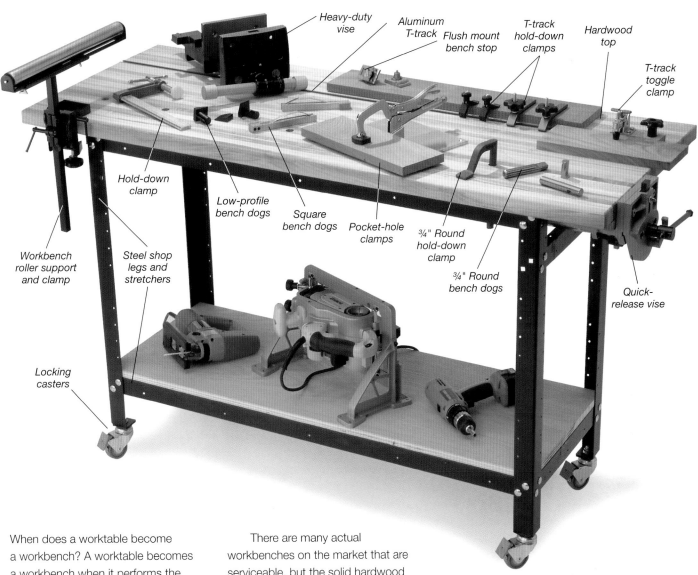

Heavy-duty vise

Aluminum T-track

Flush mount bench stop

T-track hold-down clamps

Hardwood top

T-track toggle clamp

Hold-down clamp

Low-profile bench dogs

Square bench dogs

Pocket-hole clamps

¾" Round hold-down clamp

¾" Round bench dogs

Quick-release vise

Workbench roller support and clamp

Steel shop legs and stretchers

Locking casters

When does a worktable become a workbench? A worktable becomes a workbench when it performs the function of a workbench. And that is where a woodworker's method of work begins to define the answer.

While the table shown above is not a workbench in any traditional sense, it might just be the answer to many regular Joe (or Jill) woodworkers' needs as they learn the craft.

There are many actual workbenches on the market that are serviceable, but the solid hardwood top and metal frame components we assembled above (for under $300) are even less expensive and will serve quite well. Drill some dogholes, mount a vise, and you have a useful addition to your shop. Add to that the bounty of accessories available, and your woodworking just got a lot easier.

Jointer Basics

For flattening and straightening stock, the jointer is an essential tool. Maintaining a jointer isn't difficult, and operating it properly is easy once you know how. Here's a short primer on how to use your jointer and keep it in tip-top shape.

by Bruce Kieffer

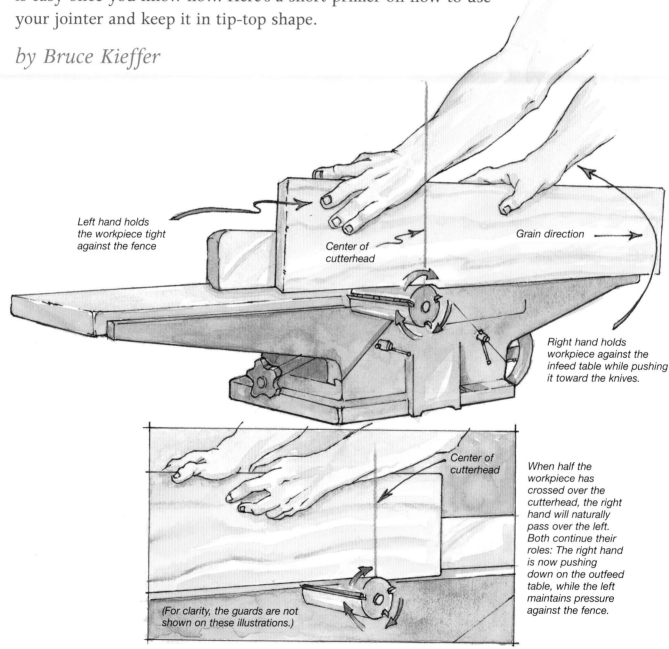

Left hand holds the workpiece tight against the fence

Center of cutterhead

Grain direction

Right hand holds workpiece against the infeed table while pushing it toward the knives.

Center of cutterhead

(For clarity, the guards are not shown on these illustrations.)

When half the workpiece has crossed over the cutterhead, the right hand will naturally pass over the left. Both continue their roles: The right hand is now pushing down on the outfeed table, while the left maintains pressure against the fence.

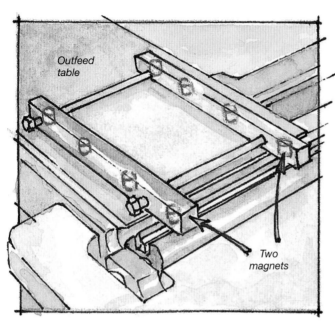

Step 1: *Magnetized bars help set the jointer knives flush with the outfeed table. The bars hold the knives in place while you tighten the set screws.*

All the craftsmanship in the world won't help you build better projects if the boards you start with are not straight and true. To make them so, most woodworkers usually turn to their jointers. Here's a short course on how to keep your jointer in tune, as well as a few tips that will help you get the most from this dependable shop workhorse.

Three Steps to Success

Tuning up your jointer won't take very long—there are really only three key steps to it. But before they can be performed, you should be comfortable with the basic operation of the machine. If you've only scanned the manual that came with your jointer, this is an excellent opportunity to give it a thorough read.

While you're reading, have a pro sharpen the knives. Even if you've been a woodworker for more years than you care to remember, leave planer and jointer knives to the experts—it's just too tricky trying to keep those long edges straight without the proper equipment.

Before you reinstall the knives (most jointers have two or three), be safe and unplug the machine. The easiest way to align the knives is with a set of magnetized bars that are available at most hardware stores (see Step 1 at left). These magnets stick to the outfeed table with one end protruding over the knives. Because they're magnetized, they pull the

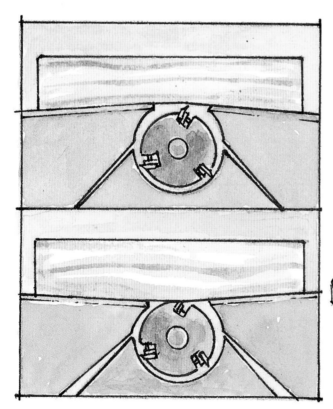

Step 2: *You can tell if your infeed and outfeed tables are parallel by jointing test edges on some long scrap. Usually adjusting the infeed table will take care of any problems.*

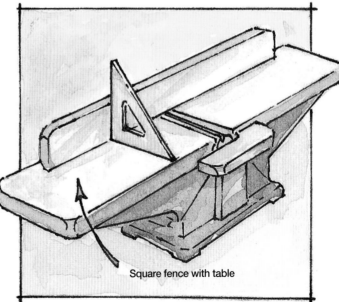

Square fence with table

Step 3: *Use a 90° triangle to square your fence with the outfeed table. Once it's perfect, adjust the fence gauge accordingly.*

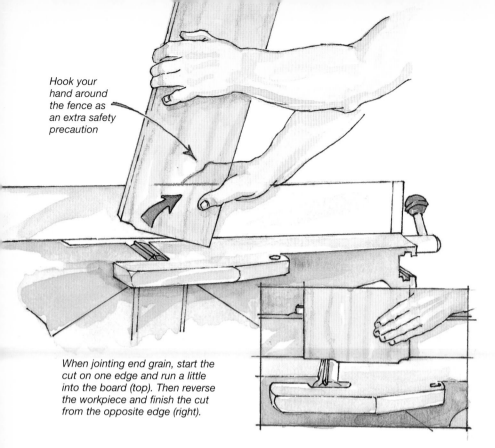

Hook your hand around the fence as an extra safety precaution

When jointing end grain, start the cut on one edge and run a little into the board (top). Then reverse the workpiece and finish the cut from the opposite edge (right).

A Quick Fix for Small Nicks

Every woodworker enjoys saving a few dollars, especially if doing so doesn't have any impact on the quality of the work. When newly sharpened jointer knives get nicked by an unusually hard knot, there's no need to resharpen them right away. Just move one knife a little to the side so the nicks no longer line up.

Addressing End Grain, Snipe and Feed Direction

Jointing end grain can be tricky. To do so without tearing a huge chunk out of the trailing edge of a board, stop feeding after an inch or two, reverse the board and complete the cut from the other end. But don't try this with narrow (less than 4") or long (more than 48") boards.

"Snipe" is the woodshop word for that annoying little concave cut that jointers tend to leave on the end of a pass. Either the outfeed table is lower than the knives (see how to fix this in the tune-up section above), or the workpiece is too short. In the latter case, just hot-melt glue a piece of scrap to the end of the board, let it dry, then make your cut.

Finally, a word about feed direction: To avoid chipping or chatter, make sure you feed the wood into the knives so the grain pattern widens toward the trailing end.

knives up to the level of the outfeed table and hold them in place while you tighten the set screws.

Test your knife installation by placing a straight stick on the outfeed table and then rotating the cutterhead manually (use the pulley to avoid getting nicked by the sharp knives). The stick should move exactly the same distance with each knife. Repeat the process along the full length of each knife to make sure that all the cutters are in line.

To see if the jointer's infeed and outfeed tables are parallel, joint two long boards and hold the jointed edges together: If their centers touch and there are gaps at the ends, one or both of the tables are low near the cutterhead. If the ends touch and there's a gap in the

center, then one or both are high near the cutterhead (see Step 2). Adjust only the infeed table (except in severe cases), then keep testing until the jointed edges rest against each other with no gaps.

Finally, adjust the fence so its gauge reads 90° when it makes a 90° cut. Use a square to make the initial fence setting (see Step 3), then make a test cut on a board and check it with the square. Adjust the fence as needed until the tool consistently makes 90° cuts. When it does, you can adjust the fence pointer to read 90°. Most jointers have a stop bolt that holds the fence at 90°. Even though this is a fairly reliable index, it's still a good idea to check your fence for square every time you change its setting, just to be sure it's dialed in at 90°.

QuickTip

Never a Dull Moment with Two Sets of Jointer Knives

High-speed steel jointer knives—standard-issue on most jointers—will stay sharp a remarkably long time. But, sooner or later, they'll need a fresh grinding. Buy a second set of sharp knives before your current ones get dull. That way, you'll have new knives to install when your old ones come out for sharpening.

Tip One: Occasionally you may need to swing the guard of your jointer out of the way for operations like leg tapering (see below), which can create a dangerous situation for the hand holding the guard. To give yourself something secure to hold on to, fasten a cabinet door knob to the guard—it will keep your fingers well clear of the knives.

Tip Two: Build a sturdy push pad, like the one shown above, for your jointer. A hand plane knob and a cement-float style handle give both hands good purchase, and a friction-fitted replaceable stop below supports the trailing end of boards as you joint them.

1½"

A conventional pushstick like the one shown at right doesn't provide enough workpiece control, and your feed hand could be in danger. The modified two-handled push pad (above) is a better alternative.

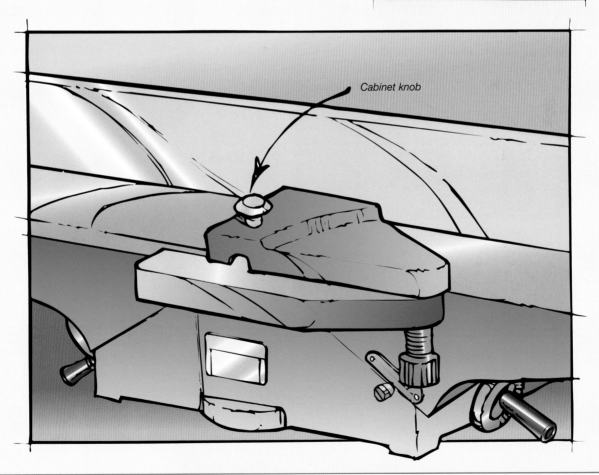

Cabinet knob

Secrets of Surfacing Stock

The relationship between your jointer, planer and table saw is critical to properly preparing stock. Whether you are cleaning up rough-sawn lumber or correcting cupping, warping or twisting — you need all three tools (and a set of winding sticks) to succeed.

by Jeff Jacobson

Here's the deal ... planers do not flatten wood, they surface wood. Put a rough-sawn twisted or warped board through a planer and you get a smooth, twisted or warped board. So, how do you deal with those deformed pieces of valuable lumber? You could use a hand plane to flatten the wood, or you can use the combination of a jointer, planer and a saw (in this story a table saw). With these three tools working in concert, you will make short shrift of snaky stock. To do so, you'll need to follow the basic steps shown here.

A word about jointers. As indicated, a jointer is the key to dealing with distorted lumber. By face jointing, you can deal with cups and twists. And to that end, you can't truly face joint anything wider than the width of your jointer's cutterhead. A 6" jointer will handle up to a 6" wide board; 8" jointers, an 8" wide board, etc. Jointers are also one of the more dangerous tools in a shop. If you get your finger tangled up in a jointer head, the motion of the cutter will pull your finger into the head with great power. Always use guards and safety gear when using a jointer. The space available here is insufficient to adequately cover jointer safety in detail. Proper use of your tools is an individual responsibility.

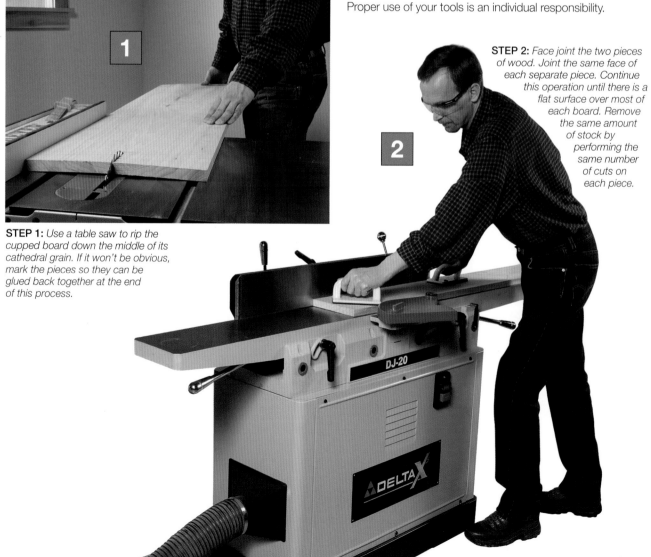

STEP 1: *Use a table saw to rip the cupped board down the middle of its cathedral grain. If it won't be obvious, mark the pieces so they can be glued back together at the end of this process.*

STEP 2: *Face joint the two pieces of wood. Joint the same face of each separate piece. Continue this operation until there is a flat surface over most of each board. Remove the same amount of stock by performing the same number of cuts on each piece.*

The Consequences of Wood Movement

Cupping

Warping

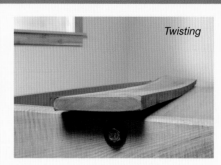
Twisting

As freshly cut (green) wood dries, the cells that make up the wood fibers actually shrink. The problem is that the fibers shrink almost twice as much in one direction (tangential) as they do in the opposite direction (radial). Depending on how the grain or wood fibers run through the length of a board, this shrinkage differential will cause the wood to distort. Once a board is dry, that shrinkage can be addressed and corrected. Cupping and warping are two of the easier distortions to correct.

Twisting is the mother of all board distortions. Fixing a twist is tricky because material needs to be removed in an asymmetrical fashion. Also, more stock usually needs to be jointed away in order to harvest usable material.

Five Steps to Correcting Cupping

Often, wide boards with beautiful cathedral grain are significantly cupped. Visually, the board would be a perfect selection for a tabletop or desk, but it's too cupped to use. So, how do you flatten the board but retain its visual integrity? Follow the five steps starting at left. (For a narrow board 8" or slimmer — depending on how wide your jointer is — you can start on step 2.) And remember, once a board is properly dry its tendency to distort will abate.

STEP 3: *Move to your planer and begin surfacing the stock. Continue until you have a smooth flat surface on both faces of each board. Because you face jointed the boards, their faces are now parallel to each other.*

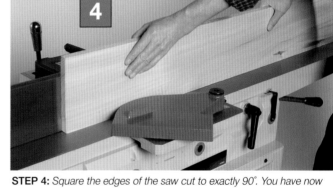

STEP 4: *Square the edges of the saw cut to exactly 90°. You have now re-formed the two sections of your wide cupped board into two perfectly flat boards with prepared glue-joint edges.*

STEP 5: *Glue the pieces back together, taking time to ensure that the grain matches at the glue joint, the glue-up is flat and the edges are properly aligned. You now have a flat, stable, wide panel.*

STEP 1: *Evaluate segments of the warped board to access whether you can get your desired part out of the piece. A template of the part (on the saw table) is very useful during this process.*

STEP 2: *After you cut out the piece of stock appropriate for your part, face joint the piece. For safety's sake, the piece should be at least 16" long. It is better to waste a bit of wood than get hurt.*

Fixing Warps and Twists

As with the example of cupping, when you decide to fix a specific problem of wood distortion, it should be with a goal in mind. In this example, the goal is to harvest a specific part from a board that is warped. It only makes sense that if you have to straighten 18 lineal inches, the task will be easier and waste less material than removing material to straighten 36 lineal inches. For that reason, the evaluation phase of this process is best done with specific parts in mind. The limitation to producing useable parts from a warped board is the thickness of the wood required to make a specific part. The full dimension of the part must exist within the volume of the wood you are machining. If, by reason of the wood's curvature over its length, you need to remove so much material that the board's thickness is less than that of the part, you need to find another piece of wood or move to a different segment of the warped board you are looking at. The curvature of a warp will not be uniform down its length, so you might be able to produce a specific part from one section of the board, but not another.

For all of these reasons, the first step in dealing with a warped board is evaluation. When you have determined which segment of the overall board can produce the part you want, cut that section out. As the next step is face jointing, do not cut out a piece that is too small to safely face joint ... 16" is a minimum safe length.

STEP 4: *Plane the stock flat with parallel faces. The length of the piece is important here, too.*

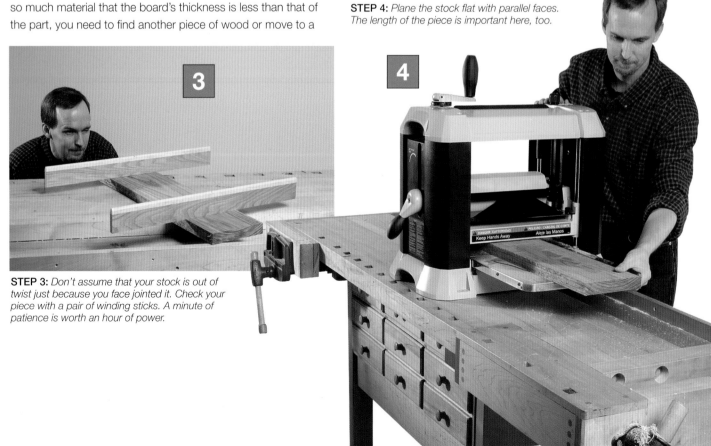

STEP 3: *Don't assume that your stock is out of twist just because you face jointed it. Check your piece with a pair of winding sticks. A minute of patience is worth an hour of power.*

After that, the process is very similar to that described in "Five Steps to Correcting Cupping." The only caveat is that you'll need to check the board for twist after you face joint. Do this with a pair of shop-made winding sticks (photo 3 of the second sequence). Proceed through the steps and you will end up with a flat, parallel and square piece of wood from a warped source.

Dealing with twisted boards is essentially the same as the process of dealing with warped stock. The key difference is how you address the face jointing. See the sidebar at right.

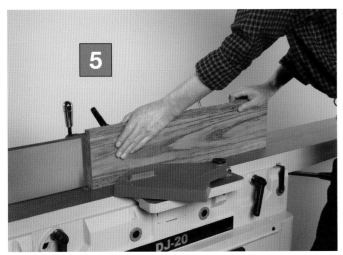

STEP 5: *With the stock flat and the faces parallel to each other, joint the edges square. The piece is now ready to be formed — from warped board to useful stock in five simple steps.*

Twist and Shout

In the front view photo at left, the colored lines indicate differing planes or levels on the face of this twisted piece of persimmon wood. The white lines indicate the level farthest from the mean. Yellow is next, with magenta representing the lowest level of the board. The goal of face jointing this board would be to remove the white outlined area first. Next, move to the yellow area. When you get to the magenta plane, the board's face will be essentially level or flat.

Side View   *Front View*

Think of the surface of a twisted board in terms of a topographic map. The colored contour lines in the picture above represent the hills and valleys. The goal of face jointing in this case is to level off the hills. Use your jointer to take off the high points a bit at a time. As with a twisted board, it is always more effective to flatten smaller, piece-specific, sections of the board.

Resawing: Basic Hows and Whys

Lumber sure isn't getting any cheaper. When you need a thin slice, turn to your band saw and a wide blade to create it. Resawing is also the way to transform highly figured stock into mirror-image panels. If you've never resawn before, here's how.

by Linda Haus

Blade drift is the constant concern of resawers. A proper saw blade coupled with a point fence are the first steps towards accuracy. Then, as you cut, make left and right adjustments as shown above.

Point fence

So you can use a band saw to slice thin pieces of wood from bigger pieces of wood...what's the benefit? Why not buy your wood sliced thin to begin with, or just plane or sand it to thickness? Here are five good reasons:

First, you'll get the best use out of expensive or beautifully figured wood.

Second, you'll be able to create book-matched, slip-matched or swing-matched panels.

Third, you'll have a method to efficiently use salvaged or reclaimed lumber of large dimension.

Fourth, you will be able to create your own lumber from a tree…or even from firewood!

And fifth, when you get good at it, you can begin to make your own handmade plywood (see Handmade Plywood).

Equipment Makes a Difference

To get started with resawing, you'll need a band saw of sufficient power and with a large depth of cut. Any motor smaller than 1 HP and depth of cut less than 10" will limit your effectiveness. (A typical 14" band saw has about a 6" maximum cut…so you'd be limited to a 12" wide book-matched panel or less.)

We also recommend using a point fence of some sort. By having a single point to register the cut (placed adjacent to the cutting edge of the saw blade), you will be able to swing your stock left or right to correct for blade drift. You might be able to get away with using a standard fence once in a while, but if you're trying to slice off a ¼" piece of expensive hardwood, and your blade drifts toward the fence, you are powerless to correct it.

Speaking of saw blades; the rule of thumb for resawing is "the wider the better." Wider blades, ¾" and larger, cut straighter, which is the goal. Also, fewer and larger teeth per inch make for better resawing.

The question that readers ask is, "Can you resaw using a narrow band saw blade?" The answer is, sometimes, yes. If your band saw is well tuned and the wood is acceptably dry and without internal stresses, a narrow blade can work. More often than not, however, an ordinary ¼" or ⅜" blade will only lead to more wandering in the cut. It's not designed for a heavy-duty task such as resawing.

When it comes to resawing blades, think wide and dentally challenged. Fewer teeth per inch allow the blade to remove sawdust more effectively. And if you are slicing through a 10" or 12" board, you can imagine how much waste that makes. Wider blades track better and cut straighter; exactly what you want when resawing. If your machine will accept a ¾"- or even 1"-wide blade, you'll have the ideal width for resawing. These wide blades can be costly, but for routine resawing they're really the way to go. Even if you don't opt for an expensive "specialty" resaw blade, stick with at least a ½" open-toothed blade to enhance your resawing activity.

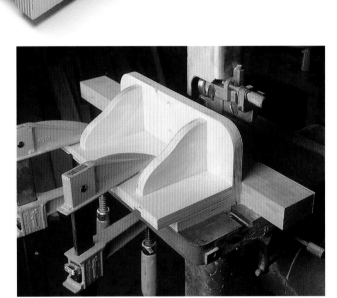

A point fence, like the adjustable shop-made version above, is the key to being able to adjust for blade drift as you resaw. This example fits into the saw table miter slot.

Resawing by the Numbers

Here's a step-by-step primer on resawing:

1. Square up and surface two faces of your lumber. While it's possible to resaw rough-cut lumber, your work will be more accurate and easier to control if you first prepare the stock.

2. Use a point fence. You can easily make or buy one. Many of the larger band saws come standard with a viable point fence.

Handmade Plywood

Creating your own plywood gives you total control of a project's appearance and wood species. The core material on the lid of this display box for example, is actually plywood, but it appears to be a piece of solid wood. The way to accomplish this is to use successive sheets of resawn veneer, sandwiched around the inner plywood core. Then, wrap the edges with hardwood strips of the same wood species. Resawing give you the flexibility of creating custom veneered plywood from any wood species you desire. This capability expands your plywood surface options immensely and allows you to create custom veneers that match the rest of your project perfectly. It's an economical and efficient way to make the most of your lumber and design possibilities.

Baked-in
hardwood
edge

⅛" Plywood core

Resawn and
book-matched
hardwood veneer,
laid up from
successive flitches

By resawing hardwood to create custom plywood, all
the surfaces of this project appear to be made of solid
wood. It's a great illusion and savvy design approach.

3. Set the fence to the thickness of the stock you require. Be sure to accommodate the saw kerf in your planning. For example, it's impossible to get three ¼"-thick pieces of stock from a ¾" piece of wood. The two saw kerfs eat up close to ⅛" of wood.

4. Adjust the saw guide to the width of the board you are resawing.

5. It is a good idea to scribe a line the width of the slice you are removing on the visible edge of the board. This will help you keep the saw blade exactly where you want it during the cut.

6. Use a push stick to finish the cut, in order to keep your fingers clear of the blade.

7. If you are making multiple resaw cuts in a piece of lumber, decide whether you need to run the sawn face of the stock over your jointer or not before beginning the next resaw pass.

8. Use a planer with a slave board to remove the saw cuts from the faces of the resawn slabs. Don't run stock thinner than ¼" through your planer without a slave, or it could get caught in the feed rollers and shatter. Or use a sander to smooth the slab.

When choosing resawing blades, think wide and dentally challenged, as with the wide blade at right. At a minimum, stick with a ½"- or ⅝"-wide, open-toothed blade, (middle). Thin blades (left) are really designed for cutting curves, not resawing.

QuickTip

Sliding Outfeed Supports

A couple dining table slides and rollers are all it takes to make a retractable outfeed platform for your table saw. Simply attach the slides to the bottom of the saw's tabletop and mount the rollers on a board stretched between them. When not in use, the slides can be pushed in and out of the way (right).

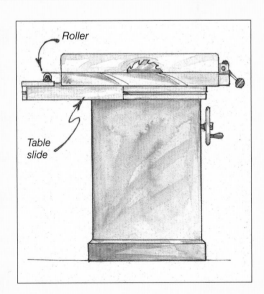

Roller

Table slide

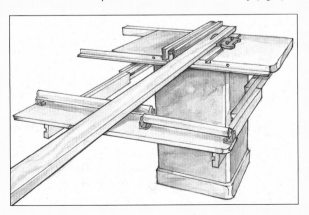

The Secret to Resawing Success

Slicing a board in two through its thickness is one of those nifty ways to create a pleasing book match, get more mileage out of your thick lumber and create perfectly color-matched workpieces. If you have a band saw or both a band saw and table saw, resawing is a cinch. Try it to expand your design and material options.

by Bruce Kieffer

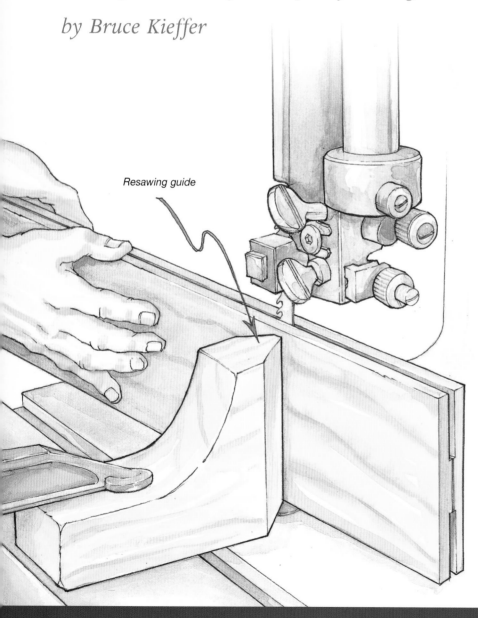

Resawing guide

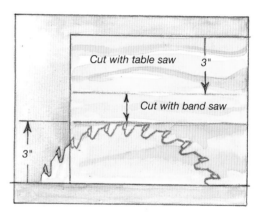

Take advantage of both table and band saw when resawing. Use the table saw to cut away most of the waste and the band saw to finish the cut. The table saw blade kerfs will serve as guides, keeping your band saw cut straight.

Contrary to what some people may believe, resawing will seldom save you money. But there are excellent reasons for resawing: To match wood grain and to match wood color. It's not a complicated procedure, either. In fact, resawing is similar to ripping, but you cut your board to thickness instead of to width.

As with most shop techniques, the pros have developed several different approaches to resawing. Most use a band saw, while some prefer their table saw. But both methods have their limitations. Resawing on a band saw is confined to boards that will fit

Book Match

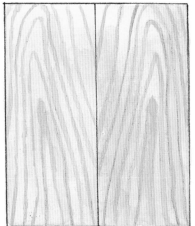

Slip Match

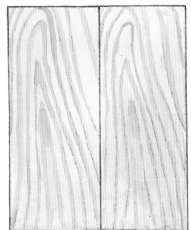

Swing Match

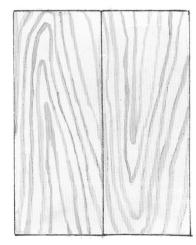

Grain Matching: *In a book match (left), every second leaf is turned over so that the figure always matches perfectly at the joint, like facing pages in a book. In a slip match (center), the leaves are placed side by side, like cards in a game of Solitaire. A swing match (right) takes a slip match one step further by flipping or swinging every second leaf end for end.*

under the blade guide (about 6" on most band saws) and it's difficult to keep the blade straight. Resawing on a table saw is limited to boards twice as wide as the cutting height of the blade (about 3" on most 10" table saws), but you have to make two cuts and settle for a wider kerf.

There's also a way to combine both methods, taking advantage of the strengths of both tools. Using a table saw first, cut part way through both board edges. Then finish the cut on a band saw, guiding the blade through the wide kerfs made on the table saw. It's easier to manage the blade tracking issues on a band saw if you remove most of the waste first.

If you use only your band saw, you'll find it easier to resaw when you use a ½" wide, 3 tooth per inch (tpi), hook tooth blade (see "Blade Basics," page 51). This type of blade makes a rough but straight cut quickly. Start with the presumption that you will have to thickness plane, or at the very least sand, any wood you resaw. Figure you'll lose ¼" for each resaw. In other words, resaw to ½", then plane down to ¼",

easily and efficiently removing all the saw marks.

For optimal cuts, your band saw should be in tiptop shape. So before you start resawing, tune it up according to the owner's manual.

What to Watch Out for

Wide boards that are thinner than ¾" are hard to keep upright when you resaw. To combat this, you can make and use a resawing guide like the one shown on page 48 to support those

*Quick*Tip

Tension Release

Tensioning and releasing the tension from band saw blades is a chore. This simple solution will work on most 14-inch saws. Buy a short length of ⅜-16NC threaded rod and a nut that fits it. Drill and pin the nut onto the tension adjustment rod, or immobilize it there with epoxy. Replace the tension screw on the saw with the threaded rod. Then you can use a regular ⁹⁄₁₆-inch socket driver to adjust the tension.

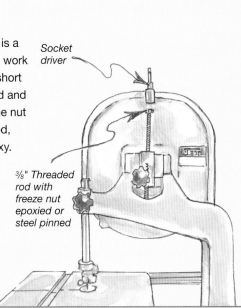

Socket driver

⅜" Threaded rod with freeze nut epoxied or steel pinned

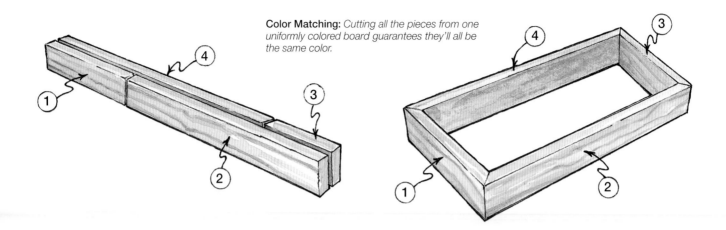

Color Matching: *Cutting all the pieces from one uniformly colored board guarantees they'll all be the same color.*

boards. Another thing to be aware of is that band saw blades tend to wear unevenly on the sides of the teeth. Using an unevenly worn blade will cause the saw cut to wander off center. You know this is happening if you find yourself feeding the board across the saw at an angle in order to follow your cut line. If the wandering seems excessive, it's time to buy a new blade.

One more word of caution: Don't be surprised if you resaw a straight board and the resulting pieces are warped. This is caused by internal stresses that are released when the cut is made. Most of the time the warp is minimal, and generally it can be remedied when you plane to remove the saw marks. Plan for some amount of warping and you won't be disappointed.

*Quick*Tip

Drawing a Smooth Curve

An old band saw blade works wonderfully for drawing smooth curves. Drive nails at key spots along the waste side to guide it along. If you're fresh out of old band saw blades, a stiff piece of electrical wire will also do the trick.

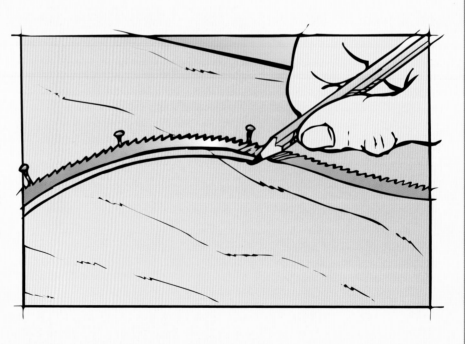

Blade Basics

For woodworking, the three most popular band saw blades are the standard, skip and hook tooth.

Standard tooth blades have the most teeth per inch (tpi). More teeth mean smoother, but slower cuts because the smaller gullets (the spaces between the teeth) can't remove the waste as quickly as other tooth patterns.

Skip tooth blades have half the number of tpi of a standard blade with the same size teeth, and the gullets are twice as wide. You'll make faster cuts, but they'll be rougher.

Hook tooth blades feature evenly spaced teeth that are hooked so they have a more aggressive cutting angle, and the gullets are deeper, too.

A ¼"-wide, 6 tpi, hook tooth blade will suffice for 99% of your band sawing. The narrow width allows you to cut a tight radius while the 6 tpi make relatively smooth cuts. And the hook tooth pattern cuts quickly, which will never be a problem if you sand your band sawn edges to finish them.

For the other one percent, buy a ¼"-wide, 10 tpi, standard tooth blade when you want really smooth cuts, and a ½" wide, 3 tpi, skip tooth blade when resawing boards with just the band saw.

Standard *Skip* *Hook*

Grain Matching

Grain matching adds a lot to the appearance of your finished projects. By splitting the thickness of a board, and then flipping the pieces open like a book, you'll get a grain match called a book match (see Grain Matching, page 49). It's a sure sign of intentional, good design if used prudently.

If you slide the pieces apart instead of flipping them open, and then set them next to each other, you'll get a slip match. And if you flip one piece end to end, and set it next to the other piece, you'll get a swing match. Each type of grain match pattern can be useful, depending on the look you want.

Color Matching

Resawing is a good way to get a color match for things like face frames and tabletop edging. It's hard to color match wood that comes from different boards even though they're the same species. But if you resaw thicker boards, (see Color Matching on page 50) you'll at least double the amount of color match you can get from one piece of perfectly color-matched wood.

Will Resawing Save You Money?

Resawing probably won't save you money. You might spend less money today, but not over the long run. If you use your leftovers now, you'll have to buy more wood for your future projects. Before you go to the lumberyard and

buy what you need for your next project, check to see what boards you have on your lumber rack. If you have thick pieces that you're willing to turn into thin pieces, resaw them to get the thinner pieces you need.

Most of the time, resawing actually costs you more money. Thicker lumber costs more per board foot than thinner lumber. If you took an 8/4 board and resawed it to get two ¾" pieces, they'd cost more than if you just planed down two 4/4 boards. That's because the lumber yield goes down for manufacturers by cutting lumber thicker than usual. Grain and color matching are well worth the added cost, but be sensible when you consider resawing your more valuable thicker boards for the sole purpose of making a greater quantity of thinner boards.

Four Methods of Casework Joinery

Once you eliminate the frills from a complicated casework project, building it becomes a simple matter of constructing a series of boxes. We asked expert woodworker and instructor Lonnie Bird to walk us through the usual options and theories behind casework construction, and here's what he has to say.

by Lonnie Bird

Have you ever wanted to build a chest of drawers or dressing table but just weren't sure how to begin? Perhaps you saw a photo of a china cabinet in a magazine and you wanted to reproduce it but felt it was beyond your reach. Although large-scale casework projects can seem somewhat intimidating, building them is really nothing more than constructing boxes. Once you gain an understanding of the methods involved, construction becomes much easier.

Drawers, which are also boxes, are fit within the casework and slide on wooden rails or runners. Doors are often added as well to keep the contents of the chest hidden from view, although sometimes doors have glass panes, or "lights," specifically for displaying the contents of the case.

The challenge when constructing any casework is to keep it square. As you can imagine, it's much easier to fit doors, drawers, and molding to a box with 90° corners than to a trapezoid or a parallelogram. But that becomes easy, too, once you realize that parallel sides of the box must be exactly the same length.

Understanding Methodology

Over the centuries, cabinetmakers have developed a number of ways to construct casework, and each method has its own advantages. By understanding the various methods of construction, you can design your own casework to suit your needs. Once you've constructed the case or box, you can add feet, moldings, doors, and other details to give your design distinction.

For the purpose of discussion, I've divided casework into four separate categories: frame-and-panel, post-and-rail, box construction and face frame. Although these categories work well for getting a grasp on case construction, cabinetmaking is too diverse to always fit neatly into categories. Sometimes you'll find it necessary to combine construction techniques from two or more types.

Frame-and-Panel

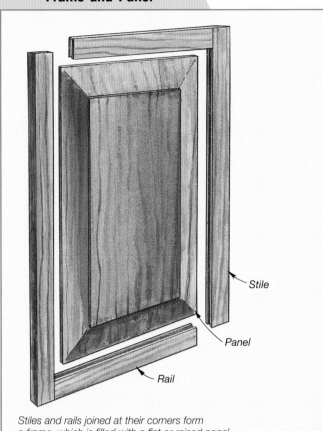

Stile

Panel

Rail

*Stiles and rails joined at their corners form
a frame, which is filled with a flat or raised panel.*

Frame-and-Panel

Frame-and-panel casework is simply a
series of wood panels surrounded by
a stile and rail framework. The paneled
framework is joined at the corners to
create a box. Probably the most familiar
example of this timeless design is the
rolltop desk. Mass-produced in large
numbers around 100 years ago, the
rolltop desk was once a common sight
in America's offices. These massive oak
desks featured a large, spacious writing
surface supported by a pair of chest of
drawers. The space between the chests
provided a knee-hole. A frame-and-
panel assembly covered the knee hole
at the back of the desk to provide
a finished appearance.

Positioned on top of the writing
surface was another paneled
framework, which housed a series of

small drawers, pigeonholes, and other storage areas. The inside edges of the framework were grooved to provide a track for the canvas-backed tambour, which rolled down to secure and hide the contents. Although the rolltop desk is an elaborate example of casework, not all frame-and-panel casework is that complex. In fact, it can be as simple as a storage chest with a hinged lid.

Construction: Successful frame-and-panel casework begins with well proportioned panels. Rectangular panels look best; panels that are square (or close to square) tend to look boxy and somewhat clumsy. To proportion panels for a pleasing effect, I use simple mathematical systems. Ratios of small whole numbers and numbers derived from the Fibonacci series (see box on page 55) have universal appeal.

The proportion reflected in this sequence is akin to the Golden Rectangle. First discovered by the Ancient Greeks, the Golden Rectangle has been used to develop proportions for everything from architecture to credit cards. The ratio, 1 to 1.618, is also a foolproof method for sizing panels in frame-and-panel casework.

The framework surrounding the panels is typically assembled with mortise and tenon joints. The inside edges of the frame members can be left square or "stuck" with a simple molding profile that is mitered or coped at the corners. The panels can be raised or beveled along the edges or simply left flat.

Once assembled, four sub-assemblies of framework are joined at the corners to create a box. Although a simple butt joint has sufficient strength, adding a tongue and groove joint at the corners helps with alignment during assembly and glue-up. The assembled box is usually supported by bracket feet or some other type of short base to lift the box off of the floor. After assembly of the casework, doors, drawers, and lids are added for detail.

Post-and-Rail

Another time-tested method of case construction is known as post-and-rail—sometimes referred to as leg-and-rail. Post-and-rail construction is a good choice when the case is positioned high off the floor. Dressing tables, tall chests and sideboards are just a few examples of furniture that use this type of construction. The posts are used as legs to elevate the case and are usually embellished to eliminate the plain, square look; a tapered leg is a simple, yet elegant option. Other versions include turning or compound curves such as cabriole legs.

Construction: Typically with post-and-rail, a set of matching posts are joined with wide boards to create a box. This construction method is very similar to the methods used to join tables and beds. The posts are mortised to accept tenons, which are cut on the ends of the case sides. Often, four posts are used,

Post-and-rail is the best case construction method when your case is going to be elevated off the floor. The posts serve as legs and are typically tapered, turned or carved, as in the example shown here, to embellish the overall appearance.

but if the case is very wide, as with a sideboard, additional pairs of legs may be added for more support. At the case front, a framework of rectangular openings is created to allow the fitting and installation of doors and drawers. The top rail of the framework is usually turned on edge to create a broad surface for dovetail joinery. A single, wide dovetail is sawn on the end of the top rail. This fits into a corresponding dovetailed socket on top of the leg post. Lower rails are joined to the legs with double tenons. Doubling the tenons creates twice the surface area for glue and significantly adds to the strength and rigidity of the case. Vertical frame members—stiles—are either dovetailed or tenoned into the horizontal rails. The back of a typical case is also a thick, wide board, or several boards glued together with several tenons cut on the ends that fit within mortises in the legs. Dividing the wide joint into a series of smaller ones strengthens the leg mortises and helps avoid splitting of the case sides during seasonal changes in humidity.

The Box Method

The box method is the technique that you probably used the first time you built a small cabinet, tool chest or jewelry box. As the name implies, four planks are simply joined at the corners to create a box. It's undoubtedly the least complicated method—and one of the most widely used. Because of its flexibility, the box method can be used for a variety of designs and furniture styles. The completed case could rest low to the floor on bracket feet or be positioned at eye level on a post-and-rail base.

Although the basic design of this construction method is quite simple, it functions well within complex furniture designs. The slant front desk, for example, has an upper corner cut at an angle that supports a hinged lid. The lid folds down to form a writing surface and expose an elaborate arrangement of pigeonholes, drawers, doors, and hidden compartments. The entire assembly rests on bracket feet that lift it a few inches off of the floor and raise the writing surface to a comfortable height for working.

Right-sized Rectangles

The Fibonacci Series is figured by adding the successive number to the number that precedes it. The successive terms are 1, 1, 2, 3, 5, 8, 13, 21 and so on.

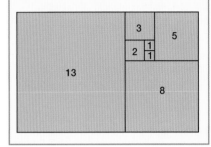

Construction: Construction of the box method can be as simple as butt joints and nails—or as complex as half-blind dovetails. When deciding which joint to use at the corners, I consider the material, the overall size of the box and how it will be used. I'll often fasten the corners of diminutive boxes with glue and nails. Afterward, I'll cover the entire box with a figured veneer to decorate the box and hide the simple construction.

I always construct large furniture casework with dovetails. Even though the joint is often hidden by molding, the strength is unmatched and ensures the

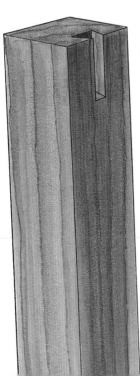

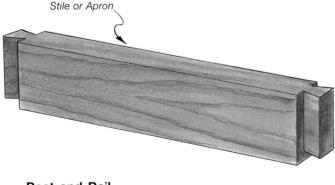

Stile or Apron

Post

Post-and-Rail
When you start thinking of furniture in terms of its most basic forms, even complex pieces become easier to understand.

Adding a face frame to a box stiffens it and creates resistance to racking. It's a good option for casework with doors, as it frames the doors visually. The stiles provide a place to mount the hinges.

longevity of the piece. Splined miters are also a good choice for small, decorative boxes which won't be subjected to a great deal of stress. An added advantage with miters is they allow the wood grain to flow in a continuous pattern around all four sides of the box.

If the case is to have drawers, the dividers and partitions can easily be joined with a sliding dovetail that fits snugly within a mating socket in the case side. Drawer runners are typically joined with mortises and tenons to the front and back dividers, creating a strong, rigid framework for drawer support.

Backs on these cases are let in to a rabbet, which is cut along the back, inside edges of the box. The back is usually made up of a series of random width boards that are nailed to the rabbet in the case. The edges of the backboards are also rabbeted to allow each board to overlap the next. A quirk bead may also be shaped along the edges to dress up the backboards and hide the seasonal wood movement that occurs between them.

The finest casework of this type sometimes has a frame-and-panel back. Although considerably more work, the rigid framework adds both strength and stiffness to the case and the frame-and-panel design provides a more finished appearance, especially if the casework will be viewed from all sides instead of just the front.

Adding a Face Frame

Still another method of casework construction is to attach a face frame to the box in the previous example. Our old friends, stiles and rails, return to create the face frame. The assembled frame is then glued (and occasionally nailed as well) to the front edges of the box.

Adding a face frame to a box gives the box greater stiffness and resistance to racking. It's also a good option for casework with doors. The face frame "frames" the doors visually, and the stiles provide a place to mount hinges. The top rail of the face frame often is sized wider than the stiles and bottom rail to provide an area for application of a crown molding.

A Few Embellishments

Once you've settled on a method of case construction, you can choose to dress it up or dress it down. Plain furniture styles, such as Shaker and Arts & Crafts, use simple lines, such as straight or tapered legs, subtle curves and sparse moldings. In contrast, period furniture styles use compound curves, elaborate gooseneck moldings, and perhaps some carving.

Other Casework Variations

Some forms of casework don't seem to fit into any particular category. For example, corner cabinets don't really have sides; they're simply a face frame with canted corners. The back edges of the corner are rabbeted to accept the backboards.

Most examples of tall furniture casework are built in several sections. For example, a period tall chest has a post-and-rail lower case that supports a dovetailed box upper case. This design combines the best of both casework methods: the lower case is visually lifted from the floor and supported by cabriole legs and the box construction of the upper case is straightforward in

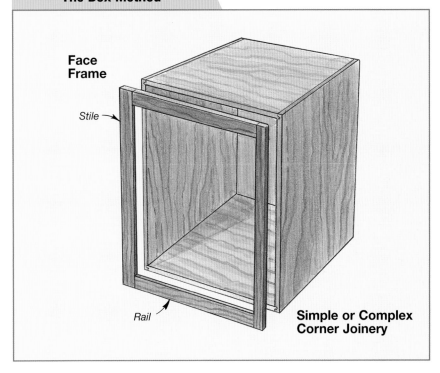

The Box Method

Face Frame

Stile →

Rail

Simple or Complex Corner Joinery

construction and is easily fitted with partitions, dividers and drawers.

Still another unusual example is the tall case clock, sometimes referred to as a grandfather clock. Its tall, elongated case is really three separate boxes stacked upon one another. The base and middle section, or waist, are simple face frame boxes. In contrast the hood, which frames the dial and houses the works, is an elaborate mix of construction methods.

QuickTip

Choosing Configurations and Styles of Machine Casters

If you're considering mounting casters under a machine, the ideal setup is to have two fixed casters at one end and two swivel casters at the other. That way, you can steer in much the same fashion as an automobile does. All four wheels should have locks, so the machine can be immobilized during use. They should also be sized correctly: casters are rated as to the weight they can carry, so four 30 lb. casters can, in combination, tote a total of 120 lbs. Err on the side of caution and use heavier casters than you really need.

The Versatile Dowel Joint

When choosing joinery for your next project, don't overlook the humble dowel joint. Here are some tried-and-true tips to ensure your success.

by Jeff Greef

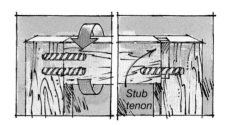

Figure 2: *Wood tends to twist, and the only way to resist this force in a frame joint is by using at least two dowels or a tenon and a dowel.*

Every time we begin a new project, we all face some tough decisions, not the least of which is choosing the best type of joinery. Depending on the application, not every joint has to be complex. One of the simpler options you may not employ enough in your woodworking is the dowel joint. In some situations, it's the perfect choice.

Doweling has been a standard technique in the furnituremaking trades from the time that accurate boring tools first became available. The advent of drill bits and drill presses made dowels an efficient and economical alternative to other interlocking joint styles.

Dowels do offer speed, ease of installation and versatility, but often at a price when it comes to strength.

But in many applications, dowels are strong enough. Remember, most of our projects don't have to support a loaded dump truck for the next twenty years.

Where Are They Used?

Dowels excel at aligning edge to edge joints in solid-wood panels. While there are no limitations on the use of dowels for this purpose, it pays to keep a few technical details in mind. In edge to edge joints, dowels cross the grain of the lumber and can, if glued in, restrict

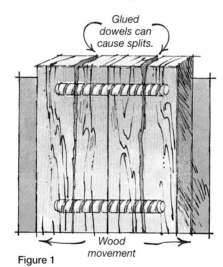

Glued dowels can cause splits.

Figure 1

Wood movement

the natural movement of the wood (see Figure 1). Since a well jointed and glued edge is plenty strong on its own and gains little strength from the addition of dowels, use them for alignment purposes only. And in anticipation of wood movement, never glue the dowels in the holes. Incidentally, dowels are just as useful for aligning edge to edge joints with man-made materials like plywood and particleboard.

In frame construction, the width of the rails can determine the effectiveness of a dowel joint. Generally speaking, any frame joint requires at least two dowels to resist the rotational force that can ruin an assembly (see Figure 2). If the frame is made up of narrow stock, there may not be enough room for two dowels, in which case a mortise and tenon joint makes a better choice.

In a few instances a single dowel is sufficient, but the joint must utilize some other means of resistance against rotational force. In a door frame, for example, a stub tenon keeps the pieces from twisting while the addition of a dowel increases the gluing area and improves the strength of the joint (see Figure 2). Windsor chairs, which gain their stability from having a large number of single dowel joints, provide another example.

It's easy to overlook another obvious benefit of dowel joinery: appearance. On many projects it's preferable that the joinery remain hidden, and dowels make this easy to accomplish.

Dowels are ideal for light-duty carcase joinery.

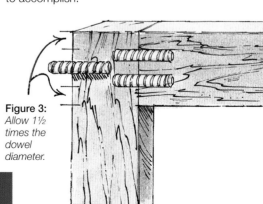

Figure 3: *Allow 1½ times the dowel diameter.*

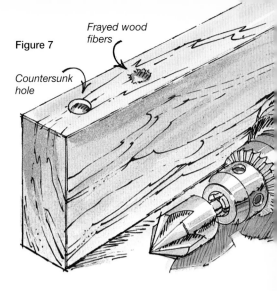

Figure 7

Frayed wood fibers

Countersunk hole

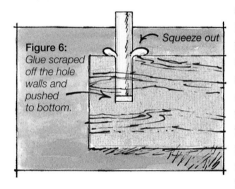

Figure 4:
A properly sized dowel leaves plenty of stock around the hole.

More on Joint Mechanics

The spacing, size and number of dowels in a joint is critical to its final strength. Dowels situated too close to an edge or to each other are more likely to cause a split in the surrounding wood. Allow a minimum space of one dowel diameter between the edge or end of a board and the first dowel hole (see Figure 3). Better yet, if you have the room, leave twice the diameter. This rule of thumb also applies to the spacing between dowels. If you expect a joint to withstand lots of stress, fit as many dowels as you can within these spacing guidelines.

The size of the dowels used in a joint will help determine just how much weight or force the joint can withstand. Both the gluing area and the dowel strength increase with the dowel diameter, but as the dowel holes get larger they may come too close to the edge of the lumber. In edge to edge

joints, ¼" diameter dowels work fine because you won't really need them to bear any of the load. In frame and miter joints made of ¾"-thick stock, ⅜" dowels provide the most strength and gluing area you can get without sacrificing too much material in the lumber (see Figure 4).

The fit of a dowel in a hole is critical to the success of any dowel joint. Since most wood glues require lots of wood to wood contact, a loose-fitting dowel will have a greater risk of failure. On the other hand, holes that are too small lead to increased pressure on the wood as the dowel is driven in, making a split much more likely.

Prior to boring dowel holes in your projects, always drill test holes in a scrap piece. This way you can switch

Figure 6:
Glue scraped off the hole walls and pushed to bottom.

Squeeze out

drill bits or alter your dowels to ensure a perfect fit. You'll find that the best joinery dowels are readymade pins that are cut to length and feature spiral or straight flutes along their sides (see Figure 5). Long dowel rods may be cheaper, but their diameters are less consistent than you'll find with dowel pins, the savings are really very minimal and you give up a lot of convenience.

Fluting serves two purposes. First, flutes allow air and glue trapped in the hole to escape as a dowel is driven in. This relieves the pressure that builds up in the holes. Second, fluting helps keep glue on the hole walls and dowel pins for better adhesion. Unfluted dowels tend to scrape the glue off the walls and force it to the bottom of the hole (see

Figure 6). This makes driving in the dowel very difficult and can lead to a split in the wood as hydraulic pressure builds up. Even if you're able to seat the dowel in the hole, the result is often a glue starved joint. In a frame and panel, this means the joint may never hold together.

In addition to the doweling tips already mentioned, follow two more little steps to ensure success with your joints. To guarantee that the joint members make full contact along the seam, countersink the dowel holes slightly (see Figure 7). This prevents any fibers raised during the drilling process from jamming between the boards and provides a reservoir for excess glue that might otherwise interfere with the fit of the joint. Second, drill all your dowel holes about ¹⁄₁₆" deeper than needed. Holes drilled just deep enough for the dowels leave nowhere for excess glue to go, often leading to a split in the wood. In addition, if your dowels are a hair longer than expected, they can prevent your joint members from closing properly.

Once you get around to assembling the joints, be sure to apply glue to both the dowels and the holes. For thorough glue coverage, use a smaller dowel or toothpick to spread glue on the walls of the holes, and use a small brush for coating the dowels. Both yellow and white glues work well. Remember, good wood-to-wood contact and thorough glue coverage are two keys to all successful joinery.

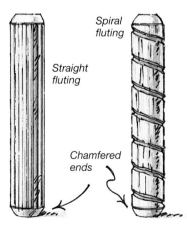

Spiral fluting

Straight fluting

Chamfered ends

Figure 5: *Chamfered ends and flutes make dowel pins easy to drive in and help keep glue on the walls of the holes.*

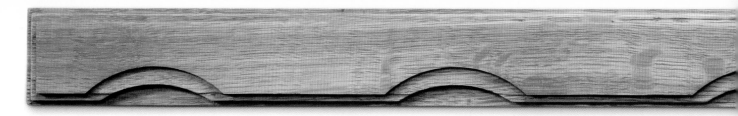

Biscuit Joiners

They're not just for face frames anymore …

by Rob Johnstone

Figure 2: *When biscuits become wet with glue, they expand in their slots. This increases the glue joint area and creates a bit more of a "grab" on the mortise walls. Close tolerances make for better glue joints.*

As creatures of habit, we tend to categorize tasks and even tools into comfortable little niches. When most of us think of biscuit joints, they are often considered for their ability to join end grain to edge grain, as when forming face frames; or aligning long butt joints, as when gluing up panels. But biscuits and the biscuit joiners that cut their slots are much more versatile than those obvious bread-and-butter uses. For example, with the use of specialty biscuits, you can form very handy knockdown joints. And speaking of specialty biscuits (see Figure 1), there are biscuits that hold edges together without the benefit of clamps, transparent biscuits for solid surface work and even hinges that can be mounted in surface mortises shaped by your biscuit joiner. That's versatility.

How They Work

Biscuits are compressed wooden wafers (there are wood fiber biscuits, too) that come in different specific sizes. When they are inserted into their mortise and come in contact with glue, the wafers expand (Figure 2), filling the mortise and even "grabbing" the mortise walls to a degree with their expansion pressure. As you would expect, the closer the tolerances, the tighter the fit, and the better this joinery system works.

The advantages of this joinery approach are obvious. Setup is quick (Figure 3): biscuits are much easier to align than dowels and much quicker than chopping and cutting traditional mortise and tenon joints. And, while the strength of a mortise and tenon cannot be beat, often, biscuit joints are more than sufficiently strong to do the job. In Figure 4, shelf locations are created when their biscuit mortises are cut. This is a perfect example of the fast setup and sound joinery of the biscuit system.

No-clamp biscuits

Solid surface biscuits

Knockdown biscuits

Biscuit hinges

Figure 1: *Specialty biscuits are versatile.*

Figure 3: *Here's a trick that will provide accurate setup and save you time. Create an assembly of setup blocks (photo below). For each common thickness of stock that you work with, make a block with a biscuit slot perfectly located for various joints. Use these blocks to set your joiner in a jiffy (below left).*

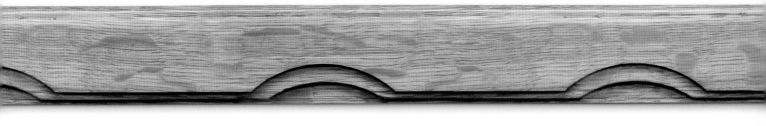

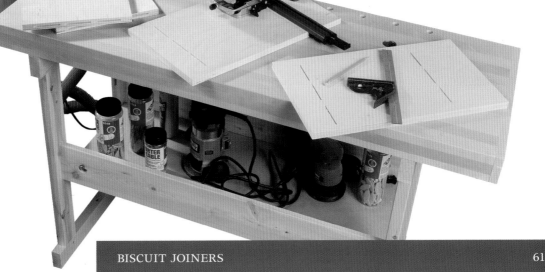

Figure 5: *Biscuits come in several sizes to accommodate different sized stock and joints. The #20 biscuit above is fine for the 3½" wide toe-kick, but the #10 is correctly sized for the 1¾" mitered picture frame.*

Toe-kick with vertical miter

Picture frame with horizontal miter

#20 Biscuit

#0 Biscuit

#10 Biscuit

FF Biscuit

To increase the strength of a biscuit joint, there are a couple of easily employed tricks. Most common is the double biscuit joint, where you offset two separate biscuit mortises and use a biscuit in each slot. Create a variation of that joint by forming a double-wide single mortise on each face of the joint. Then put two well-glued biscuits into the mortise and proceed as normal. The biscuit swelling will increase by a factor of two, and the biscuits will also bond together to form a moon-shaped loose tenon.

Miters and Square Corners

One joint that the biscuit excels at is the miter joint (see Figure 5). In vertical miters, biscuits replace a traditional spline with the added advantage that they can be completely hidden within the miter joint. With very small biscuits (size FF, for example) picture frames (an example of a horizontal miter) are easily fabricated, and their miters are considerably stronger than traditional end grain to end grain glue-ups could ever hope to be.

With that said, care must be taken to select the proper size biscuit for the job. In some tasks, such as a mitered toe-kick, if the biscuit mortise was exposed on either edge of the assembly, there would be no big problem. This is not true of a picture frame. For that reason, it is always a good idea to check your setup with scrap lumber. On vertical miters, the mortise should be located very close to the inside edge of the miter ... this allows significantly more depth in the cut before you break out of the opposite face of your material.

Figure 4: *Locate and form shelf joints for a simple shelved casework project. Use a clamped-on straightedge to guide the biscuit joiner.*

Miters: Horizontal and Vertical

Clamp your vertical miter stock back-to-back, and you won't need to set your joiner fence at 45°. Set the biscuit slot close to the inside edge of the miter to avoid cutting through the opposite face.

Biscuits must be wholly captured within their face and are best located in the center of a horizontal miter joint. Biscuits add considerable strength to these traditionally flimsy miter joints.

Figure 6: On stock narrower than ¾", you may need to adjust placement of the biscuit slot with a spacer or jig. Biscuits used in this type of joinery add control during glue-up in addition to the strength of the joint.

Joining 90° corners in casework, especially when using manufactured sheet goods, or even with small boxes, is another arrow in the biscuit joiner's quiver. As shown in Figure 6, a 90° jig can be a very useful adjunct for this technique, adding a level of stock control without the need for clamping.

Aligning Long Butt Joints

While there remains controversy in regards to whether biscuits add strength to a long butt joint in solid material, there is no argument about the help they provide in aligning the joint. An area where biscuits do absolutely add strength to this sort of joint is where you are gluing plywood to solid wood. In this case, the benefit is clear. On these long joints, use the largest biscuit size you have. Another tip: If you are joining MDF in this manner, whether solid wood to MDF or MDF to itself, the new fiber biscuits are your best bet to prevent the shape of the biscuit from telegraphing through the material as they expand.

Fancy Tricks

For 99% of its life, a biscuit joiner will simply do its designed task of cutting mortises for biscuit joints. But even this plain-Jane tool can shine with a bit of creativity. For example, the Eastlake style molding running across the top of these pages was made using only a biscuit joiner and a table saw. I laid out the spacing for the

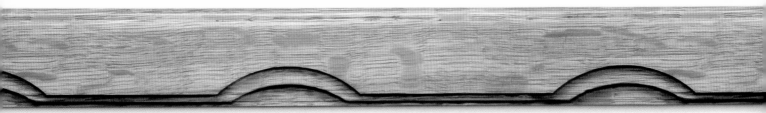

half-ellipse patterns and then began milling the largest half-moon shape (at the maximum cut setting) into the surface of the stock — in this case, white oak. Next, on exactly the same marks, I cut the second half oval at the #10 setting a full blade thickness deeper. I followed up on the table saw, cutting successive rabbets on all four edges of the stock to the depth of each half oval. A bit of sanding and a classic molding is created using a biscuit joiner.

Figure 7: *Using biscuits to align a long glue joint is a common and useful technique. This is especially true if you are joining solid wood to plywood or MDF.*

Make this Eastlake Molding

After preparing ½" thick by 2" wide stock, the author laid out the half-moon pattern on the face of the molding with simple cross marks. With the joiner set at its widest cut, half ovals were cut at each cross mark down the length of the molding.

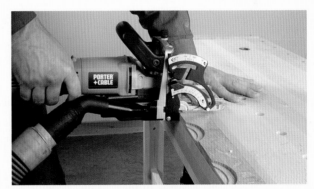

Use the same cross marks to register the second half-moon detail. Now the joiner is set to cut #10 biscuits, and the depth of cut is a full blade thickness deeper. Hold the joiner firmly in place during the cut.

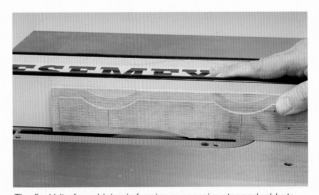

The final bit of machining is forming successive stepped rabbets around the molding. The rabbets are cut to match the depth of each half oval detail. It all comes together to create the lovely design running across the top of this article.

Two Fast and Easy Biscuit Joints

Get more mileage out of your biscuit joiner by adding offset and T-joint options to your joinery repertoire.

by Bruce Kieffer

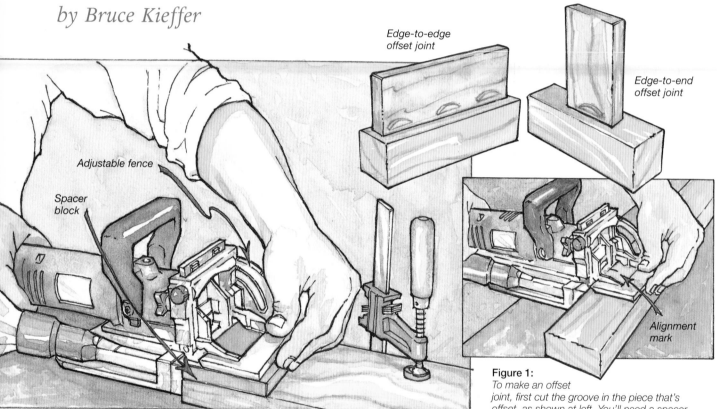

Edge-to-edge offset joint

Edge-to-end offset joint

Adjustable fence

Spacer block

Alignment mark

Figure 1:
To make an offset joint, first cut the groove in the piece that's offset, as shown at left. You'll need a spacer block to raise the joiner fence a distance equal to the offset. Then, without changing your settings, remove the spacer block and cut the groove in the non-offset piece, as shown above. With this technique, you can make both edge-to-edge and edge-to-end offset joints as shown at top.

Anyone who owns a biscuit joiner is familiar with standard edge-to-edge joints. However, if you'd like to add another dimension to your biscuit joinery, offset and T-joints are two more good candidates. Neither joint is hard to cut; they just require a little more setup than edge-to-edge joints.

Offset joints are used to assemble two pieces of wood in the same plane, just like edge-to-edge joints, but in this case the two workpieces are not flush with each other. One piece is aligned a predetermined distance above or below the other piece. Offset joints are handy for making slatted outdoor furniture, Craftsman designs or whenever you want to create a shadowline between table legs and aprons.

Using a biscuit to assemble an offset joint is faster and more accurate than using dowel pins. The only limitation is that the workpiece has to be at least 2¼" wide (to fit a No. 0 biscuit). Offset biscuit joints can be made on both edge-to-end as well as edge-to-edge joints, as you can see in the offset joint illustrations above.

T-joints, on the other hand, are most often used to assemble stationary interior shelves in cabinetry. Biscuited T-joints (see T-joint illustrations on the next page) are much faster than cutting dadoes, and when you're trying to calculate the length of the shelf, you no longer have to compensate for the depth of the dadoes. Instead, the length

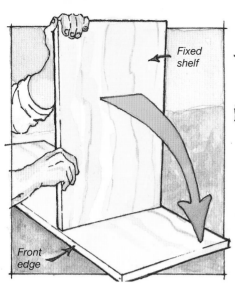
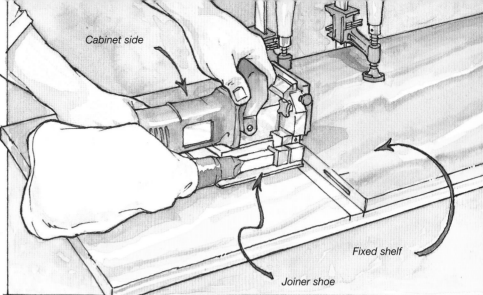

Figure 2: *The first step to making a T-joint is to set the shelf upright as shown here so the top, bottom, front and back are all oriented correctly. Now lay it down on the cabinet side as if it were hinged.*

Figure 3: *Once your orientation is correct, align the front edges of the shelf and cabinet side. Now clamp the pieces together and, with the adjustable fence removed or tilted away, cut the grooves in the end of the shelf.*

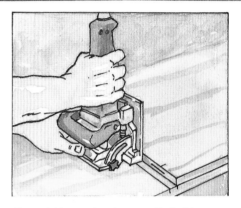

Figure 4: *To complete the second half of the T-joint, hold the biscuit joiner upright and press the shoe tight against the end of the shelf. Now plunge the joiner down to cut the grooves in the cabinet side.*

of the shelf is just the inside dimension of the cabinet. This makes cutting the cabinet parts less confusing.

Another important benefit is the fact that a biscuited T-joint has more tensile strength than a standard butt joint. This means it is more resistant to being pulled apart. The tradeoff is that it has less sheer strength than a dado joint, so the shelf can't bear as much weight.

How to Make Biscuited Offset Joints

The first step in making these joints is determining the offset distance between the two faces. Using 3/8" as an example, cut a spacer block from scrap wood 3/8" thick and slightly longer and wider than the biscuit joiner's adjustable fence. Mark the groove registration lines (the ones used to align the biscuit joiner) on the faces and edges of the pieces being assembled. Then set the spacer block on top of the piece that will be offset and set the biscuit joiner fence on top of the spacer block. Adjust the fence so the groove will be cut in the center of the offset piece (see Figure 1). Tighten the fence and cut the groove.

Now, without readjusting the height of the biscuit joiner fence, set it on the other piece (without the spacer block) and cut that groove (see Figure 1).

Assemble the two pieces and you'll see that they are offset exactly 3/8" from each other. Remember, the key to making these biscuited offset joints is using a spacer block as thick as the offset.

How to Make Biscuited T-Joints

To illustrate this joint, use a stationary cabinet shelf as an example. First, lay out and mark where the shelf meets the cabinet side. Then set the shelf upright and align it within the drawn lines so the top, bottom, front and back are all oriented correctly (see Figure 2).

Now lay the shelf down on its side just as if it were on a hinge. Make sure the end of the shelf is lined up with the marks you drew on the side, then align the front edges of both the shelf and the side. Clamp these two pieces together.

On the top end of the shelf, mark registration lines at 4" to 6" intervals. Use these marks to align the biscuit joiner and cut the grooves, starting with those in the end of the shelf. To do so, simply remove the adjustable fence from the front of your biscuit joiner, (or tilt it all the way up, if that's how your's works).

Now set the bottom of the biscuit joiner—the shoe—on the cabinet side, snug in the 90-degree corner created by the end of the shelf and the inside of the side. Align the center mark on the

biscuit joiner with the registration marks on the shelf, then cut the grooves in the end of the shelf (see Figure 3). Now you can cut the grooves in the cabinet side, leaving the pieces clamped exactly as they are. Set the biscuit joiner's shoe upright and against the end of the side, again snug in the corner. Align the center mark on the bottom of the shoe with the marks on the shelf, hold the shoe tight to the end of the shelf, and cut the grooves in the cabinet side, as shown in Figure 4, above.

With a little practice, you'll wonder how you ever got along without these two joints. In fact, your old doweling jig may start to get pretty lonely. One last hint: Save your spacer blocks as you make various sized offset joints. A collection in 1/8"-thick increments makes joint setups quick and easy.

Moving Beyond Dowels and Biscuits

Wood joints need to be engineered strongly enough to hold two workpieces together for a long time—hopefully forever. Once you've got this base covered, joints also serve an important aesthetic function, adding complexity and elegance to your designs. Practice making these advanced joints to expand your joinery repertoire.

by Hugh Foster

Once students in cabinetmaking school have mastered the various versions of the basic butt joint, they are often required to perform an exercise in more advanced joinery. Using pairs of hardwood cutoffs, they repeatedly construct a wide variety of common joints until they reach perfection (or at least the instructor's view of it). Then the joint goes home with them to their own shop, where it becomes a useful

working model (and sometimes a reminder of their humble beginnings).

This exercise in jointmaking isn't a bad idea for all of us to try, even for those of us who didn't learn our craft in the classroom. A good place to start is with the simple lap joint. Once you've mastered that one, you can move on to the dovetail lap (which naturally leads to more demanding joints like the sliding dovetail). This mechanical joint opens

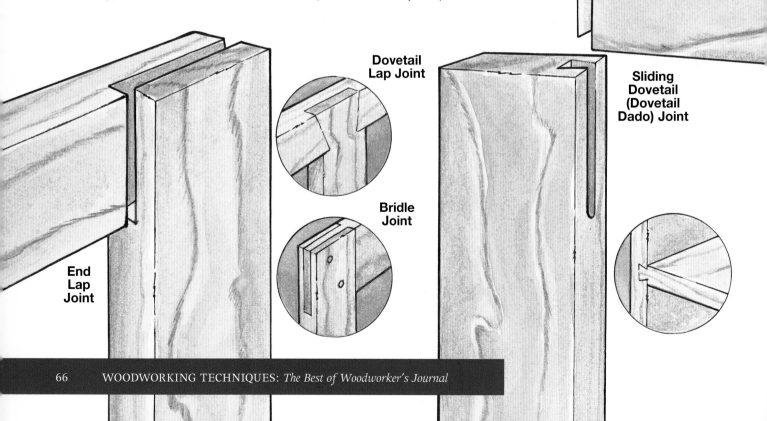

End Lap Joint

Dovetail Lap Joint

Bridle Joint

Sliding Dovetail (Dovetail Dado) Joint

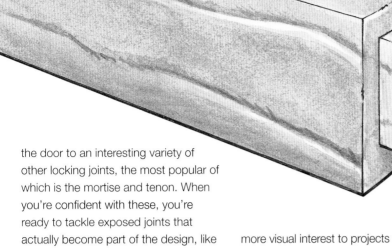

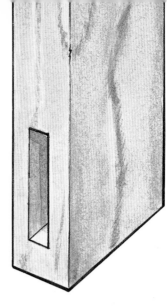

Mortise and Tenon Joint

the door to an interesting variety of other locking joints, the most popular of which is the mortise and tenon. When you're confident with these, you're ready to tackle exposed joints that actually become part of the design, like the through wedged tenon. But we're getting ahead of ourselves here, so lets get back to that basic lap joint.

Making Lap Joints

There are many varieties of lap joints, but all are characterized by the fact that one member laps over the other. This usually happens in such a way that the pieces end up flush when assembled. End lap joints are made by cutting rabbets at the ends of two pieces, then joining them at right angles (see previous page). With just a bit of extra effort, these can be cut as dovetail laps which tend to lend

more visual interest to projects than the standard square lap.

A bridle joint results when you cut two lap joints in opposite faces of the workpiece. Bridle joints are stronger than doweled or even mortised joints because of their larger gluing area. They are also referred to as open mortises. Inserting pins across the glued joint creates a mechanical connection for greater strength. Years ago, pin holes were made slightly offset so the dowels drew the joint tight when driven home. Given the strength of modern glues these days, pins in lap joints serve more of a cosmetic than functional purpose.

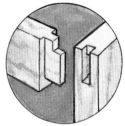

Haunched Tenon Joint

Wedged Tenon Joint

QuickTip

Straightening Twisted Lumber

Rough lumber with a diagonal twist can be difficult to straighten, unless you use this trick. Joint the edges of the board and set it on a flat surface. Shim the two high corners, then rip two guide rails from scrap stock: their height should be the same as the highest spot on the shimmed board, and they should be cut from straight hardwood. Finish nail these in place, keeping the nails as close to the center of the guide rails as possible, so they never come in contact with the planer knives. Then run the assembly through the planer (or a wide belt sander equipped with a coarse grit belt), alternating the sides: the top should be up on the first pass, down on the second, and so on, until the board is flat. The guide rails will keep the board perfectly aligned.

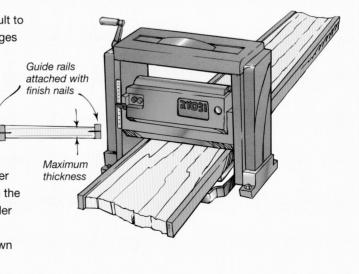

Guide rails attached with finish nails

Maximum thickness

In this unique mechanical joint, two small wedges are inserted in tenon slots before the joint is assembled. As the joint is drawn together they contact the back of the mortise and spread the tenon. To accommodate this locking action, first pare back the side walls of the mortise with a sharp chisel.

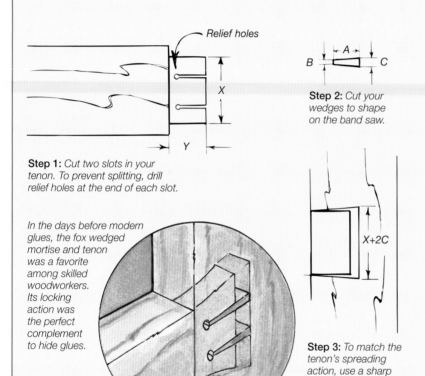

Step 1: Cut two slots in your tenon. To prevent splitting, drill relief holes at the end of each slot.

Step 2: Cut your wedges to shape on the band saw.

Step 3: To match the tenon's spreading action, use a sharp chisel to reshape the mortise into a wedge.

In the days before modern glues, the fox wedged mortise and tenon was a favorite among skilled woodworkers. Its locking action was the perfect complement to hide glues.

the end of the dovetail. You should be able to install all but the last inch or two of the tailpiece without resorting to a mallet.

Milling Mortise and Tenon Joints

In their various forms, mortise and tenon joints range from simple to very complex. They can be cut with hand tools, a mortising machine, table saw or a router, and tenons may have square or round edges. When you need extra strength, increase the gluing surface by adding haunches, or by doubling up and using two mortises and a pair of matching tenons.

Cutting a mortise looks harder than it really is. You can use a pair of guides that run against the faces of the workpiece to automatically center a router bit on an edge. Mortises can also be drilled to depth and cleaned out with a chisel or milled with a mortising jig on a drill press. The matching tenons are typically cut on the table saw, using a zero-clearance insert to stop thin stock from falling through. The workpiece can be machined vertically with the help of a tenoning jig, or held against the saw's fence on each pass, depending on its size. You can also mill the tenon face-down on the saw table backed up with your saw's miter gauge.

The time-honored method for making mortise and tenon joints is to start with the mortise, which usually is cut to a fixed width based on your router bit or drill bit's diameter. Once the mortise is completed, cut the tenon to fit it.

Mortise and tenon joints are especially attractive when the tenon's end grain shows through the open mortise. Just be sure to cut your tenons $\frac{1}{16}$" longer than the mortised piece and sand them flush after assembly. You can

Building Sliding Dovetails

Sliding dovetails (see page 66) are often referred to as dovetail dadoes. Unlike run-of-the-mill dadoes, they're usually pretty enough to leave exposed. To make this dado, remove most of the stock with a straight bit, then finish up with your dovetail bit. Hogging out the waste with a straight bit places less stress on the dovetail bit, which is considerably more fragile. When making

the matching tail, expose the cutting edge of your bit from the fence and cut one half of the tail at a time, moving the fence to adjust the size. More bit exposure creates a thinner tail; less exposure increases tail thickness. Adjust the bit height accordingly so the tail seats all the way in the dado slot. Just be sure that your workpiece doesn't vary in thickness. If you want to hide this joint, stop the dado short and notch take this joint to the next level by cutting a kerf in the tenon and adding a wedge to the exposed end, as shown on page 67.

Fox Wedged Mortise and Tenon

Primarily a furnituremaker's joint, the fox wedged mortise and tenon is a mechanical locking joint that gets stronger and tighter as it is clamped. Some advanced woodworkers don't even glue this joint because they feel it simply doesn't need it. As shown in the tint box on the facing page, the mortise is first cut square, then opened into a wedge shape with a chisel. The tenon is slotted for a pair of wedges and, as clamping pressure draws the joint together, the wedges are driven into the slots. This forces the tenon to spread, filling the wedge-shaped mortise. As you may expect, layout is critical with this joint. You'll have a real problem if the wedges are too thin (the tenon won't grab), or too thick (the mortise gets full before the shoulder is snug).

Be sure to make plenty of these sample joints in scrap stock, then cut them open to check your results. You'll save on expensive stock and learn how to perfect one of the most elegant mortise and tenon joints around.

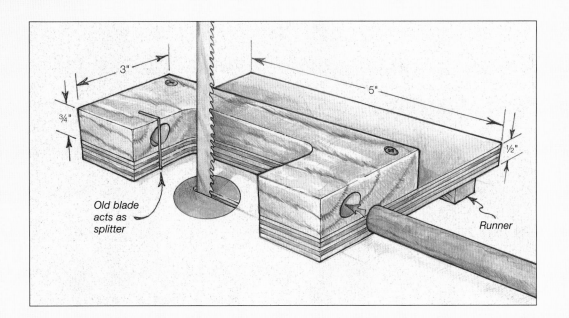

Old blade acts as splitter

3"

¾"

5"

½"

Runner

No-Twist Dowel Splitting

To split dowels on your band saw, use guide blocks like the one shown here with holes drilled for each size dowel. Screw these blocks to ½" plywood bases. Make a 2" x 2" cutout in the jig, then draw a line through the dowel guide hole and make a ¼"-deep band saw cut. Epoxy part of an old band saw blade into the cut, to act like a splitter and prevent your dowels from twisting. A runner attached to the bottom of the base fits in the miter gauge slot and guides your cut.

The Easiest Centered Mortises

Here's a pair of fail-proof jigs to help you center a mortise on any sized workpiece easily and accurately.

by Rick White

There isn't much to this mortising jig, but it's been one of contributing editor Rick White's favorites for years. It's a mortising guide that automatically centers itself on just about any board. With it, you'll cut perfect mortises every time, right down the center of your workpiece. All you need is a plunge router and a straight bit the width of your intended mortise. If you clamp scrap shim to one side of your stock, you can even form an off-centered mortise. Like most of the jigs that earn a spot in his shop, flexibility and ease of use are key.

The jig is just a simple, ⅜" thick Plexiglas™ router base, with ten holes drilled in it. Two of these holes are occupied by ⁵⁄₁₆"

Rick White's favorite router mortising jig consists of an acrylic plate with a pair of bearings that press against either side of a workpiece, automatically centering the bit.

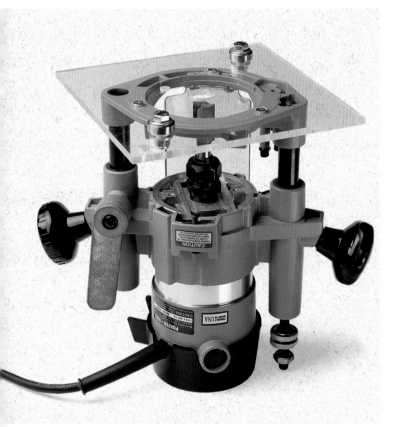

bolts that hold ⁵⁄₁₆" ID bearings in place with the help of a washer and aircraft nuts. The bearings can be moved to any set of mated holes to accommodate various board thicknesses. Three holes are used to mount the base to the router, and the last larger hole is for the bit.

To change the width of a mortise, just change the bit to one of a different diameter. You can even leave this base on the router permanently as a replacement for the original base if you wish. In that case, you'll just have to remove the bearings when you're performing other tasks. For such a simple jig, it's amazing how often Rick reaches for it.

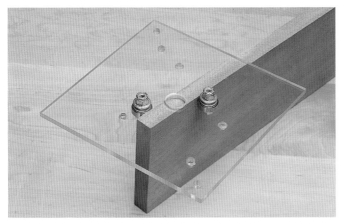

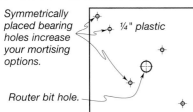

Symmetrically placed bearing holes increase your mortising options.

¼" plastic

Router bit hole.

Drill extra bearing guide holes closer together for mortising narrower stock. This allows you to get closer to the ends of a board.

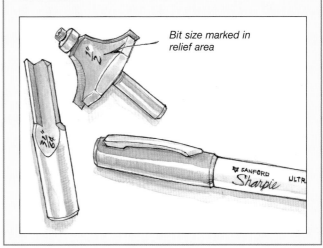
Another Take on a Mortising Jig

When it comes to jigs, there's almost always more than one design that skins the same cat. Mortising jigs are no exception. Master woodworker Ian Kirby favors the jig shown here, which he scratch-builds from scrap wood to suit the particular mortises he needs to rout. The jig consists of a base with a pair of rails screwed to it that straddle the workpiece he's routing on either side. He clamps the workpiece in place between the rails, then screws a four-sided cage on top of the rails, sized to fit the width of his router base and long enough so the router mills the length of mortise he needs when it travels from one end of the cage to the other. With this setup, the jig keeps his workpiece held securely and the router positioned precisely over the center of the workpiece. Plus, there's no chance of the bit wandering off course with the router trapped in place along the cutting path.

While you can create mortise and tenon joinery by hand, a carefully made router jig will tackle mortises in a fraction of the time. The key is to devise a jig that holds the workpiece securely, centers the router over the work and helps control the router's cutting path.

How to Cut Dovetails by Hand

Dovetail joints are a woodworking hallmark. Next time you need to make some, keep your router jig on the shelf and try cutting them by hand. You can do it—really!

by Chris Inman

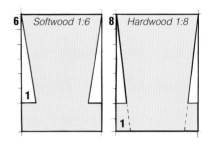

Dovetails are one of the most beautiful woodworking joints, and their exceptional strength makes them the joint of choice for building fine furniture. Cutting a set of pins and tails does take practice, but then there isn't any operation in woodworking that doesn't require practice to do well. Following the step-by-step approach outlined on the next page will lead you to mastery of this essential joint.

Always remember that one of the keys to cutting dovetails successfully is taking great care during the layout stage of the project.

Traditionally, dovetails were used on the best furniture, but they were usually covered with moldings or hidden by some other means. Today, dovetails are used for their decorative appeal and are exposed on carcasses, drawers and structural members.

From many years of experimentation, cabinetmakers have found that the best angle for dovetails is 83°(1:8), unless they're working in softwood which calls for an angle of 80.5°(1:6). If you make the tails too sloped their tips will be weak and will likely break off. If the angle is too straight the strength of the joint will be jeopardized. It's important to remember that the pins give the dovetail joint its

Figure 1: *Set your marking gauge so it's 1/64" more than the thickness of the boards you intend to join, then lay out the shoulder lines on the faces and edges of the stock. Make sure your material is square before you begin.*

Figure 2: *Lay a ruler diagonally across the workpiece, aligning an inch mark with each edge. Now use the ruler to space out the center lines for each pin. Use a square to help draw the lines from the ruler marks to the end of the board.*

Figure 3: *Extend the pin center marks with a square, then measure to each side of the lines to get the pin sides. Set your bevel gauge and scribe the angle for the pins on the end of your stock. Shade the waste areas to avoid cutting the wrong parts.*

Figure 4: *Hold your board in a vise to cut the pins with a fine-toothed handsaw. Cut in the waste areas as you just brush against the center of the scribed lines. Find a good rhythm by cutting all the angles going one way first, then the other.*

Figure 5: *Once all the pin sides are cut, slip a coping saw into the kerfs and cut across the waste areas to create the gaps for the tails. Keep the saw blade at least 1/8" away from the shoulder line and be careful not to cut into the pins.*

Figure 6: *Clamp a board along the shoulder line to align your chisel. For the first few taps hold the chisel vertically, then slightly undercut the rest of the shoulder until you reach the middle of the board. Next, flip the board to chisel the other side.*

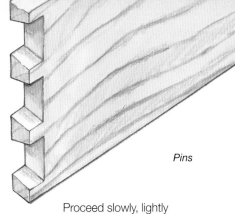

strength—the short grain in the tails has strength only when supported by an adjoining pin. Always use a sharp knife or awl to lay out the joints. A pencil line is too thick.

When cutting the sides of the pins and tails, splice the layout line with the saw blade, keeping the bulk of the kerf in the waste areas. Spend some time just learning to cut a line this way. The type of saw you use is unimportant, although it should have very fine teeth. Western-style saws cut on the push stroke and generally leave a wider kerf. These saws work well in combination with a coping saw, which is used to remove the waste once the angles are cut. Japanese saws, on the other hand, cut on the pull stroke and leave a very thin kerf. Since the kerf is too thin for a coping saw blade to fit, you move right into removing the waste with your chisels. Try both methods, if you have the saws, to see which one you like best.

Tails

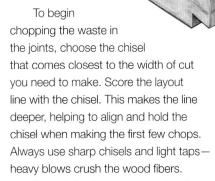

Pins

To begin chopping the waste in the joints, choose the chisel that comes closest to the width of cut you need to make. Score the layout line with the chisel. This makes the line deeper, helping to align and hold the chisel when making the first few chops. Always use sharp chisels and light taps— heavy blows crush the wood fibers.

If any fitting is necessary after the joints are cut, it's usually best to pare across the grain with a sharp chisel. Always cut from the outside corners toward the middle, otherwise you'll risk tearout as the chisel exits the wood.

When assembling the joints, use a steel hammer for a positive blow.

Proceed slowly, lightly tapping the pieces together. If you have to strike the workpiece with force, the joint is too tight and should be pared. Drive the joints together only 2/3 of the way during the test fits. Each time you assemble the joint you'll crush some fibers, so don't overdue the fitting. When the fit is right, pull the pieces apart until you're ready to glue them together.

Dovetail joints don't need much glue if they fit properly. Spread a thin bead on the leading edge of each tail and pin, and as the pieces go together the glue will spread across the joining surfaces. Don't put glue on the shoulders or faces of the joints—too much glue means lots of clean-up time.

Figure 7: Transfer the pin locations to the other board from the inside of the joint. This keeps the natural tendency of the awl's force against the pin (when marking from the outside the awl follows the wood grain away from the pin).

Figure 8: After the tail angles are scribed on the inside face of the board, use a square to mark the end grain. Lay out the outside angles with your bevel gauge then shade the waste areas as a safeguard against making a mistake.

Figure 9: Hold the tail stock in a vise and use your saw to first define each kerf, cutting straight into the wood no more than 1/32" on the waste side of the lines. Now the saw will hold firmly during the first few strokes of each angled cut.

Figure 10: Cut the tail sides, then use a coping saw to remove the waste. Pare each shoulder after clamping on the straight edge. Remember to make the first few taps with the chisel straight into the wood, then undercut the rest.

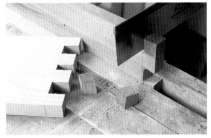

Figure 11: Cut off the waste at the outside shoulders with your fine-toothed saw and clean up the shoulder with a chisel. With the same chisel reach into each pin and tail gap to remove any minor bits or humps that might impede the joint's fit.

Figure 12: Tap the tail piece onto the pins with a steel hammer, but don't force the pieces together. If binding occurs, find out where it is and pare the high spots in the joint. Don't drive the joint completely together until final assembly.

Gluing Secrets Revealed

Gluing up stock is such a part of woodworking that it's sometimes easy to overlook. For many, it's a process to work though and get behind you...until you run into trouble. Then you start looking for a better method. To help out, we've put together some of the Journal's favorite gluing tips.

by Rob Johnstone

What would we woodworkers do without our trusty—and usually underappreciated—wood glues? Can you imagine veneering, bent-laminating or installing blocking without glue in the process? But, even a mainstay like glue can cause problems, particularly when it creeps or shows an ugly blotch right in the middle of a fresh coat of stain. So, in the mix of all the other tricks of this trade, there are a good number of gluing secrets worth sharing. Here are a few we've either gleaned from readers or discovered ourselves over the years. Hope you find them helpful.

As With Most Things, Use It or Lose It

The usual precautionary talk about shellac is that it's got a short shelf life. Thankfully, modern glues last longer, but even they have a logical limit. If it's been awhile since you last popped the top on your yellow wood glue, squeeze out a bead on scrap and check its condition. It should dispense fluidly and with even coloration. If the glue seems gummy, pitch it and buy a fresh bottle.

Likewise, if you're a fan of the new polyurethane liquid glues, buy them in small quantities and toss them after they reach the expiration date on the bottle. Polyurethane glue will slowly absorb water from the atmosphere and begin to cure in the bottle. It's an unpleasant surprise when you need to use it and a costly lesson to lose most of a bottle to time.

You may have noticed on the label that yellow wood glue can be subjected to several freeze-thaw cycles without losing its full adhesive properties, but it's still a good idea to store your glue at room temperature during the winter months. If you forget and need to use glue that's still at December garage temperature, warm it up first or it will leave a chalky residue on the wood as it cures.

Just a few drops of a fluorescent compound like Blacklite added to your glue will allow you to see glue marks and smudges clearly. The errant glue will stick out like a sore thumb(print) under a black light.

Glow in the Dark Glue

Chris Marshall, one of WJ's contributing editors, clued us in to this keeper. Mix some Blacklite™ glue additive to your favorite glue, and those stray glue marks and fingerprints will shine out a warning under a black light. (See the photo on the opening

5 glue-up quick tips

One: When using polyurethane glue, moisten both surfaces of the joint with water just before clamp-up.

Two: For best results when working with oily woods such as teak or cocobolo, wipe down the glue joint with acetone or alcohol before applying the glue.

Three: Hide glue has absolutely no glue creep once it has cured. Neither does epoxy or polyurethane.

Four: Cut one long side of an old credit card with a pinking shears to create a serrated edge. Use it to apply glue evenly to large areas, similar to a trowel.

Five: When gluing wood with epoxy, a rule of thumb is: the longer the open time of the epoxy, the better the bond will be.

Woodworking glue

page.) Just one ounce per gallon of glue will do the deed. In this case, an ounce of prevention is worth a perfect stain job. And one more thing: some glues already have fluorescents (the stuff that glows under a black light) in their standard formulation. Franklin's HiPURformer™ is one example. So get your old black light out of the attic (and while you're there, grab those tie-dyed T-shirts, too; they're back in style), and put it to use in your shop.

If you tossed the black light before Reagan took office, another option for finding those glue blotches is to wipe the wood with mineral spirits after sanding. The dampened wood will reveal the glue, and mineral spirits won't raise the grain in the process. It's also a good way to see sanding scratches.

Big, Flat and Far too Wide

It seemed so easy in your head…gluing that wide panel to a wooden substrate…but then you're stumped as to how to clamp the thing until the glue sets. Rats! Don't fear: Rick White, the Journal's only practitioner of "White Magic," will help you pull a rabbit out of your…um…hat. As demonstrated in the photo below, combine square areas of contact cement surrounded by your woodworking glue. The contact cement acts like a clamp until the glue cures. As Rick says, this is really useful when you are fighting gravity in a vertical application. No muss, no fuss. It is a bit like magic after all: look Ma, no hands (or clamps)!

Dangerous Curves—The Jig is Up

Wood, given its druthers, grows pretty much in a straight line…and sawyers prepare stock in the same manner—straight and true. This is all well and good until a woodworker gets it into his head to build a non-linear project, like a round picnic table, for example. How do you get that straight stock to go in a circle? The easiest way is dry-bent laminating. John English, a regular contributor, used that technique to build up the curved apron for a Spanish cedar table years ago in the magazine. Clamping three ¼" pieces of stock around a jig and using waterproof glue, he had a perfectly shaped table apron in no time. One key advantage to curved laminations is that there is almost no springback…the glued-up curve stays true to the jig's shape.

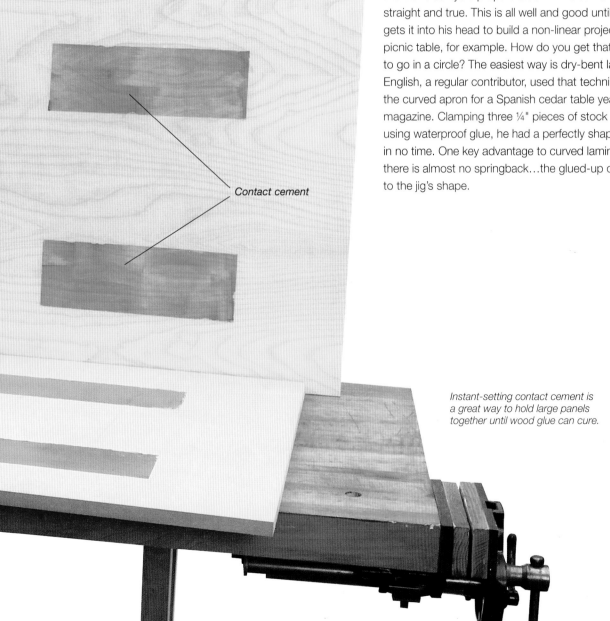

Contact cement

Instant-setting contact cement is a great way to hold large panels together until wood glue can cure.

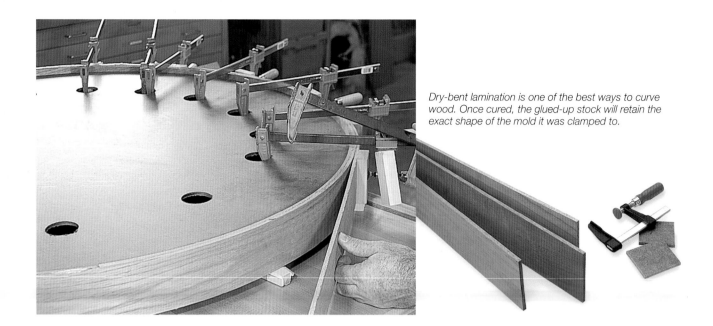

Dry-bent lamination is one of the best ways to curve wood. Once cured, the glued-up stock will retain the exact shape of the mold it was clamped to.

Quick! Hide the Edges

Hardwood veneered plywood or MDF are the mainstays of modern cabinetmaking. These manufactured panels are durable, dimensionally stable and beautiful. But their edges are ugly. The question is, how to hide those edges and make the panels look good? Journal editor Rob Johnstone has trimmed panel edges using every trick in the book, but his favorite is one that may surprise you. He glues a hardwood strip between the panels and then rips the glued-up pieces apart on the table saw—leaving exactly ⅛" of solid hardwood on the panel. By clamping the panels to the hardwood strip, you get a much better glue joint. Now you can use a ⅛" bearing-guided roundover bit in a router (Rob prefers a laminate trimmer) to clean up the slightly oversized edging, and the panels are perfect. Plus, the ⅛" hardwood edge is much more durable than a thinner veneer…ironed on or glued.

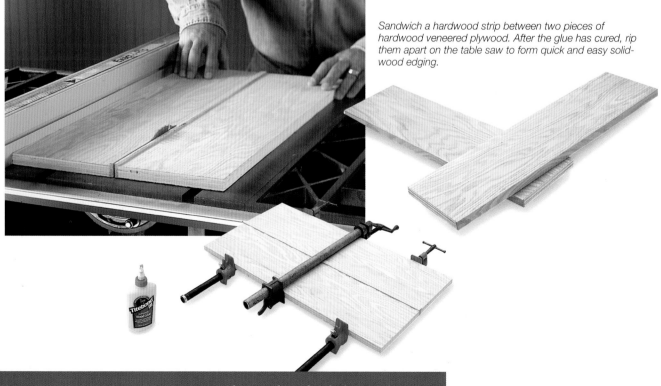

Sandwich a hardwood strip between two pieces of hardwood veneered plywood. After the glue has cured, rip them apart on the table saw to form quick and easy solid-wood edging.

Wavy veneer can be hard to handle, but Mike McGlynn's ironing trick tames this trying task.

The Heat is On—With Yellow Wood Glue

Contributing editor Mike McGlynn is seemingly an endless well of slick woodworking techniques. Attaching veneer, especially wavy veneer, is a particularly trying piece of work in most cases. But Mike uses regular woodworking glue and a household iron to make short work of that task. Simply apply the glue to both the veneer and the substrate (in this case, a plywood shelf with its edges trimmed with mahogany to match the crotch-grained mahogany veneer) and let the glue dry completely. Then place the glued faces together and, with a very hot iron (see the photo above), smooth the veneer in place. It will bond immediately and not move a micron—just like contact cement. So be sure to have it where you want it when you start!

Clear Plastic Clamps for Perfect Miters

Linda Haus, our techniques editor, has never been fond of making miter joints (who is?). Her advice for great-looking miter joints on small to medium sized boxes is to use 3M-brand packing tape to align the pieces and roll them into

a perfect box. The tape has great strength and just the right amount of elasticity for the job. It is also clear, so as you apply clamps to the box and square up the assembly, you can visually check the miters. This technique also keeps most of the glue squeeze-out inside the box which, in most cases, is preferable. Linda's toolbox is never without a roll of this clear plastic clamp.

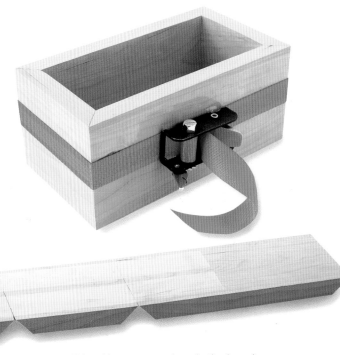

Clear packing tape

Linda Haus uses 3M packing tape as a clear plastic clamp. It allows her to roll up a mitered box to create perfect corners.

Getting a Grip On Clamping

by Rob Johnstone

The variety of clamps available to the woodworker is expanding all the time. New features and accessories all make the process of clamping easier. But the most important fundamental steps to successful clamp-ups are well-formed and -fitted glue joints, a complete test run (dry test) of the clamp-up (ever more important as the subassemblies become more complex) and an appropriate glue or adhesive for the task at hand.

Starve a Joint —Feed a Failure

A simple but critical clamping point is the application of the glue. Too much, and you've got a big mess and the glue surfaces are likely to slip and slide into misalignment. Too little, and the joint is prone to failure. If you apply too much pressure to the clamp-up, the results will be the same as if you failed to apply sufficient glue to the joint ... the glue will squeeze out of the joint and it will effectively be "starved."

The Fan Effect

When you're edge gluing, the pressure generated from each side of the head of a clamp spreads out at 45° until it encounters the glue joint. As you can see in the photo on page 82, these fans of pressure will determine how many clamps are required for an effective glue-up. In the example, one clamp would not have been enough, but the three pressure fans generated overlap to a degree that's a bit excessive. Also demonstrated in the photo

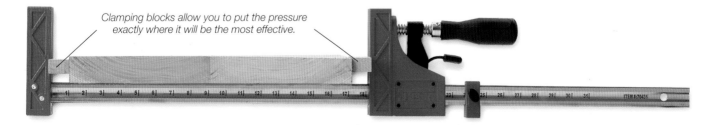

Clamping blocks allow you to put the pressure exactly where it will be the most effective.

Fans of pressure extend from each clamp head until they reach the glue joint. In the example at right, the fans overlap more than they would need to, but clearly, a single clamp would not have applied pressure along the entire length of the joint.

is the practice of alternating clamps on opposite faces of the panel. This helps to keep the panel flat, but you need to check the glue-up with a straightedge of some sort to be confident that the boards are correctly aligned.

Clamping blocks are another way to control your glue-up. The blocks allow you to place the clamping pressure exactly where you want it to close the joint and keep the panel flat. (See photo, below) You determine where the blocks must be placed during your dry clamp test. Glue blocks also protect the edge of your panel from metal clamp heads, but that's a side benefit.

Tongue-and-groove Joints

Tongue-and-groove joints add another wrinkle to the clamping game. Not only do you need to apply pressure to the edge of the panel to draw the joint together, but it's best if you can squeeze the joint together onto the tongue. Again, clamping blocks come to the rescue.

Use clamping blocks and a C-clamp (positioned as shown in the photo at right) to squeeze a tongue-and-groove joint tight (photo above).

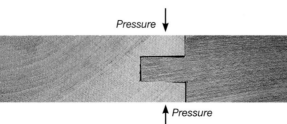

Pressure ↓

↑ Pressure

Dry-bent laminations are gluing technique that can be exceptionally useful.

Accuracy When Gluing Up

Because the result of gluing and clamping a subassembly together is more or less permanent, it is essential that once your clamps are set you verify that all the pieces are square, flat and properly aligned. Measure across the diagonals of any square or rectangular aspect of your piece ... the measurements should be exactly the same. Use a straightedge to check that the subassembly is flat. A good set of winding sticks is a practical way to make sure your subassembly is not twisted in any way. You only have one chance to get it just right ... take your time and be sure all is well.

Dry-bent Laminations

The technique for creating curved shapes — for elements like table skirts or chair legs — is called dry-bent laminating. It is very simple in concept. Create a form matching the shape you desire. These forms can get quite large. Use very thin strips of wood — thin enough that they bend very easily — and, as always, test clamp them in your form. After the dry test, apply a thin coat of glue to each strip of wood, and clamp them tightly in the form. It's a good idea to wax the clamping faces of the form. When the glue dries (and it will take several hours to cure), the glued-up strips will retain their curved shape. In addition, the product you have created will be very strong, as a result of the multiple laminations.

There are three simple keys to accurate and effective gluing and clamping: preparation, preparation and preparation.

Alternative Clamping Methods

For the resourceful woodworker, clamps are everywhere.

by Stephen Shepherd

There's an old saying that a woodworker's wealth can be measured by the number of clamps he or she owns. With today's bewildering variety of clamps and holding devices, it's easy to forget that early woodworkers managed quite well without any of them. Instead, they relied on their wits and a repertoire of clever, low-tech clamping methods to hold parts in place while the glue was drying.

Since those days, technological advances have added even more of these alternative clamping methods to the resourceful woodworker's tool kit. Most are cheap, if not free, and readily available. More important, alternative clamps are often the best or quickest way to handle awkward or unusual clamping situations.

Go Bars

A go bar is a piece of springy wood that can be bowed between the workpiece and a ceiling joist of the shop to apply clamping pressure in the middle of a large piece of work where a regular deep-throat clamp will not reach, Figure 1. For example, piano manufacturers use go bars to apply pressure in the middle of large wooden soundboards.

Typically, go bars are made from strong, dense, springy woods such as ash, oak, osage orange or hickory. They must be thin enough to flex and to supply enough spring pressure, and they must be long enough to reach from the workpiece to the ceiling with a few inches to spare. The ends are usually sharpened to a blunt point in order to concentrate pressure and prevent skidding.

To use a go bar, first apply glue to your workpiece and position it under a suitable ceiling joist. Place a scrap of wood on the work to protect it, then spring the go bar between the joist and the work. You can increase the pressure by adding more scraps between the go bar and the workpiece, or by adding more go bars.

Figure 1: *Sometimes the simplest and best way to clamp something is with a little creativity and one of these ingenious alternative clamping methods. The hardwood go bar shown here is applying spring pressure to this large panel assembly.*

Hose Clamps

Round automotive hose clamps can be of great value in the shop, especially for repairing broken spindles, round tenons and other round or turned work. I've also used them to make collet chucks for the lathe and to attach conduits and fixtures to support columns in the shop.

Hose clamps are available in sizes from ¼" to 4" and larger, and I try to keep a supply of various sizes in stock. When using them for repair work,

I usually place a piece of waxed paper between the clamp and the work to prevent the metal from discoloring the work and to keep the clamp free of glue.

Joiner's Dogs or Pinch Dogs

Joiner's dogs, Figure 3, are probably the quickest and simplest way to join two boards. Made of iron or steel, joiner's dogs have two pointed legs that are tapered on the inside, so when you drive them into the end grain of two adjacent boards, they pull the boards together. You can use them on other types of joints as well.

The biggest disadvantage of joiner's dogs is that they leave holes in the work. If you are using them to join panels, the best way to eliminate the holes is to make the panels longer than necessary and trim them to size after the glue dries. If you are clamping groundwork for veneer, the veneer skin will cover the holes.

Nails and Screws

Nails and screws are usually used to hold things together permanently, but they can also serve as temporary clamps until the glue dries.

Headless brads, finishing nails and carpet tacks may all be used to hold parts together temporarily. Cut nails can be used as impromptu wedge clamps due to the wedge-shaped design of the nails.

Screws have the dual advantages of allowing you to precisely control the location and amount of pressure and of being easy to remove once the glue has dried.

Figure 2: *Hose clamps of various sizes are indispensable for repairing small round parts such as chair tenons.*

Figure 3: *These iron joiner's dogs (pinch dogs) have tapered legs that pull boards together when driven into end grain.*

Figure 4: *Rubber bands are particularly useful where band clamps are too big or bulky to do the job.*

Wooden Pegs

Wooden pegs, both straight and tapered, may also serve as clamps and clamping accessories.

The draw-bored mortise and tenon joint is one prime example. To make this joint, you first cut the mortise and tenon. Then, with the tenon removed, drill a peg hole through the mortise. Next, position the tenon in the mortise and mark the hole location on the tenon. Remove the tenon and drill a hole slightly offset toward the tenon shoulder. When you reassemble the joint and drive a tapered peg into the hole, it draws the tenon tightly into place. Often, these joints were assembled without glue. In many traditional shops, tapered pegs are used to secure assemblies and glue-ups to the workbench or a clamping board. A clamping board is a stout, flat board (or boards) with many holes to allow for a wide variety of clamping arrangements. Simply place pegs in appropriate holes and drive wedges between the pegs and the workpiece to apply pressure where needed.

Rubber Bands

Rubber bands, Figure 4, of various sizes are excellent for repairing small or irregularly shaped pieces, such as broken fretwork. They also come in handy for assembling small boxes and other projects. Choose the size or number of bands you need to provide the right amount of pressure. Rubber bands won't mar the surface of your work, and glue doesn't stick to them.

Sprung Boards

This is a technique often used by musical instrument makers to edge-glue two boards, particularly thin ones such as guitar or violin soundboards. First, you attach two cleats to a workbench or base board, parallel and slightly closer together than the total width of your glue-up. After applying glue to the edges to be joined, place the outer edges against the cleats, with the glued edges forming a peak where they meet in the center, Figure 6. Press down on the peak to flatten and clamp the edges together, using a weight to prevent the assembly from springing back. You may need to experiment to determine the ideal spacing for the cleats to get the right amount of pressure.

Upholstery Springs

Sections of coil springs from discarded upholstered furniture can be fashioned into clamps that are serviceable and useful for a variety of jobs, Figure 7.

Coils that are made of better steel can be difficult to cut. If diagonal pliers or end cutters don't work, try bolt cutters. Cut the coil on a bias to produce points on the ends. The points will hold themselves in the wood even at odd clamping angles such as mitered picture frames.

The downside of coil spring clamps is that they produce holes in the wood. In some cases, you can protect your workpiece with clamping blocks or wood scraps. If you need to repair a hole, you can usually swell it shut with hot water or steam.

Figure 5: *A clamping board and wooden pegs can adapt quickly to any shape. Wedges exert pressure between the pegs and the work. Creativity is the key to using any clamping process, standard or alternative.*

String, Rope and Twine

Any time a piece of string will be in contact with glue, it pays to wax it prior to use. Just run the string over a piece of beeswax a few times to coat it adequately.

String and blocks. A piece of string and eight blocks of wood make the ultimate, one-size-fits-all, picture frame clamp, Figure 8. The continuous loop of string ensures proper clamping pressure at all the miters until the glue dries. You may need to use two strings to distribute the pressure properly on wide frames or boxes. I've even seen this method used for cabinet carcasses.

You can use any kind of string, twine or cord that will take a bit of stress. Loop it around the frame and tie a knot to form a fairly tight loop, leaving enough slack to get the eight blocks of wood between the frame or box assembly and the string.

Place two blocks between the string and each side of the frame, in the middle where the string is looser. With that done, slide the blocks outward toward the corners of the frame. This tightens the string and directs the pressure to the mitered corners. Then, you can further direct the pressure by sliding the individual blocks.

Tourniquets. The tourniquet is probably the first clamp ever invented. It certainly is a primitive and elegant clamping solution for square, rectangular, oval and round objects, as well as for awkward or oddly angled assemblies such as chair legs, Figure 9.

I prefer to make my tourniquets with soft cotton rope. It will stretch, yet it doesn't mar the surface like hemp or manila rope does.

Figure 6: *Instrument makers have long used this sprung board arrangement to join thin book-matched panels together without clamps.*

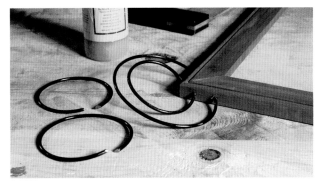

Figure 7: *Upholstery coil springs make great impromptu clamps for mitered assemblies and other odd angle joints.*

Figure 8: *This classic method of clamping frames needs only a piece of string and eight small blocks of scrap wood.*

Figure 9: *Nothing beats a tourniquet for awkward clamping jobs like chair leg assemblies. All you need is cotton rope and a wooden toggle to twist it.*

To create a tourniquet, I tie a loop in one end of the rope, wrap it around the work a couple of times and tie it through the initial loop. Then I insert a stick, or "toggle," between the ropes and twist them to shorten the rope and apply pressure. When the tourniquet is tight enough, I block the toggle to prevent it from untwisting.

"Serving" string. String works well for wrapping around pieces such as veneered columns to hold the veneer in place while the glue dries. This technique also works well for restoration and repair work for round, oval or odd shapes where other methods will not work.

But, wrapping (or "serving") the string around and around the work can be time-consuming and clumsy; so, the traditional craftsman often made a "serving mallet" that acted as a bobbin and a tensioning device for the string.

Wedges

The wedge is by far the most common and time-honored method of applying force, and one of the handiest tools ever invented, since its principle underlies many kinds of joints and clamping devices found in woodworkers' shops.

Dovetail joints, for example, are open mortise and tenon joints that rely on their wedging action to remain tight and square while the glue dries.

Wedges are also used to secure tenons in their mortises or sockets, either as blind-wedged (fox-wedged) tenons totally enclosed in blind mortises, or as through tenons, where the exposed end is wedged with one or more wedges to keep the shoulders tight and prevent the assembly from racking.

On solid seat construction in Windsor chairs, the wedges are wider than the tenon. This extra width locks into the wood to prevent the leg from rotating in the socket.

Many clamp designs are based on the wedge principle. The thread on a screw clamp is actually an inclined plane, a variation of the simple wedge. Another popular type of clamp, the cam clamp, is essentially just a circular pivoting wedge.

Wedges may also be used in conjunction with other clamping devices to add specific pressure to a certain area. For example, if you are using a spanner beam to exert pressure in the middle of a large workpiece or assembly, you might use a wedge between the beam and your clamping block to push it down a little tighter.

As mentioned earlier, many craftspeople use wedges in conjunction with pegs in a workbench or gluing or clamping board, where they can exert just the right pressure in just the right place. I keep a small container of various sized wedges near my workbench and use them on a daily basis.

Wedges used in pairs ("folding wedges") are great for applying uniform, controlled pressure, even in many places where clamping is impossible by any other means.

Unlikely Clamps

With a little ingenuity, you can make a clamp out of just about anything. Here are a few examples:

Drill press: If your drill press has a tightening device to lock the quill, you can use it to clamp a glued-up assembly until the glue dries. If your table has a rack and pinion, you can also place the work under the chuck and crank up the table to apply the pressure.

Lathe: Position the work between centers and advance the tailstock screw to clamp the work.

Jacks: The new scissors jacks work great for certain applications, as do the very old screw jacks from Ford Model A and Model T automobiles. For heavier-duty clamping jobs, you can use a house jack. I once needed to hold a lathe in place while turning a rather large chunk of wood, so I rigged up a couple of 4 x 4s and a house jack to apply pressure between the ceiling beams and the ways of the lathe.

Tires and inner tubes: I have seen small trailer tires used to glue up round rings of laminated veneer. First, you wrap the glued-up layers of veneer around the deflated tire. Then, bolt a two-part wooden caul around the veneer, and inflate the tire to force the laminated wood against the caul. Deflate the tire to release the clamping pressure. You can do the same thing with inner tubes from cars, trucks and bicycles. They are thin and can

Figure 10: *When used in pairs, wedges provide an elegant way to apply direct, parallel clamping pressure without clamps.*

be used as long tubes by cutting near the stem and sealing both ends. Used against fences or cauls, the air pressure can apply specific clamping pressure until the glue dries. Deflating releases the pressure and glue does not usually stick to the rubber.

Doors: Of all the unlikely clamps, I have actually used a spring-hinged door to clamp a small repair on the edge of a box. The box was delicate and the pressure from the self-closing hinge was just enough to do the trick. Of course, I couldn't move the door until the glue dried.

Tape: Tape can be very handy for a lot of clamping situations. Masking tape, painter's tape, packing tape and duct tape all have their uses in the shop, Figure 11. Masking tape in particular is useful for applying edgebanding, purfling and inlays. Its ability to stretch enhances the clamping pressure. Painter's tape is the best choice if you need to protect the surface of the work from the tape adhesive.

Weights: What could be simpler than harnessing gravity to do your clamping for you? Anything of mass such as rocks, bricks, barbells, canvas bags full of sand, or chunks of iron can be used to clamp two pieces of wood together. Always use a clamping pad to avoid damage to the finished surfaces.

Wire: Brass, copper or iron wire can be wrapped, twisted and tightened around an unusual shape to hold it in place. Iron or baling wire will react with the glue and leave a mark, so use wax paper or other protection between the iron and the wood. Select the gauge of wire that is appropriate for the particular application.

Miscellaneous clamping helpers: I have used a piece of foam rubber as a clamp to provide pressure on delicate, uneven gluing where just a little pressure was required.

I have also used a sponge for the same purpose. Paper clips, binder clips and clothespins can also provide limited clamping

Figure 11: *Masking tape and other kinds of tape are useful for controlled clamping operations like gluing inlay banding into the edge of a mirror frame.*

pressure for small gluing jobs. I have even used one of those small food-saver vacuum units to vacuum veneer small pieces.

And on and on it goes …

As you can see, the list of alternative clamps and methods is limited only by your imagination. I have nothing against regular clamps — I use them all the time. But I've learned to think out of the box when it comes to clamping the many odd and different kinds of joints and assemblies that an active woodworker is likely to see. By mastering a few principles and rules of thumb, it's amazing how easily and efficiently you can adapt unlikely items and materials to your clamping needs.

Flattening A Glued-Up Panel

Woodworking isn't like machining metal. Tabletops and panels don't always end up perfectly flat. Here's what to do to get them darn close.

by Peter Korn

There's just no two ways about it—perfection is an elusive standard for woodworkers. Even after painstaking efforts at choosing lumber, orienting the grain, milling and jointing the stock, then gluing and clamping it together, we will still occasionally suffer the whims of machinery and nature. Boards cup, jointers snipe, planer beds and knives are imperfectly ground, glue creeps…If you've put a hand to wood, you know the list.

Few woodworking operations offer more chances for imperfection than making a tabletop. Try as you might, you may still end up with a 1/32" difference between some boards, and the threat of cupping always lurks around the corner. With this kind of a beginning, how can we expect to make a perfectly flat tabletop? Well, the answer is to work for something more within our reach—flat enough.

Hand Planing a Panel

Before you start planing, be sure to allow the moisture absorbed into the wood from the glue to evaporate for a couple of days. Failing to do this will only lead to wasted effort, since the joints you'll work so hard to flatten today will continue to shrink and become narrow depressions tomorrow.

Once the extra moisture evaporates, set to work on the tabletop. Wherever the grain allows, a well tuned bench plane is the best tool for flattening a glued-up panel. The bench plane family includes a range of sizes, all with the same design. The #03 smoothing plane, at 9" long, is the shortest in the family, while the #7 jointer plane is the longest at 24". A 9" or 10" smoothing plane like the one shown in Figure 1 is often the best choice for flattening a panel.

A sharp plane blade cuts so cleanly that it leaves the wood's surface clearer than even the finest abrasive could. This assumes, of course, that your plane is

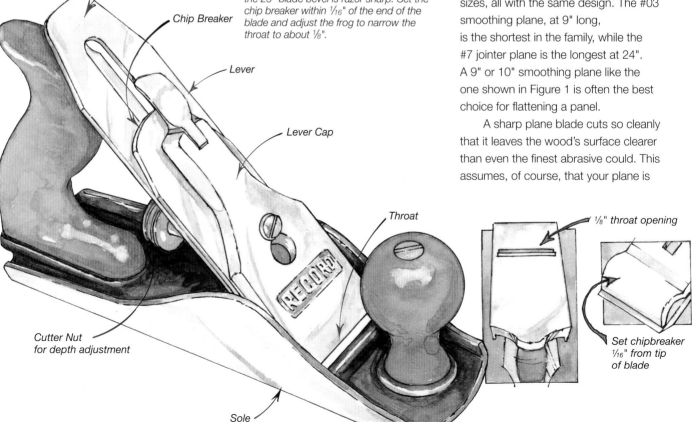

Blade

Chip Breaker

Lever

Lever Cap

Throat

Figure 1: The key to good planing is a well-tuned tool. Be sure the sole is flat and the 25° blade bevel is razor sharp. Set the chip breaker within 1/16" of the end of the blade and adjust the frog to narrow the throat to about 1/8".

Cutter Nut for depth adjustment

Sole

1/8" throat opening

Set chipbreaker 1/16" from tip of blade

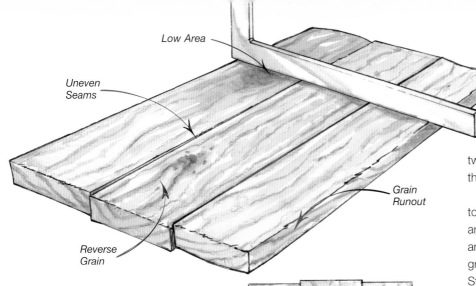

Low Area

Uneven Seams

Reverse Grain

Grain Runout

Figure 2: *Hold a straight edge on the panel and mark the high spots (above), then plane the ridges going with the grain. If your blade loses touch with the wood, expand your planing area and turn the tool about 30° (right), which shortens the contact area of the sole and permits the plane to reach deeper into the hollow.*

well tuned. If it's not, spend an hour or two on maintenance first.

When starting to work on a glued-up panel, first put a long straightedge across it to get a feel for its contours (see Figure 2). Once you know the lay of the land, plane the ridges with a smoothing plane. Go with the grain and take fine shavings to limit tear-out and maintain control. If the grain is too difficult to plane, use a cabinet scraper instead. As the plane creates a slight hollow, the iron may lose contact with the wood before the joint is completely level. If this happens, plane a wider and longer area taking parallel, adjacent strokes to even out the dip. To get a bit further into a hollow, try holding the plane at an angle to the work, while still planing in line with the grain. This shortens the contact area of the plane sole so it cuts into a slightly smaller radius.

When the plane sole begins to skim the lower board, slow down and proceed cautiously. Chances are, you probably couldn't arrange all the boards in your panel with the grain oriented in the same direction, so the grain of the lower board might run opposite the

Dip Area

first board. If you begin to tear out the lower board, stop planing immediately and finish up with a scraper. If there's no tear-out, continue planing until the seams are smooth.

Scraping the Surface Smooth

Scrapers take fine shavings with or against the grain (although not across it) with no tear-out. A cabinet scraper is better than a hand scraper for tabletops because it has a sole and maintains a fairly flat surface (see Figure 3). Overzealous application of a hand scraper might leave noticeable dips. Scrapers are notoriously intimidating to the uninitiated, but they're fairly easy to use and quickly become indispensable.

Sanding as a Final Step

Sanders are less precise at creating flat surfaces than cutting tools like planes and scrapers. However, belt sanders remain popular for flattening a panel for

two reasons; they're power tools and they require minimal skill.

If you insist on using a belt sander to flatten a panel, remember that they are aggressive and easily create ridges and dips of their own. Start with a 150-grit belt to limit the chance of a mistake. Start the sander off the wood, ease it down like an airplane onto a runway, and keep it moving with the grain at all times. Watch out for the ends of the panel where a belt sander can easily remove more wood than you want. Then finish up by hand-sanding to 180- or 220-grit.

How Flat is Flat Enough?

So how flat should a tabletop be? The answer depends on the type of finish you plan to use and your own aesthetic sense. The glossier the finish, the more the light will reveal any idiosyncrasies in the surface. Conversely, an oil-type finish can make a surface look flatter than it is.

As to the degree of perfection, that's an individual choice. Keep in mind, though, that there's no compelling reason for handmade furniture to imitate the impersonal perfection of manufactured goods. A few minor imperfections testify to the sweat equity that goes into every project.

Figure 3: *Since a cabinet scraper (below) has a sole, it maintains a flat surface better than a hand scraper (right).*

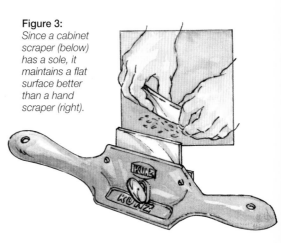

Bread courtesy Bread Alone,
Boiceville, NY. www.breadalone.com.

Butt Joints and Breadboard Ends

Butt joints are basic in appearance, but they're actually sophisticated in execution.
Breadboard ends are a flawed technique ... but woodworkers like how they look.

by Ian Kirby

Three primary joints are used in furniture making: dovetail, mortise-and-tenon and butt. Dovetails are regarded by some to be the epitome of fine workmanship. They join wide boards at the corners to make boxes. Mortise-and-tenons are the workhorse joints of frames and rail-and-leg structures. Butt joints are an anomaly in that the parts don't interlock as in the other two systems; they're simply boards glued together on edge. Butt joints may seem simple, but they have a singular, important purpose: to make wide boards from narrow ones.

The simplicity is deceptive here, because the edges of a quality butt joint must be smooth and in total contact. To illustrate how total the contact must be, I'm reminded of my early days of making

furniture when the common adhesive was hide glue prepared in a water jacket double boiler.

Once the edges of two boards had been planed and met the various tests for accuracy, one board was clamped in the vise. Very hot and consequently very thin glue was brushed quickly onto both edges to be joined. The second board was now placed on the board in the vise, glue edge to glue edge. The top board was pressed down hard against the first, then slid a few inches forwards and backwards lengthwise. This squeezed out the excess glue, which was rapidly cooling and becoming sticky. The trick was to align the boards correctly before the glue set. The result was called a "rub joint."

After about 15 seconds, we released the vise and lifted the assembly by the top board. Since no clamps were used to compress or distort the wood in any way, the integrity of the joint depended entirely on the joining edges being smooth and in total contact.

Another example of the attainable accuracy of the contact edges is a stunt I would pull for audiences at woodworking seminars. I would make a butt joint, put water on both edges, squeeze the parts together and lift the assembly by the top board. Water alone would hold the parts together, albeit temporarily. It underscores the potential holding power of accurately prepared edges.

Making a Butt Joint

Take two adjacent boards and fold them together as though they were hinged at the intended joint. The hinge can be either side. Clamp the folded pair together in a vise.

Plane the paired edges so they are flat in length and width. The plane should be set for a fine cut to produce .003" shavings.

Checks may be made with a straightedge alone because if the paired edges are flat across their thickness, they need not be square. The out-of-square angles on the two boards will cancel each other when you remove the boards and stand one edge on the other. Nevertheless, I go for square as well and check the paired edges with a try square.

Steps Toward a Proper Butt Joint

In my experience, there are seven steps to making a correct butt joint:

- Compose the pieces
- Record the composition
- Plane edges, assess total contact
- Dry clamp to prepare for glue
- Apply glue and clamps
- Scrape off dried glue
- Plane the wide board flat

Composing the Pieces

If only two pieces of wood are involved and you can use any face, top or bottom, and any edge, left or right, there are many arrangements to choose from. Your task is to find the best-looking combination that minimizes the joint lines and blends the grain pattern effectively.

Recording the Composition

Once you've made your choice, record the arrangement of the boards by marking random lines across each joint or drawing a large chevron across the entire assembly with a soft pencil.

Flattening the Edges

I'm using a hand plane to make a butt joint in this article. The length of the edge that you can make accurately is about 2.5 times the length of the plane. This is the reason planes come in different lengths. However, for all but the shortest joints, a #7, 22"-long plane is my plane of choice. Its ample heft and length promote more accuracy than shorter planes.

How smooth? Glue is more effective on a smooth surface than a rough surface. The surface produced by a sharp hand plane is the smoothest you can get.

How flat? Aim for zero to .005". In practical terms many butt joints stick together quite well beyond this tolerance. You can attribute this mostly to glue strength and the increased contact provided by a row of clamps tightened down on the joint. We will never know the internal stress that the glue must counteract when the clamps are removed, but it makes us look good in spite of ourselves.

A hand plane produces arguably the most effective butt joint, but you can also make good joints with a table saw, a jointer or a router, depending on wood species and sophistication of your equipment.

Glue causes things to stick together in two ways: mechanical adhesion and specific adhesion. Mechanical adhesion occurs when glue enters the porous

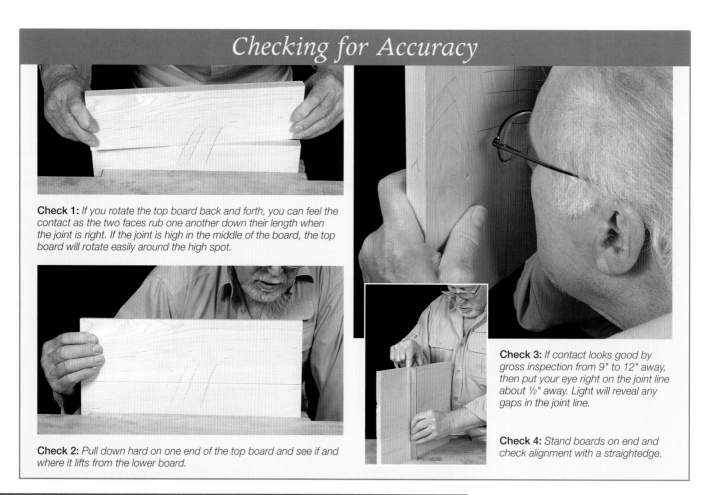

Checking for Accuracy

Check 1: *If you rotate the top board back and forth, you can feel the contact as the two faces rub one another down their length when the joint is right. If the joint is high in the middle of the board, the top board will rotate easily around the high spot.*

Check 2: *Pull down hard on one end of the top board and see if and where it lifts from the lower board.*

Check 3: *If contact looks good by gross inspection from 9" to 12" away, then put your eye right on the joint line about ½" away. Light will reveal any gaps in the joint line.*

Check 4: *Stand boards on end and check alignment with a straightedge.*

surface of the wood and acts like a myriad of tiny dowels or connecting hooks. Specific adhesion is the molecular force of attraction between the glue and the surface of the wood.

It used to be thought that mechanical adhesion was all-important, but in fact that accounts for only a small percentage of the glue line strength. The joint will only be as strong as the molecular forces that are able to operate at the interface, so the best results come from the smoothest glue line faces.

Checking the Joint

Clamp one piece in the vise and stand the other piece on it edge to edge. If the series of checks that

I show in "Checking for Accuracy" prove positive, it's on to the next joint or procedure. If any of the checks are negative, it's back to square one: you'll need to plane the surfaces further.

Reinforcing a Butt Joint?

You may be familiar with two methods that are believed to make a butt joint stronger, the most common being a spline. Splines are strips of solid wood, preferably the same material as the board, inserted into a groove cut along each joined edge. Now come the questions: How wide and deep should the groove be? What material should the spline be? How tightly should it fit the groove? The answers are overshadowed by two other considerations. First, cutting the spline grooves will remove a significant percentage of the area where the glue's specific adhesion can take place, thereby weakening the joint. Second, even if the interfaces of the joint are correctly made

and it is tested to destruction, it will fail at the bottom of the groove where you have reduced the board's thickness.

In light of these two points, if you still believe that a spline truly helps, keep it thin: a 1/8" saw kerf is enough. Make the spline a snug push fit and its width about three times its thickness in each board.

Another option is to use joining plates, more familiarly known as biscuits these days, which improve upon the spline method in several ways. For one, the groove is intermittent rather than continuous, which preserves more area for the glue's specific adhesion to occur. Second, the biscuits are made of European beech, a particularly strong wood. Third, because the grain of the biscuit runs on the bias, it is angled across the joint line, resulting in greater strength. Fourth, the biscuit is compressed at the

Gluing Up With Biscuits

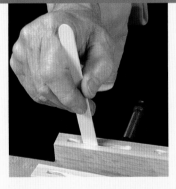

Deposit glue in the slots, wet the slot sides with a paddle and remove excess glue. Then roll glue on the two edges to coat the mating surfaces.

Wet the biscuits with a paddle and insert them in the slots.

Assemble the two boards, aligning them with the chevron mark that recorded the composition. Repeat the procedure to include the third board, if applicable.

Position the clamps alternately above and below the assembly. This will counteract the tendency for the boards to buckle as you apply pressure.

same time it is stamped out: a biscuit snugly fits in its 4mm kerf when dry, but when wetted by the glue, it swells, causing internal pressure and a strong resistance to being pulled apart.

Preparing to Glue

Once you've satisfactorily planed the edges, you can glue and clamp the joint together. Begin by assembling the clamps, arranging the boards, and closing the clamps with the joint dry. It's easy to determine the correct number of clamps to use by plotting the pressure fans for each clamp. The fans radiate out from the clamp heads at 90°.

Applying Glue Correctly

Glue cannot work unless it wets the wood — and that's not as simple to accomplish as it may sound. The best method is to

To facilitate cross-grain planing, trap the workpiece firmly on three sides: the bench stop, a board clamped in the vise and a board clamped to the bench.

roll a thin layer onto each surface. Roller pressure wets the wood and ensures that a thin glue layer is deposited on each face, resulting in a controlled and limited squeeze-out.

A common but definitely poor method is to squeeze a bead onto one edge and rely on clamp pressure to spread the glue. The thickness of the bead causes the pieces to slide out of alignment, and squeeze-out is often excessive and spotty. Limited or no squeeze-out indicates there may be no wetting and, therefore, no adhesion.

Between these best and worst methods of applying glue, we typically use brushes, paddles, and even fingers as applicators. Don't use your fingers: they contaminate the glue with residual oils, making it less effective. Wet fingers also get glue in places where it shouldn't be.

Flattening the Board

The first across-the-grain cuts clean the board and reveal the machine marks.

Here's a shaving from a slightly curved blade when planing across the grain: thick in the middle, thin on the outside edges.

Check for flat in length and width as you proceed, using a straightedge. Continue planing until you see no light underneath.

Periodically check for twist by sighting across the top of a pair of winding sticks.

For a simple butt joint without splines or biscuits, a roller is the only required applicator. The butt joint with biscuits shown in "Gluing up with Biscuits" requires a more complicated glue application procedure, which is described in the photo captions.

Flattening the Board

Once the glue has cured — about two hours for PVA glue — unclamp the board but let it rest for another five or six hours so it will be strong enough to resist the stresses of further planing.

The board must now be made flat in length and width, to thickness, and to dimension. The way boards are flattened by hand is to plane across the grain. Counter-intuitive as it may seem, this method produces flatness and smoothness impossible to achieve any other way, and it underscores the unique capabilities of the humble hand plane once again. Refer to the photos in "Flattening the Board."

Clamp the workpiece firmly to the bench. Set the plane for a fine cut and lubricate the sole with a few strokes of candle wax. Begin on one edge. You will hear and feel the plane click and catch where it cuts the high spots. Make about six strokes in the same place, then move over a plane width and repeat. Lighten the cut when you start producing a continuous shaving as the plane travels across the board. Continually brush the workpiece clean of shavings. Keep checking for flat with your straightedge. Check for twist early in the flattening stage with winding sticks, and make the appropriate adjustments. As you steadily lighten the cut, the shavings will become ever finer. When they reach the near-dust stage, the board is as smooth as you can make it with a plane. In the case of a breadboard, or a benchtop surface, the job is done. If the work is a piece of fine furniture, you can turn to finer grits of sandpaper, starting at #250, before applying the finish.

Are butt joints simple? Not really. But learning to make them correctly provides you with a good opportunity to improve your hand-planing skills.

Breadboard Ends: A Flawed Technique Lives On

There are various stories about why the breadboard end came into being. The popular one, of course, is that it keeps boards flat. It doesn't, no matter how well constructed: if the center pieces are determined to cup, nothing will stop it from happening.

A cursory inspection of any breadboard end will show that shrinkage leaves the once flush edges at odds. No surprise here, since the base board shrinks and expands in width and the end board remains constant in length. In short, it's an example of cockeyed technical thinking; it doesn't work. However, aesthetically it has become a widely-accepted practice because it frames the long grain of a tabletop or a breadboard attractively.

Breadboard ends first appeared when hand tools ruled the shop, so it's no surprise that the end piece was applied as a tongue-and-groove. Because a hand plow plane can't make a stopped groove, the through groove on the end board was married to a tongue on the base board made with a shoulder plane.

Once shapers and table saws became the norm, the hand tool method was replaced by a loose tongue. Having a joint comprised of three separate pieces enabled makers

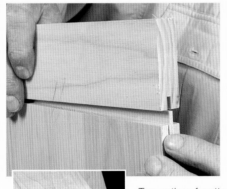

Two options for attaching breadboard ends are loose tongue (top left) and biscuits (right). The inset photo shows the flush-fitted biscuit option at bottom while at top is the loose option embellished with 1" ebony inserts. The end board extends beyond the main board, and the inserts — extending proud of the end board — have been modeled by a file to follow the shapes of the main board and end board.

to hide differential shrinkage by having the end board project from the base board and the spline project still farther. The detail could be further emphasized by using a different wood for the spline. This technique was widely used by the architects Charles and Henry Greene.

Now, biscuits allow us to dispense with the spline, but the shrinkage problem remains. Again we can resort to slightly different dimensions of the parts. The end result is the retention of a technique, which, although flawed, persists simply because we like its appearance.

Frame-and-Panel Doors

Sooner or later, your projects will lead you into the realm of door-building. Rectangular panels in frames seems pretty easy, but the final result can be disappointing if you don't consider design along with building technique. Here's a sensible overview of door design that provides insight and options for making attractive, harmonious cabinet doors.

by Ian Kirby

Frame-and-panel doors nearly always look pretty good. The reason is that harmony automatically results from the construction: as you can see in the drawings on the next few pages, all the lines follow the architecture of the frame. Nevertheless, if you build without paying attention to proportions and details, the door probably won't look ugly, but it also won't look its best. Many small considerations at the planning stage are what makes a door really pleasing to the eye.

Why Frame and Panel?

Let's begin by looking at the reasons why we use the frame-and-panel. It's our time-honored solution to the fact that solid wood changes in width and thickness in response to moisture in the air. By making a frame out of narrow pieces of wood, the wide panel trapped in a groove inside the frame is free to expand and contract. A broad beveled edge—called the field—disguises the movement and thins the panel to fit its groove. This system is very old, and people are totally comfortable with how it looks. When we make doors from plywood or MDF that don't shrink or expand, we often rout out shapes that imitate solid-wood frames.

Design by Drawing & Building

Draw what looks best to you, then build a full-size sample in wood. Look at it in room light to see how the shadows fall. It'll probably look good, but if you don't like the effect, it's easy to experiment and revise the shapes to make the composition more harmonious.

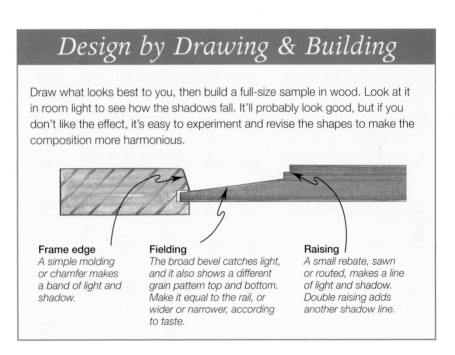

Frame edge
A simple molding or chamfer makes a band of light and shadow.

Fielding
The broad bevel catches light, and it also shows a different grain pattern top and bottom. Make it equal to the rail, or wider or narrower, according to taste.

Raising
A small rebate, sawn or routed, makes a line of light and shadow. Double raising adds another shadow line.

Raised and fielded all around isn't the only good solution. You can get the same benefits from a panel that's fielded on two sides only, a flat panel, or an overlay panel. And by adding muntins, you can make panels with any width wood. You'll see these variations in the drawings on pages 102 and 103.

When you want to design a door, you actually face two sets of decisions: how it is going to look, and how it is going to be made. Although techniques affect appearance, it's a mistake to allow technique to take over. When that happens, everything comes out looking the same. You need to be able to make whatever you design, which usually means choosing or modifying your techniques to suit your design decisions. It's worthwhile not only to explore all the alternatives made possible by techniques you know, but also to look for new techniques because they will open

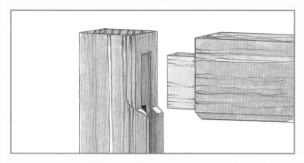

Chamfered Edge, Mitered Shoulder

A chamfer creates a simple band of light or shadow. Try sawing or planing a steep chamfer, 12 to 15 degrees. Any inside edge molding can be mitered by cutting back the shoulder line on the stile to the inside edge of the molding.

Routed Edge, Coped Joint

A complex routed edge makes lots of lines and shadows. A matched set of router bits cuts both parts. Any frame molding can be coped by cutting back the rail shoulder so it fits over the molding on the stile. The coped joint has no tolerance for miscut parts or warped and twisted wood.

Solving Other Joint Problems

Coped joints with one locating shoulder and soft curves (above) can tolerate sloppy manufacturing and wood variation. A soft molding makes soft highlights and diffuses shadows. Coping a chamfer (below) leaves a fragile feather edge. It's better to miter chamfers.

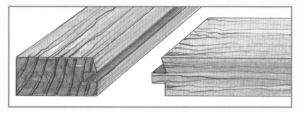

up more design possibilities than you currently have available to you.

For example, compare making a door with a cope and stick router bit set plus a panel-raising bit, to making it with the table saw. The bit set creates enough of a joint to hold the frame together; it makes matching grooves for the panel, and it molds the inside edge of the frame. Its companion panel-raising bit forms the field and the tongue that fits the groove in the frame, and it also might mold the raised portion of the panel. This tooling gets the whole job done. The trouble is, big door or little door, you can't adjust anything. For all their advantages, router bit sets take control of how the door looks. The table saw, on the other hand, can shape any size groove, rebate, and chamfer, and it is easily jigged to saw fields up to nearly 3" wide. Such details as beads, roundovers and coves can be routed after shaping on the saw. Shop-jigged techniques like these require more know-how than bit sets, but they give you control of dimensions, proportions and details.

Design and Technique Considerations

Design is the process of achieving a good-looking result within realistic limitations. The available technology is one kind of limitation. Two more are function and form—the cabinet has to close, so it needs doors; the cabinet is this big, so the doors have to fit. But the foundation under every design problem is neither form nor function. It's economics, which in woodworking means getting the best out of the wood and tools you've got. Of course, it would be nice to buy some spectacular wide planks for panels, but what about the stash of beautiful 6" boards you've been storing for longer than you care to admit?

One way to make a panel out of narrow boards is to glue up the width you need, but maybe the figure makes a lousy edge-to-edge match, or maybe there still isn't enough width, so you add a narrow strip, and now the figure and color don't match: a real distraction. A better alternative is to build door frames with a dividing strip, called a muntin, as shown on page 102. Although muntins typically tenon into the rails, there's no technical reason why this has to be. They can be cut the same length as the stiles with short rails in between, a small technical change that can have a large effect on overall door appearance.

Making a muntin is no more difficult than gluing up a panel, plus it hands you another design choice: to raise or not to raise. While a raised panel is traditional, it's not the only solution. With narrow pieces of reasonably dry wood going into a modern interior, movement is not such a big issue, so a flat panel is another good alternative.

Retain the flat panel by a rabbeted edge. The width of the rabbet and the location of the frame groove give you control over the shadow lines. If you want less shadow, move the panel groove closer to the front of the frame. For a deep, dramatic shadow, move the groove toward the back.

Working with Light and Shadow

To work out proportions and frame details, draw the door in front elevation, full-size. The drawing shows you a lot, but it can't portray the effect of light and shadow on the different levels of frame and panel. In the real world, you don't see in elevation view. You always see in perspective and it changes as you move or as the door opens and closes. What you see also depends on the light you see it in. The only way to assess the effect of light and shadow is to build a full-size mock-up and look at it in the room.

If it looks terrific, great; build the doors. However, if your mock-ups aren't as dramatic as you expected, the reason is likely to be depth, or the lack of it. Increasing visual depth

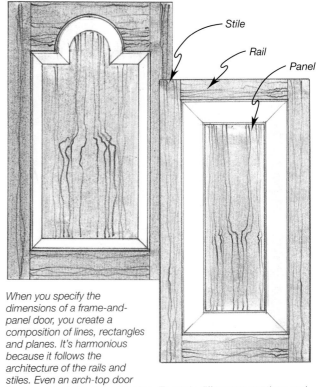

When you specify the dimensions of a frame-and-panel door, you create a composition of lines, rectangles and planes. It's harmonious because it follows the architecture of the rails and stiles. Even an arch-top door is symmetrical about a center line. To study different proportions and details, draw frame-and-panel doors full-size. You can't get a sense of proportion without a visual reference.

*Quick*Tip

Retrofitting Option for Euro Hinges

Someday you may need to replace a set of worn-out butt hinges on a cabinet door with Euro-style cup hinges. Provided the cabinet doors are ¾" thick, it will be easy to find suitable cup hinges. If, however, your cabinet door is thicker than ¾", here's a way to retrofit thicker doors to work with standard cup hinges: Simply rout out an area in the door back for each cup bracket that reduces the door's thickness to ¾". Then bore and install the hinges as usual. Try to keep the routed area as small as possible for neater appearance. You may also want to stain the exposed wood in this area to help blend it in with the rest of the finished wood.

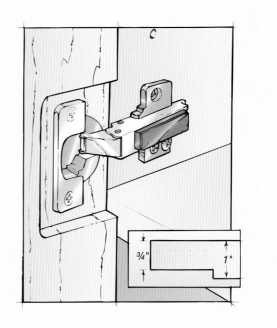

Flat Panels

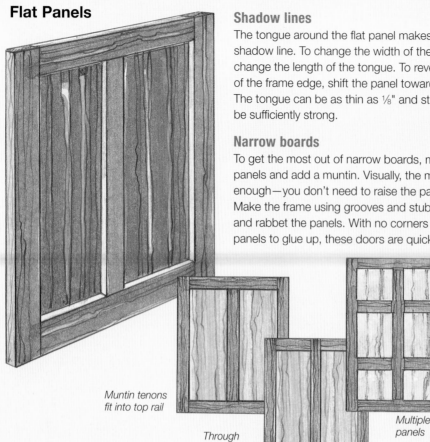

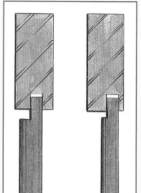

Shadow lines

The tongue around the flat panel makes a deep shadow line. To change the width of the shadow, change the length of the tongue. To reveal more of the frame edge, shift the panel toward the back. The tongue can be as thin as 1/8" and still be sufficiently strong.

Narrow boards

To get the most out of narrow boards, make flat panels and add a muntin. Visually, the muntin is enough—you don't need to raise the panels, too. Make the frame using grooves and stub tenons, and rabbet the panels. With no corners to fit and no panels to glue up, these doors are quick to make.

Muntins

A muntin divides the frame to fit narrow panels. The muntin can be held between the rails, or it can follow the form of the stiles. For a different look, divide the door into small panels with rails and muntins. Proportion the muntins to suit the frame.

Muntin tenons fit into top rail

Through muntin with short rails

Multiple panels

Fielded on Two Sides

Narrow Boards

To use narrow boards, add a centered muntin. The double-raised effect of two small rebates also enriches the composition. These details are easy to saw and rout.

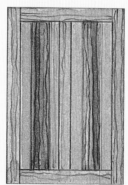

Centered muntin

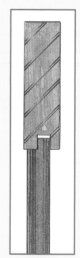

No Shadow Lines

Raising and fielding two sides of the panel, instead of all four, simplifies how it looks and how it's made.

To avoid a shadow line top and bottom, size the panel's tongue to fit the groove in the frame and make the front surfaces almost flush. The telling detail is the little diagonal line where the bevel crosses the inside edge of the frame.

Double-raising

Overlay Panels

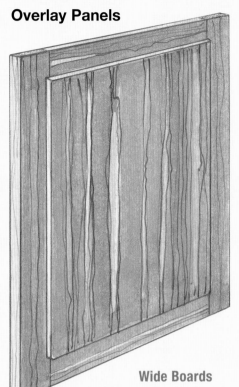

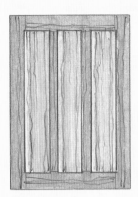

Narrow panels

Multiple Panels
To enrich the composition, and to get the best out of ordinary wood, divide the overlay panel into a number of smaller ones. This is another way to make wide doors with narrow wood.

Edge Details
Grooves retain the overlay panel in its frame. To highlight the edge of the panel, chamfer it, or scratch a little bead.

Square panels

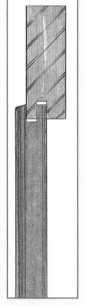

Wide Boards
An overlay panel is a good way to showcase wide, highly figured boards. There is no raising or fielding to disrupt the patterns in the wood. Because the panel stands proud of the frame, it casts dramatic shadow lines. Visually, the panel comes forward, while the frame recedes backward.

makes stronger shadows. You can do it in a number of ways: enlarge the molding, move the panel backward in the frame, change the width of the raising or, on a flat panel, change the width of the rabbet.

You'll soon notice that from most viewing distances, all you see of any molded profile is light and shadow, and simple profiles often work best.

A chamfer or a little rabbet doesn't seem like much of a molding, but it makes a sharp line of light. Until you get quite close to them, complex profiles look about the same as simple ones: lines of light and shadow.

As for the panel itself, raising and fielding is one solution, and a flat panel is

a second. Fielding two sides instead of all four lies in between the two. You get the visual strength of the vertical fielding, without cross-grain busyness at the top and bottom. Since the wood doesn't move in length, just make a square tongue to fit the groove, with a tight (shadow-free) shoulder line.

To get the most out of highly figured wood, try making an overlay panel. The overlay panel comes forward and the frame recedes. With wide boards, make a single panel. With narrow boards, either glue up or else add muntins to divide the frame. The highlights and shadows created by the two levels of panel and frame are dramatic.

Moving Beyond Technique
Learning to see light and shadow is the key to making frame-and-panel doors. To take control of visual effects, you have to take a step beyond technique and focus on design and aesthetics. The next step is to turn the process around by modifying your techniques to achieve the visual effects you want. This is design at its most practical level. It's very satisfying to work out a solution that not only gets the most out of your materials and shop time, but also produces a set of cabinet doors that really do look their best.

How to Make Tambour Doors

All it takes is a piece of cotton artist's canvas and plenty of glue to turn a pile of slats into a genuine tambour door. The construction process is easy, and the end result can add a unique door style to your next casework project.

by Chris Inman

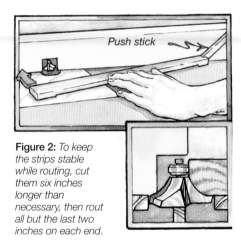

Figure 2: *To keep the strips stable while routing, cut them six inches longer than necessary, then rout all but the last two inches on each end.*

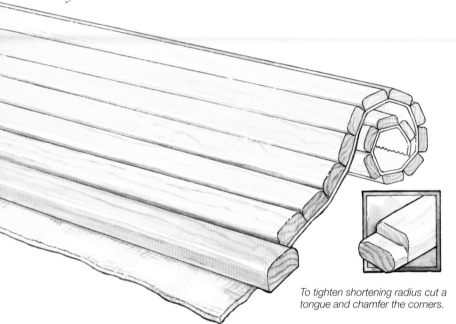

To tighten shortening radius cut a tongue and chamfer the corners.

Mention tambour and most people immediately think of a rolltop desk. However, this type of door is actually suitable for a wide variety of cabinets, and what's more, making a tambour panel is easier than building a common frame and panel door.

If you're unfamiliar with tambour, a quick review will help clear things up. A tambour door typically consists of narrow wood strips glued to a cloth backing, although some doors are made with wood strips connected by a wire cable or even linked together with sophisticated interlocking joints. The cloth-backed type is the easiest to make in the home shop. With the cloth acting like a hinge connecting all the pieces, the door is capable of turning gradual corners. Once the tambour has been made, it's installed in a cabinet with two parallel grooves that guide the panel into its open and closed positions.

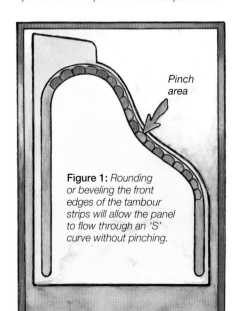

Figure 1: *Rounding or beveling the front edges of the tambour strips will allow the panel to flow through an 'S' curve without pinching.*

Pinch area

Tambour is usually made with wood up to 1" thick, although it's important to keep in mind that tambour panels will have a more difficult time turning corners as the thickness or width of the wood strips increases—narrower strips allow a tighter turn. Increasing the width of the cabinet grooves also accommodates thicker or wider stock, as does cutting a thin tongue on the ends of thicker strips.

Most often, the cabinet grooves follow one of two patterns: a single curve or an "S" curve. In order for the tambour to glide through an "S" curve, the front edges of the wood strips must be rounded or beveled so they don't pinch against each other as the panel flexes forward (see Figure 1). Relieving the edges isn't necessary on a door used in a single curve.

Making the Wood Strips

On small projects, use thin strips for example, to make a roll-top bread box, tambour strips ¼" thick by ⅝" wide would be a good choice. Cutting the strips can be done in one of two ways. If you rip a ⅝"-thick board into ¼"-thick strips, your tambour will have a quartersawn appearance. If you prefer a plain-sawn appearance, use ¼"-thick lumber and rip it into the ⅝"-wide strips. With this second method, be sure to draw a large triangle on the face of each board before ripping so you can install the strips in the same order later on.

No matter which cutting method you choose, some of the strips will warp. It's always best, therefore, to cut about 25% more strips than you need for your panel. It's also a good idea to let your strips air dry for a few days to guarantee their stability. Once the material stabilizes, set up your router table for beveling or rounding over the front edges of the strips. Relieving the edges will create a V-shaped gap between each pair of strips on the assembled tambour, allowing it to bend forward slightly in the "S" curve, as shown in Figure 1.

Be sure to use a push stick to safely rout such small material, and make it a rule to cut the strips about

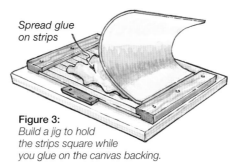

Spread glue on strips

Figure 3:
Build a jig to hold the strips square while you glue on the canvas backing.

six inches longer than you actually need (see Figure 2). If you can avoid routing the last few inches of each strip you'll always have a flat, stable surface contacting the router table while the rest of the strip gets increasingly tippy.

Making the Panel

The ideal tambour backing is lightweight artist's canvas, available at art supply stores. Cut your fabric a few inches longer than the door size and ½" narrower than the length of the slats (you don't want the fabric reaching the cabinet grooves).

To hold the strips square while you apply the fabric, build the simple framing jig shown in Figure 3. Set the strips face side down in the jig and snug them together, then lay out a line ¼" from each side edge to use as a guide for spreading the glue and laying the canvas. Often, the last strip in a tambour is shaped differently for use as a handle, so be sure it's properly positioned in the panel. Apply yellow glue to the strips with a small brush, carefully working

up to the pencil line, then lay the fabric on the wood and press it down evenly with hand pressure. After the glue dries for an hour, gently bend the tambour to break any glue bonds between the slats. Once this glue has been removed with a knife, loosely curl the tambour and set it on end so the glue cures thoroughly.

Trim off the excess canvas so about ⅛" on each end strip is revealed. To complete your tambour, install the panel in the cabinet, then cut one of the leftover wood strips ½" shorter than the rest and screw it to the fabric on the back side of the handle strip in the panel (see Figure 4). This will prevent the fabric from unraveling or coming loose from the wood.

Back-up strip

Figure 4: *Covering the end of the canvas with a back-up strip will keep the fabric from unraveling.*

Veneering a Drawer Face

Not all wood panels need to be made of solid wood or even plywood. Wood veneer applied over a particleboard or MDF core is an excellent option to mimic the look of solid wood, and you can use any interesting wood species you like. Best of all, we'll dispel a common misconception: veneering is not as hard as you might think.

by Bruce Kieffer

Veneering is one of the most challenging and interesting aspects of woodworking. In fact, many in the field consider it an art form. While there's a lot of techniques to learn on the road to mastering veneering, there's always a starting point. The best way to get your feet wet in veneering is by concentrating on a simple and practical application. Let's say you want to make a maple chest of drawers. The front of this chest will be all drawer faces, made to look like one large flat plane. To give your chest a decorative look you decide to make the drawer faces out of birdseye maple. Here's a situation where veneering is the perfect solution. You'll be doing the simplest form of flat panel veneering, requiring no joining or seaming, and you probably have most of the tools you need on hand.

Basically, a veneered drawer face like this should be made of ¾" industrial-grade particleboard edged with ¼"-thick solid wood, and then covered on both sides with glued-on veneer. Whenever you're working with veneer you must remember that you have to end up with a balanced panel. This means that whatever is applied to one side of the core is also applied to the other side. In addition, the grain of the veneer should run the same way on both sides of the core. To save on costs, the hidden inside of the drawer face can be veneered with a different grade or species of veneer.

Figure 1: *Glue and clamp the solid edging to the core, two sides at a time. The corners of the edging can be mitered or overlapped.*

Having enough clamps on hand is also critical. Your clamps should be spaced at three- to four-inch intervals on the entire surface of the core, and you should have some clamps on hand with jaws that are deep enough to reach and apply pressure to the center of the core.

Almost any glue that's made for bonding solid wood can be used for veneering. Yellow carpenter's glue works

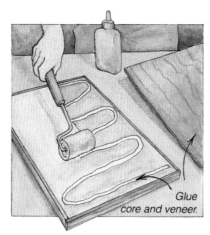

Figure 2: *Use a paint roller to spread the glue evenly on the core and the back of the veneer.*

well, but white glue is an even better choice for veneering larger surfaces because it dries more slowly. While some woodworkers contend that contact cement works fine and cuts down on clamping requirements, it doesn't generally offer enough bonding strength to hold the veneer down for an extended period of time.

Making Your Drawer Faces

For this example, we'll make the drawer boxes and faces as separate components. When they're ready to be assembled, drill ⅜" holes through the fronts of the drawers and attach the drawer faces with screws and washers. The ⅜" holes allow for minor adjustments and make it easy to align the drawer faces in their openings.

Calculate the finished widths and lengths of each drawer face and then cut your particleboard cores ½" narrower and shorter to allow for the solid-wood edging. Cut the solid edging ¼" thick, ¾" plus ¹⁄₃₂" wide, and 1" longer than the lengths you need. You can miter the ends of the edging or overlap them. In either case, once this is done, glue and clamp the edging to the core, as shown in Figure 1. When the edging is complete and the glue has dried, sand the edges flush with the core.

The next step in this process is to rough-cut the veneer. An inexpensive tool known as a veneer saw works best for this task. Lay out the areas on your veneer sheets where you will cut out the pieces for the drawer faces. Make sure to add at least 1" in length and width for overhang, which will be trimmed off after the veneer is glued in place. Carefully guide the veneer saw against a straightedge to cut the length, then the width of the veneer. Make several light cutting passes with the saw until you cut through the veneer.

Gluing and clamping the veneer to its core is simple. Think of it as though you are creating a triple-decker sandwich with plenty of mayo. Each side of the core is covered with glue, then one side of each veneer piece is covered with glue. Position these against each other, followed by a separator piece of newspaper, and finally a caul to flatten the veneer and distribute the pressure from the clamps. In this case, the cauls are ¾" particleboard panels cut to the same length and width as the veneer. Do one drawer at a time, using a roller to spread the glue, as shown in Figure 2.

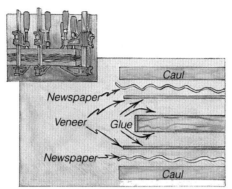

Figure 3: *Start clamping in the center of the core and slowly work the pressure out toward the edges. This method of clamping reduces the possibility of trapped glue pockets.*

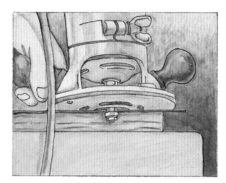

Figure 4: *Trim off the excess veneer with a piloted flush-trimming bit. Rout backwards to reduce tearout.*

Start applying pressure by clamping in the center of the drawer face and working out. This eliminates the possibility of trapping any glue pockets in the middle of the drawer face (see Figure 3). Allow the glue to cure for 24 hours and then unclamp and separate your sandwich.

Finish up your drawer by chucking a flush-trimming bit in the router and trimming off the overhanging veneer edges, as shown in Figure 4. Routing backwards, essentially pulling the router toward you, will reduce the chance of tearout. Finish-sand the drawer faces, check their fit, and make any necessary adjustments. Make sure to apply your finish equally to all surfaces of the drawer faces to properly seal them and reduce the chance of warping.

*Quick*Tip

Stretch Your Pipe Clamps
On those few occasions when you need an extra-long clamp, don't buy long pipes that will spend the rest of their lives in a dark corner. Just invest in a couple of pipe couplings and join two or more of your existing short lengths of pipe together. The couplings cost less than a buck each and are available at any home center.

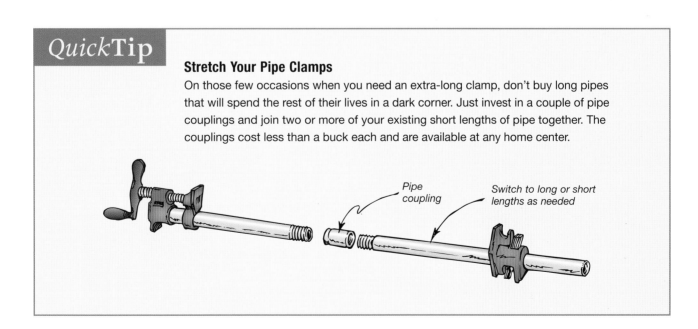

Pipe coupling

Switch to long or short lengths as needed

Veneering Wide Panels

Veneering wide panels isn't difficult, provided you apply clamping pressure evenly. Doing this doesn't require a truckload of clamps or a fancy veneering press. All you need are some scraps of oak, a few sheets of kraft paper and ordinary particleboard to create a simple, effective veneer press.

by Bruce Kieffer

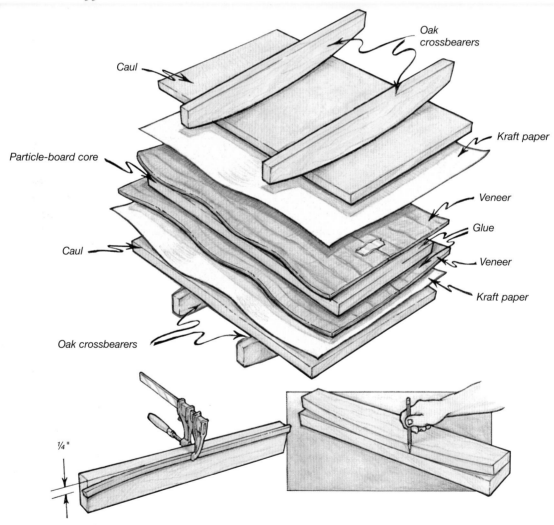

Figure 1: *To form the arc, clamp a thin wood strip to the center of an oak crossbearer and bend the strip so it is ¼" from the edge at the ends of the board. When the crossbearers are clamped onto the cauls they distribute pressure evenly over the entire width of the veneer.*

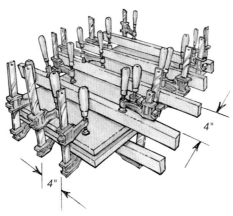

Figure 2: *Clamp the crossbearers at 4" intervals and space additional clamps around the perimeter of the assembly to hold the edges.*

Most woodworkers who start experimenting with veneer quickly face a dilemma. They need to cover a surface wider than the capacities of their clamps but they don't want to purchase a costly veneer press. Don't fret; try caul veneering. It's cheap, easy, effective, and adaptable to most of the situations you'll come across.

Caul veneering is a simple idea consisting of two easy to make wood devices known as cauls and crossbearers. Cauls are pieces of ¾" particleboard cut slightly larger than the core that's being veneered. Crossbearers are long pieces of hardwood with a slight arc cut on one side. When used together these devices transfer clamping pressure to the center of the core, across the veneer, and then out to the edges (see Figure 1). This technique eliminates the chance of trapping glue pockets between the veneer and its core.

Preparing the Veneer and Core

The first step in veneering is to splice and join your veneer sheets together, and cut the particle board core to its finished dimensions. Always remember that when you veneer you need to create balanced panels. This means you must apply veneer to both sides of the core, keeping the grain running in the same direction so that the finished panel won't warp.

Forming Cauls and Crossbearers

Oak makes the best crossbearers. Cut your crossbearers 1½" thick, 2½" wide, and 36" long (or longer if you anticipate the need to clamp wider veneer). The number of crossbearers needed depends on the length of your veneer. You'll need a set of two crossbearers at each clamping position and enough to space the sets at 4" intervals along the length of the veneer.

Cutting uniform arcs on the crossbearers is critical so they evenly distribute pressure across the width of the veneer. Draw the large radius of the arc by tracing along a thin flexible strip of wood clamped at the center of the crossbearer and held back ¼" from the edge at both ends, as shown in Figure 1. Cut away the waste and sand the sawn edge smooth. Use this finished crossbearer as a template for cutting out one more crossbearer. Clamp these two crossbearers together at the ends with their arched edges facing each other. Look at the joint between the crossbearers to see that there are no gaps and that pressure is being applied over their entire length. Make any necessary adjustments, then use these first two pieces as templates for laying out the arcs on the rest of your crossbearers. Cut out the remaining crossbearers and sand them to match in pairs.

The two cauls are cut from ¾"-thick particleboard and are made 1" wider and 1" longer than the core being veneered.

Gluing the Veneer to its Core

When faced with clamping large sheets of veneer use a slow-setting glue, like white glue, to give you more assembly time. On smaller areas you can also use yellow glue for its fast-drying qualities. Have everything ready before you begin, including tools, glue, newspaper, clamps, cauls and crossbearers. An extra set of hands also helps for larger veneering tasks.

Pour glue onto one side of the core and on one sheet of veneer, and use a 3" or wider paint roller to spread the glue evenly. Position the glued veneer on the core so there is an equal amount overhanging all the edges. Place a piece of kraft paper on the face of the veneer, then set one caul on top of the paper. Flip over this assembly and repeat these steps to glue veneer to the other side of the core. Remember to match the grain direction on both sides of the panel.

Clamp a set of crossbearers across the middle of the cauls and apply clamping pressure until the crossbearer ends touch the cauls on both sides. Check to see that the veneer sheets haven't slipped out of position. Working toward the ends of the veneer, clamp on the remaining crossbearers at 4" intervals. Place additional clamps between the sets of crossbearers near the edges of the cauls and use more clamps across the ends of the cauls at 4" intervals (see Figure 2).

Look at the joint between the veneer and the core to see if glue is oozing out its entire length. If there are dry spots, that probably means there's not enough clamping pressure, so add a few more clamps and turn the cranks a little further to bear down on the crossbearers.

After allowing the glue to cure overnight, remove the clamps, crossbearers, and cauls. Next, peel away the kraft paper, trim off the overhanging veneer edges and sand the faces of the veneer smooth. Now you're ready to use your veneered panel for whatever project you've planned.

Making Tapered Legs on a Jointer

If you think jointers only flatten wood, this simple technique for tapering stock on a jointer will surprise and amaze you. We'll take you through the basics of this easy and fun task. All it takes are a few machine adjustments, a simple push stick, wedge of scrap wood and a clamp.

by Linda Haus

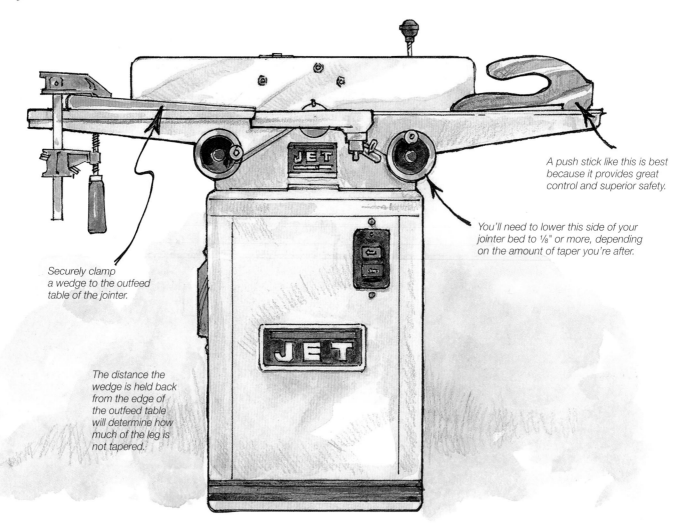

A push stick like this is best because it provides great control and superior safety.

You'll need to lower this side of your jointer bed to 1/8" or more, depending on the amount of taper you're after.

Securely clamp a wedge to the outfeed table of the jointer.

The distance the wedge is held back from the edge of the outfeed table will determine how much of the leg is not tapered.

The first time you see someone setting up to taper legs on a jointer, you may be amazed. It's like watching a car race: you don't want to see someone lose a finger (crash a car), but the apparent danger absolutely holds your attention. Actually, the technique is not only safe, but it also lets you do things you just can't do when forming legs on a band saw or table saw tapering jig.

The key to this technique is a wooden wedge clamped to the outfeed table of the jointer. The wedge becomes a ramp for the leg to climb as the cutterhead shapes the face of the stock. The leading edge of the leg forms the geometry of the cut as it climbs the wedge and the forward edge of the infeed table: the leg stock gets dragged through the cutter in a gentle arc and provides the unique style of a jointer-tapered leg.

Four Tapering Variables

The taper of the leg is affected by four variables. First, the incline of the wedge: the steeper the incline, the more acute the taper. Second, how close to the front edge of the outfeed table the wedge is clamped: the spacing sets the flat (or apron) area. Third and fourth, the length of the leg and depth of cut set by the infeed table: as you increase the leg length in relationship to the wedge, the taper becomes more gentle. As you increase the depth of cut, the taper becomes more acute or pronounced.

A shop-made plywood push stick is a must. It gives you superior control and completely protects your pushing hand as you move the stock across the cutter (no crashes!). Your lead hand is always held past the cutter, as shown in the photos and illustrations on these pages. The whole operation is also done with the guard in place, for

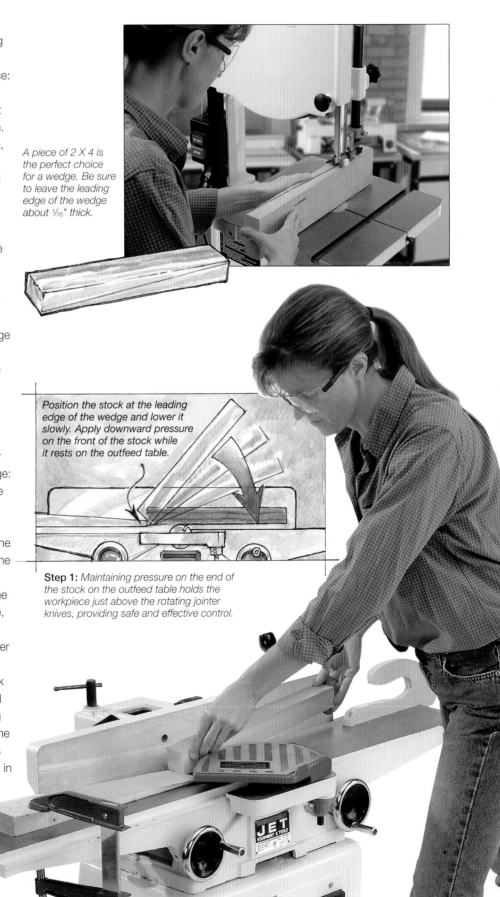

A piece of 2 X 4 is the perfect choice for a wedge. Be sure to leave the leading edge of the wedge about 1/16" thick.

Position the stock at the leading edge of the wedge and lower it slowly. Apply downward pressure on the front of the stock while it rests on the outfeed table.

Step 1: *Maintaining pressure on the end of the stock on the outfeed table holds the workpiece just above the rotating jointer knives, providing safe and effective control.*

Variations on a Tapered Theme

You can create several variations of the typical four-sided tapered leg on your jointer. For instance, you can make them with or without a foot. You can taper two adjacent faces (with or without a foot). You can start the taper high or low…you get the idea. Here are four possible legs made from stock of the same length and thickness.

This leg is tapered on all four sides and has no foot. It requires several passes and a depth of cut setting of about ³/₁₆".

This leg is tapered on four sides but ends with a foot. You create the foot by clamping a stop block in place after you've made the first few passes across the jointer.

This is a two-sided taper without a foot. It's very basic but appropriate in many situations.

It is possible to mix and match as you design your legs. Here is a two-sided taper with a foot. The back corner was chamfered to present a more delicate shape.

*Quick*Tip

Quick Bench Vise

If your bench isn't outfitted with a vise, here's a quick and inexpensive option. Take a scrap of hardwood 1" thick by 18" long by 8" wide and drill and countersink holes 1" from the top edge. Then cut a slot on both ends, 3" deep and wide enough to accommodate a set of bar clamps. Take a second piece the same size and cut slots in the same place. Then fasten the first piece to the workbench, slide in the clamps, and put the second piece on with the screw ends facing out. Now you have an extra wood vise whenever you need one.

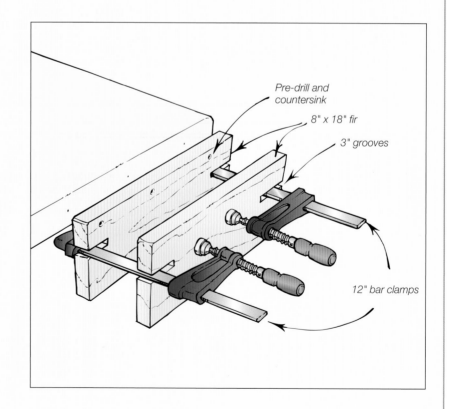

Pre-drill and countersink

8" x 18" fir

3" grooves

12" bar clamps

additional safety. (Jointers, like all power tools, are inherently dangerous. Use common sense and protective gear.)

After the wedge is made and clamped in place, the cutting process is simple. Place the "top end" of the prepared stock (cut to length and surfaced exactly square) onto the outfeed table and bump it gently against the end of the wedge and tight to the jointer fence. Hold it in place with your left hand (with gentle downward pressure) as you grab the push stick and hook it onto the other end of the leg. Rotate the infeed end of the leg toward the table, and when you make contact, move it slowly forward. The front end of the leg will lift and start riding the incline. Because you've

lowered the infeed table by ⅛" or more, you won't really start cutting until you're near the end of the leg on the first cuts. If you are tapering more than one face of the leg, spin the leg and repeat the cut. For symmetrical tapers, you need to duplicate the same number of cuts per face. Repeat the process until you're pleased with the taper. If you are leaving a little foot on the bottom of the leg, you'll need to incorporate a stop block

on the wedge after the first or second pass on each face of the leg.

You can make a variety of leg shapes and styles using this basic setup. One real benefit to tapering your legs on the jointer is, if your knives are sharp, sanding is minimal.

Easily tapered legs and virtually no sanding…simply amazing!

Stop block (optional) clamped toward back of wedge

Foot

Step 2: *Using your push stick, first lower your stock down to the level of the infeed table and then push it up the ramp. You can clamp a stop block to the back of your ramp to create a foot on your leg.*

Two Easy Ways to Calculate Cove Cuts

Using formulas to determine blade height and fence angles is easy in the computer age. Try one of these mathematically sound techniques to calculate the settings for cutting accurate coves on your table saw.

by Len Urban

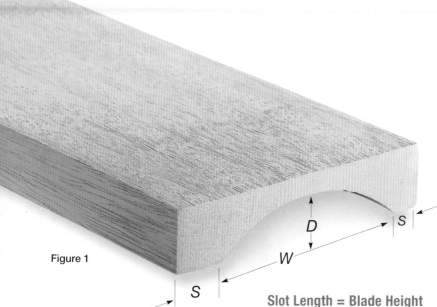

Figure 1

Setting the fence angle for cutting a cove on a table saw can be a hit-or-miss proposition. The following computer method eliminates most of the mathematics involved, yet it results in a predictable shape.

Start off by sketching out the cove molding you wish to make. Determine the cove width (W) and depth (D), and if you want it to have shoulders (S), mitered edges, and so forth. Rip sufficient stock to create the molding plus some extra stock for testing. Now you are ready to go to work.

Slot Length = Blade Height

The first measurement you need for the process is the blade height, because it creates the depth (D) of your cove cut. As an alternative to measuring the blade height from the tabletop—which can be tricky—you can raise the blade until you reach the pre-determined length of the blade slot. Since the slot length is longer than the blade is high and is easier to measure, it is the more accurate method. (Slot length, for our purposes, is the kerf left in a piece of hardboard by a 10" saw blade, as demonstrated in the photo on the next page.) Slot length can be calculated using this formula:

$$2 \times \sqrt{25 - (5-D)^2}$$

A calculator with a square root function will get you the measurement you need, or you can put the whole thing into a spreadsheet. If you use that approach, the formula bar in cell B2 should read:

$$\texttt{=2*SQRT(25-SUMSQ(5-A2))}$$

When you enter the desired cove depth into cell A2, the slot length will appear in cell B2. Remember, you'll get an answer with a decimal that you'll need to convert into a fraction. Clamp a piece of ¼" hardboard or plywood to the top of your table saw and slowly raise the blade until it creates the desired slot length, then turn off the saw and lower the blade.

Finding the Fence Angle

Next, set a compass to the width of the cove ("W" in Figure 1). Locate the pointed leg of the compass as close as you can to the lower right edge of the slot and draw an arc to the left of the slot, as shown in Figure 2. Then draw a straight line (AB) from the left edge at the top of the slot, tangent to the arc (point C), as shown in Figure 3. Next, draw a line (DE) parallel to AB (see Figure 4) at a distance equal to the width of the appropriate shoulder of the cove ("S" in Figure 1).

Figure 2: *After you have created the proper slot length in the plywood (below), set a compass to the width of the desired cove and strike an arc, as shown above.*

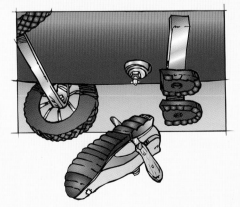

*Quick*Tip

Vibration Dampers

The heels from a tired pair of running sneakers generally have enough rubber-type material to make excellent vibration dampers for shop tools and tables. They can be custom cut with a bread knife. Use a Forstner bit to recess a bolt head and washer for mounting.

Fun with Formulas:
Woodworking with Computer Spreadsheets

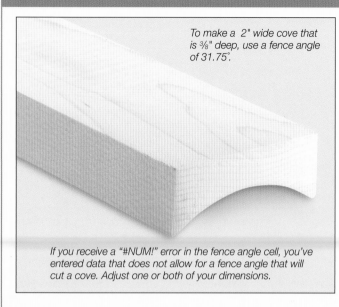

To make a 2" wide cove that is ⅜" deep, use a fence angle of 31.75°.

If you receive a "#NUM!" error in the fence angle cell, you've entered data that does not allow for a fence angle that will cut a cove. Adjust one or both of your dimensions.

Cove angle worksheet

Cove Depth (inches)	Cove Width (inches)	Fence Angle (degrees)
0.375	1.0	15.2588892595
0.500	1.0	13.2626872108
0.750	1.0	10.9429659270
1.000	1.0	9.5940763306
0.375	1.5	23.2517133839
0.500	1.5	20.1283232898
0.750	1.5	16.5437639640
1.000	1.5	14.4775244146
0.375	2.0	31.7599611836
0.500	2.0	27.3117529933
0.750	2.0	22.3128407964
1.000	2.0	19.4712370811
0.375	2.5	41.1438786223
0.500	2.5	34.9974345170
0.750	2.5	28.3319660940

There is more than one method to accomplish almost any woodworking task. When we began our cove-cutting quest, we thought all we'd need was an easy way to calculate the fence angles that would accommodate various cove requirements. After some head-scratching and reviewing some—by now—very old math books, we came up with an equation. We then turned to our trusty computer, equipped with a spreadsheet program, for help. To make it work, enter the following formula into cell C2 of a spreadsheet (see chart):

=ASIN(B2/(2*SQRT(25-((5-A2)^2))))*180/3.14159

As soon as you enter the depth of the cove into cell A2 and the width of the cove into B2, the correct fence angle magically appears in cell C2. While this fence angle is just the beginning of the process, it is a very good start!

Now, clamp a fence to the top of the hardboard with the face along line DE. Clamp a second fence to the table to create a chute for guiding the molding. Use the pre-ripped molding stock to locate the second fence. Make sure the molding slides smoothly along.

Choosing a Blade and Cutting the Coves

Any saw blade will work for cutting coves on a table saw, but blades with more teeth will leave smoother sawn surfaces than blades with fewer teeth. A fine-toothed plywood blade is ideal, if you have one.

To cut the cove, raise the blade so it just protrudes above the plywood and pass the workpiece slowly over the saw blade to make the first pass. Keep the workpiece pressed firmly down as you feed it through the chute. Safety is always a concern when using the table saw, especially in this case, since a blade guard cannot be used. The proper use of push blocks or push sticks is a must. Raise the blade a small amount and repeat the process for the second and subsequent cuts. Once you've raised the blade to the pre-cut slot length, the process is complete and the width of the cove will be equal to "W" and the depth will be dead on. Perfect shaping on the table saw.

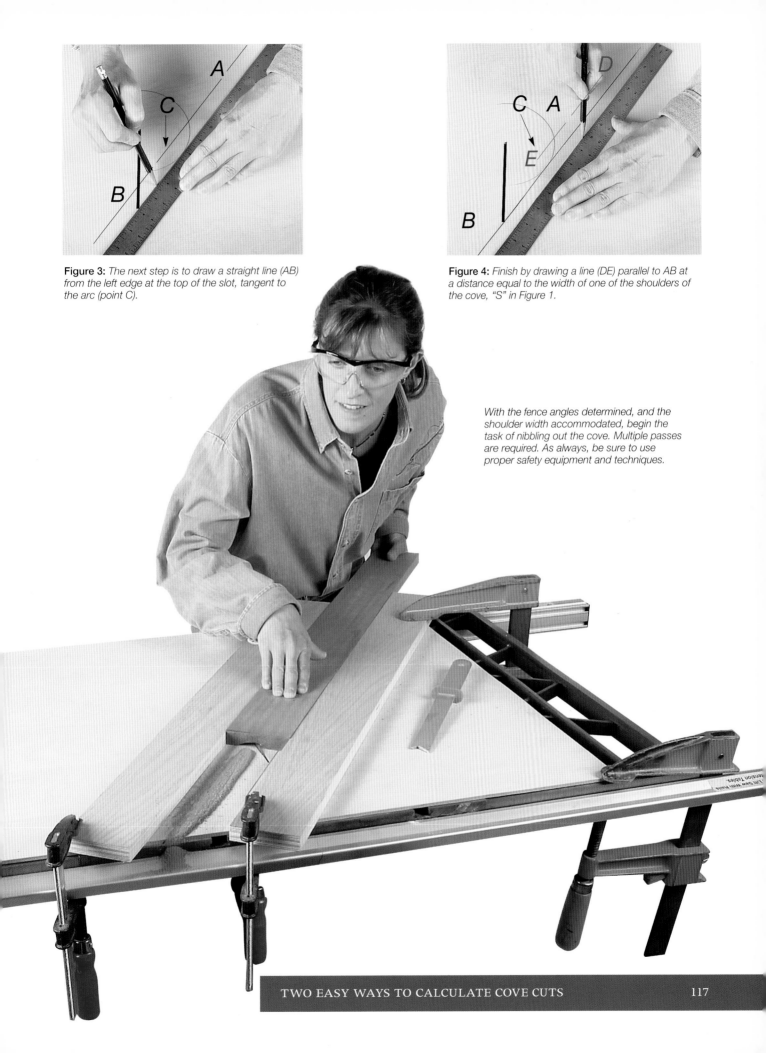

Figure 3: *The next step is to draw a straight line (AB) from the left edge at the top of the slot, tangent to the arc (point C).*

Figure 4: *Finish by drawing a line (DE) parallel to AB at a distance equal to the width of one of the shoulders of the cove, "S" in Figure 1.*

With the fence angles determined, and the shoulder width accommodated, begin the task of nibbling out the cove. Multiple passes are required. As always, be sure to use proper safety equipment and techniques.

Scroll Saw Secrets

Who wouldn't love to have a custom-made desk nameplate? This sort of signage is always a hit, and making them provides excellent practice for honing your precision scroll-sawing skills. A few pieces of scrap and a sharp blade are all it takes.

by Tom Durden

If you are just breaking into the intricate world of scroll sawing, the nameplates shown in the photo at left are great projects for learning because you end up with a useful item and pick up a lot of helpful scroll saw techniques along the way. If you're an old salt at scroll sawing already, cut a few of these anyway. You'll probably get a positive response when you give a friend one of these monikers. Mahogany is a good wood choice here; it's soft, easy to cut and looks sophisticated. And if you really want to enhance the look, do a little extra planning and select contrasting wood species to accent and offset the letters.

To get started, pick a style of print that you like. Simply go to your computer, choose a font, and print out the name. Now draw a straight line underneath the name to connect the bottom edge of all the letters. Cut the pattern along this reference line and trim away all the excess paper. Pick out the species of wood you prefer (¾" thickness) and run the edge of your stock along a jointer to give it a true straight edge. Take a moment to sand the board smooth now to reduce sanding when you're all finished scrolling. Apply your pattern using a spray adhesive or a glue stick, positioning it on the board so that the reference line is about ⅛" to 3/16" above the edge of the board. This will keep the name in one piece when you're through cutting.

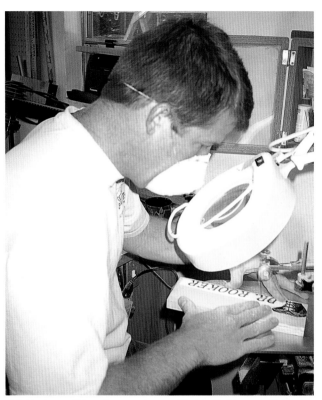

A lighted magnifying glass can be a real help with this sort of intricate work. Start at one end of the pattern and keep on cutting until you reach the other end…exiting on the reference line.

Here's a Slick Tape Trick

Usually, this is the point when you drill the holes required for your inside cutouts. Instead, here's a neat step to help you reduce burning and stretch out the life of your blades. Before drilling, apply clear packaging tape over the name. This tape is Teflon®-based and actually lubricates the blade as you cut, increasing blade life and reducing burns on the tight cutouts. With the tape pressed in place, go ahead and drill the interior access holes. Begin the cutting process by removing the inside (enclosed) areas first. Form the outside shape of the name starting at the edge of the board, beginning the cut on your reference line. Do not exit the cut until you've finished the name, exiting on the reference line as you do. You'll need the leftover piece later, so set it aside for now. Take the tape off the letters and use paint thinner to remove any leftover pattern or adhesive. Place the name on a sheet of sandpaper (to reduce the chances of snapping a letter) and sand the surface smooth with a sanding block.

Attaching the Base

Make your bases from ¾"-thick strips of wood with a classic ogee routed into their edges. For the name to look balanced, the base should be 1¾" wide and about 1" longer than the

name. If the base is slightly wide, run the edge on your joiner and route the edge again until the fit is perfect. Test-fit the name onto the base, trimming the reference line strip to length. To protect the letters while gluing the name to the base, turn to the cut-away you set aside earlier and use it as a clamping caul.

Once everything is glued and sanded, apply Watco Danish Natural Oil in a shallow tub. This is a good way to get finish into all the nooks and crannies. Allow the oil to dry completely and spray on a finish of Deft® Semi-Gloss.

Beyond the Basics

Now that you've got the basics covered, here are a few ideas to keep in mind to make your time on the scroll saw more productive and enjoyable.

Laminating Species: If you decide to try a multicolored, laminated name plate, you can really enhance the look by resawing a ⅛" piece of wood from the same species you selected for the bottom of the name cutout. Glue this ⅛" piece on top of your base. When you rout the base with the ogee bit, the top surface will be the same type and color of

Squaring Your Saw Cuts

Adjust Your Table for Square Cuts

Try the simple alignment procedure below to ensure that you get square cuts every time.

To test your cut for square, select a piece of scrap about ¾" in thickness. Place the wood flat on the tabletop and make a 1" cut straight into the wood, across the grain. Pull the wood straight back, away from the blade. Reposition the wood so your cut is facing the back of the blade. If the cut line and blade line up, then the blade will slide into the cut with no resistance: your table is square.

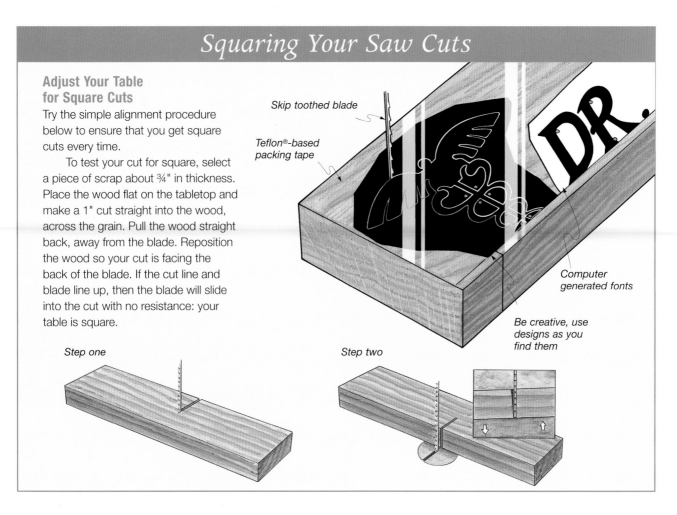

Skip toothed blade

Teflon®-based packing tape

Computer generated fonts

Be creative, use designs as you find them

Step one

Step two

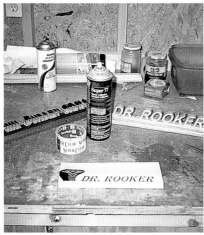

Teflon®-based packing tape joins spray adhesive as tools of the trade for delicate scroll saw work.

wood that is on the bottom of the name cutout. Adjust the cut so the shape of the ogee hides the glue joint.

Fine Details: When cutting fine details, always be aware of grain orientation. A good example is the doctor's cutout with the staff and serpent emblem (see "Squaring Your Saw Cuts"). With the grain of the wood running side to side, the staff would be unstable and break off easily. To eliminate this potential disaster, glue a section of wood (just the size of the staff design) into place with the grain running at 90° to the orientation of the strip of wood selected. Then apply the pattern to the spliced-in wood and cut as before. Also, when making

something like the teacher's cutout (the worm is made out of bubinga), be sure both woods are the same thickness to reduce sanding once the name has been cut out.

Planning ahead: We can't stress this enough…always plan ahead. The wrong gluing sequence can mean disaster. For instance, with the "Dr. Rooker" piece (shown on page 118), glue the two serpents and staffs in place first and then lightly trim the ends of the name until it fits perfectly in between. Then use a clamping caul to glue that piece in place.

Square Cuts: The best way to get reliably square cuts is to always be sure your table is at 90° to the saw blade, as discussed in the tint box on the previous page. But you also have to stick with good blades. As far as blades go, choose skip-tooth blades that include a reverse tooth configuration. Spend a little extra to be sure the blades you buy are precision ground. Once you've got a fresh blade loaded in the saw, tighten it as usual, but add an extra one-half turn to the tension knob to keep your cuts crisp.

Along with blade choice and checking for a square blade/table configuration, experiment with your saw's speed setting. Sometimes blades will cut better at a certain speed—and it isn't always the highest speed.

Dull blades: As you may expect, blades will eventually become dull. One way to detect a dull blade is when you have to start pushing harder on the wood to get the same cut. The blade will also tend to wander toward the softer grain, making it difficult to follow the line of the pattern. In some cases, the blade will burn the wood in tight turns. If it seems your blades are wearing out too quickly, check the tension of the blade.

Keep the waste piece from the name blank on hand. It will serve you well as a clamping caul when you're ready to attach the name to the base.

Apply gentle and even pressure when clamping the name to the base. Check the cutout's alignment and allow the glue to cure. The squeeze-out can be cleaned up later.

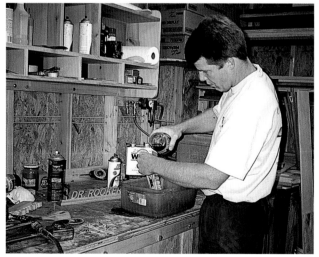

A plastic tub and a lot of polymerized oil are an effective way to apply the first sealing coat. The oil flows nicely into the scroll-sawn details.

QuickTip

Frame and Panel Benefits

Frame and panel doors don't just look pretty; they also perform a vital function. A free-floating panel is just about the only way to accommodate cross-grain wood movement, especially when you're working in solid hardwoods. Resolving the movement issue is particularly critical with inset doors: if you were to make solid-slab inset doors instead of captured panels inside frames, any expansion would make the door tighten in its opening during humid months. With a frame and panel design, the inner panel has some "slip space" in its frame to expand without causing the door to bind. For all-around good performance and great looks, use frame and panel doors whenever possible in your casework projects.

Getting Started with Letter Carving

Start simple, buy carving tools as you need them, sharpen the tools carefully, and pay attention to letter spacing. You'll be carving signs in no time flat.

by Simon Watts

Our author started letter carving for practical reasons, including its appropriate nature for apartment woodworking. The results were signs that ended up in his Canadian retreat.

Having had the run of a large, well-equipped shop for most of my life, I find woodworking in my San Francisco apartment challenging.

I have to contend with a nosy landlord, cranky neighbors and three flights of stairs. Prior to climbing those stairs every day, I had never considered taking up woodcarving — perhaps because I associated it with duck decoys, garden gnomes and other geriatric nonsense.

However, this spring, needing to replace some old signs on a house in Nova Scotia, I thought of giving it a try. My ambition was modest: learn enough to carve good-looking name boards for friends and neighbors, for boats or whatever. I looked through the usual catalogs — and saw there was a multitude of carving tools on the market and I'd better get some advice.

Furthermore, buying a gouge, chisel or adze without being able to feel the heft and balance of the tool is chancy. So I called a professional woodcarver friend who invited me to his studio. We spent a couple of hours going over his collection

of carving tools (over a thousand), "I need them all," he said "but some I may only use once or twice a year."

Not everyone has an opportunity to learn from a pro, so I thought I'd share some of my lessons and conclusions. First off, I was cautioned about taking the second-hand route. Even with familiar and respected trade names, I am told that it is asking for problems.

I decided that the faceted style of handles, usually octagonal, had a better feel than round handles (also they were less prone to roll off the bench and bite the dust — or my feet).

My friend also advised me to ignore sets and buy only the tools I needed to get started. So with his help, I made a list of essential tools and equipment — including a mallet and tool roll.

I went back to the catalogs, somewhat wiser, and decided, as a beginner, it would be prudent to buy pre-sharpened tools, already honed with the correct bevel. Suppressing my pro-British bias, I settled on the Lamp™ brand, made in Germany. I liked the octagonal, hornbeam handles, the honed and

polished edges and having the size and "sweep" (degree of curvature of a gouge) stamped into both the handle and the steel shank.

While waiting for the tools to arrive, I practiced drawing letters directly on the wood with T-square and triangle ... with poor results. The letters looked awkward and mechanical, betraying my engineering background. My artist sister was amused by my efforts and observed that it took years of practice to draw well-proportioned letters in the various styles.

I then had the good fortune to come across a book called Arthur Baker's Historic Calligraphic Alphabets. It contains 33 complete alphabets, printed in black, two or more inches high, with no grid lines or other distractions. Here was a treasure trove indeed for the novice carver. Furthermore, the author granted permission to use up to 10 of the alphabets.

I bought several other books (of marginal value), until I came across *Letter Carving in Wood* by Chris Pye. This is the best book I found: clear, detailed information combined with close-up photos and excellent sketches.

Part of the author's preparation for learning letter carving was finding the best tools for the task. As is common to woodworking, he found that the right tools made all the difference.

A sharp edge on your carving tools is critical for successful letter carving.

Eventually, one has to take the plunge, so I chose an alphabet and made several photocopies until I had enough letters. Then I cut them out and arranged them on a piece of cardboard, cut to the same size as the wooden name board.

I read and re-read the section on letter spacing (called color) and continued moving the letters around until the balance looked right. I then stuck the letters to the cardboard, photocopied a clean version, glued it with rubber cement to the wood, and began carving letters right through the paper.

This not only saves layout time but provides a mask if you plan to paint the letters, as I usually do. When the paint is dry, the paper can be peeled off or sanded down.

I was gratified by this first effort, until my sister kindly pointed out the various errors in layout — an E too close to an F, a W cramped by the adjacent letters and a forlorn looking O, marooned in space. However, the third and fourth efforts met with qualified approval, and I felt I was making progress.

Getting a good edge on a carving tool — chisel or gouge — is half the battle and takes considerable practice. Written descriptions are of marginal value, but video can be a great teacher. It was my luck to stumble on such a video by master carver Ian Agrell. Agrell is a gifted teacher. His video on sharpening carving tools is a model of brevity and humor.

So, that's how I got started — a total expenditure of about $300. I like the work: it's quiet, relaxing, has endless applications and there is no need for any of the body protection woodworkers find indispensable these days. However, after a newly sharpened chisel (my only round one) rolled off the bench and skewered my foot, I did decide to always wear shoes when I carve!

Eight Tips for Beginnners

We asked techniques editor Linda Haus to try her hand at letter carving. After several attempts she came up with the following eight tips.

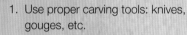

Use spray adhesive to attach your pre-printed letters to the wood. Carve pulling towards you.

At the intersection of letter segments, end the transverse, ascending and descending forms in a uniform manner.

Remove the paper and sand the surface smooth. If you're painting the carved area ... leave the paper on.

1. Use proper carving tools: knives, gouges, etc.
2. Keep your tools sharp: hone them constantly as you carve.
3. Use a proper cutting angle.
4. Don't carve too deep.
5. Print out your words/phrases.
6. Enlarge your printout on a copier. (This keeps the spacing correct).
7. Use a wood species that is easy to carve, (like basswood, butternut or alder) or close-grained softwoods.
8. Don't lose the big picture: strive for consistency in depth of cut and cutting angle on each and every letter.

Knife angle is the key to achieving uniform carved letters. About 65° is where you should start. Near perpendicular is most effective as you look at the side of the knife.

Securing your stock is an important task. You also need to be able to spin the stock around easily ... it allows you to easily pull the cut towards you.

Shell Carving Shortcut

One of the most enduring motifs in woodworking, the shell is a great introduction to carving. Here's a technique that uses the lathe to do the initial shaping and speed the process along.

by J. Petrovich

From prehistoric gravesites to Botticelli to Andrew Wyeth, the shell has figured prominently as an artistic motif.

Using a Lathe to Carve a Shell

Since most designs require more than a single carving and because most of us do not have an extensive selection of carving tools, we will do the basic shaping of the shell at the lathe. Even if you only need one shell, it's a good practice to shape two at the same time. Using the lathe is faster than roughing in the shape with carving tools and, because it produces two blanks, there is a backup…just in case.

Begin by edge-gluing two boards together, adequate to accommodate your design. The edge-gluing should be done with a paper joint. A paper joint is merely a piece of paper inserted between two glued surfaces before clamping them together. The joint is used when the attachment is intended to be temporary. Once the halves have cured, use a compass and a ruler to lay out the circle's circumference.

Cut to the outside of the line at the band saw. Leave 1⁄16 " or so of margin to remove evenly at the lathe. Glue this disc to a mounting block (use a paper

As a motif in furniture design, the shell made its greatest and most durable mark during the Rococo. No study of 18th century furniture could ignore the omnipresence of the shell. Found on chair splats and knees, on drawer fronts and aprons, the shell (along with the acanthus leaf and ball and claw foot) is at the very heart of traditional design.

Admittedly, in this postmodern world of starkness and functional simplicity, carving is not much in demand. However, for those of us who are less interested in making artistic statements and more intrigued by the craftsmanship of yesteryear's fine furniture, the shell is an excellent introduction to decorative carving.

Accurate layout is important to successful carving. The natural geometry of the shell makes it easy to draw and stylize as well. Once you have selected a style, lay it out full size on graph paper. The grid of the paper aids measurement and provides a quick reference for dealing with curves.

joint) to attach to your lathe's faceplate. Once this joint has cured, mount this turning assembly to the faceplate and to the lathe.

With the drawn profile of the shell close by, shape the blank at the lathe. Follow the steps in "Four (Turning) Steps."

Handwork to the Rescue

Once you are satisfied with the profile, remove the blank from the mounting block. A chisel works well to start the paper joint to split. Next, separate the shell halves at their paper joint using your chisel. Don't just snap them apart. Occasionally even a paper joint can resist separation enough to split the blank.

Again using a paper joint, attach the shell blanks to small boards. These boards enlarge the clamping options for your work and provide an alternative to directly clamping the work in a vise.

Next lay out the shell's rays on the blank. Marking the increments at the outer edge of the blank and at the center allows you to focus on the shape of the line as you connect the marks. Keep the lines clean. They need to be dark and thick enough to read easily.

To "lay in" or carve the lines that define the rays of the shell, use a Swiss-style chip carving knife. A more traditional approach would be to use a "V" tool, but the chip-carving knife produces a more sinuous quality of line. And though it may take a bit longer, the results merit the extra effort. If your design is more regular in shape and you want the rays to appear identical, a "V" tool may be a better choice.

With the rays separated by cleanly cut lines, it is time to shape the rays themselves. Use a skew for convex rays, and switch to a gouge or two to shape the concave rays.

Smoothing the shell is a matter of taste. For some designs leaving the tool marks is appropriate. For others you will need to blend the marks with small rasps or rifflers. This is slow going, but the handwork effort is worth it. Resist the temptation to use a power tool. Flap sanders, pneumatic drum sanders and the rest tend to blur the quality of the carving. The outer edge of the shell should be smoothed after demounting.

Demounting the carving from the clamping block is again a matter of starting a tear in the paper joint with a chisel. Once free of the board, all that remains is to clean the residue of the

The author prefers using a carving knife rather than a "V" gouge. She gets a more fluid line to her rays with this technique. Note the small board that the shell blank is paper joint-glued to: this helps enlarge the clamping surface during carving.

joint from the carving's back. Methyl ethyl keytone (MEK) works well to soften the glue, then scrape it off with a cabinet scraper. Apply the MEK with an eyedropper and keep the area moist for about five minutes. If one application and scraping does not clean the back, repeat as necessary.

Four (Turning) Steps to Starting a Clam Shell Carving

One: *With the blank mounted on your lathe, describe the center of the shell with a diamond-point parting tool.*

Two: *Next, shape the area adjacent to the center with a roundnosed scraper. Sweep it smooth.*

Three: *Switch to a skew to round over the circumference of the blank. The shell is beginning to take shape.*

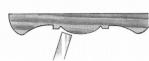

Four: *To shape the button center of the shell, a straight-edged scraper works well.*

Welcome to Curves: Dry Bending Made Easy

Straight lines are the usual convention for so much of woodworking. But don't limit your designs to flat, straight and square. Curved, flowing shapes add visual interest and excitement, and they're easy to make with this simple form-bending technique.

by Mike McGlynn

A Simple Dry Bending Form

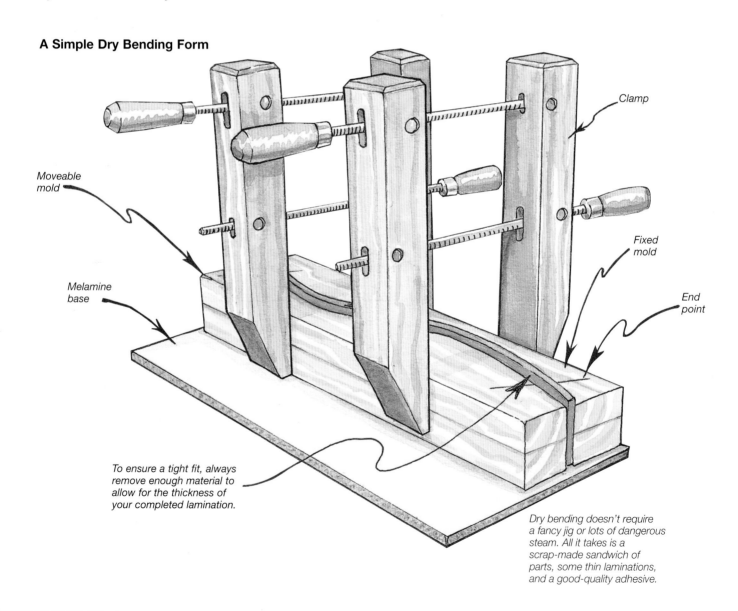

Clamp

Moveable mold

Fixed mold

End point

Melamine base

To ensure a tight fit, always remove enough material to allow for the thickness of your completed lamination.

Dry bending doesn't require a fancy jig or lots of dangerous steam. All it takes is a scrap-made sandwich of parts, some thin laminations, and a good-quality adhesive.

Figure 1: *Rip thin pieces of straight grained-wood on your band saw, using a point fence to control the thickness of your cut. Be sure you make the pieces several inches longer than the finished length required.*

Figure 2: *Next, plane the laminations to a uniform thickness of just a hair under ⅛". Do your best to avoid snipe and tear-out, otherwise these little dips will show in the final lamination. It's best to use a slave board underneath your laminations (not shown here) when your planer dips below ¼" thickness.*

Wood grows as it will, gently curving or straight as an arrow. But when we buy it from our suppliers, it's in nice flat square pieces. So, when a project or a design demands complex curves or round aprons, what do you do? The easiest and probably the strongest option is dry or laminate bending. This technique, which takes advantage of the flexibility of thinly sliced straight-grained wood and the strength of multiple laminations, has become increasingly popular since the introduction of modern glues.

The first step in making a curved shape is to create the mold. Start by gluing a couple of thick boards together, long and thick enough to capture the full length and nearly the full width of the shape you want to make. Lay out a grid work of ½" squares on this blank and sketch the shape—marking the ends of the part on the top face of the mold. Now, use your band saw to split the mold in half, lengthwise, cutting along your curved layout lines. Smooth the inside faces of the mold halves on a drum sander, making certain the faces remain square to each other. Then line both faces of the mold with clear packing tape. The tape forms a stick-free surface to prevent accidently gluing the mold to the workpiece. The last step is to attach one half of the mold to a larger piece of ¾" Melamine or waxed board to serve as a base for this bending jig. The other mold half must remain movable.

Figure 3: *After spreading glue on the appropriate surfaces, clamp the laminations into the form. Line the mold with clear packing tape to ensure full release, and use a good-quality epoxy with a long open time. Keep your yellow glue capped and on the shelf for this operation—it's not a good choice.*

Figure 4: *After the epoxy has cured, remove the blank and return to your band saw. Scribe the width of the part and stay with your point fence to rip the workpiece to the correct width you need.*

Figure 5: *If it's necessary to do further machining on a curved part, take extra precautions to ensure that the workpiece stays put when you cut or rout it and your hands are safely out of the danger zone.*

QuickTip

Routing Profiles on Curved Shapes

The day may come when you need to rout an internal profile along a curved shape. If a template won't do the trick, use a point fence on the router table and guide the workpiece carefully along the fence. Draw a series of perpendicular layout lines on the workpiece first to keep it tracking properly, relative to the fence. Keep the wood planted firmly against the fence, and feed it along from right to left as usual.

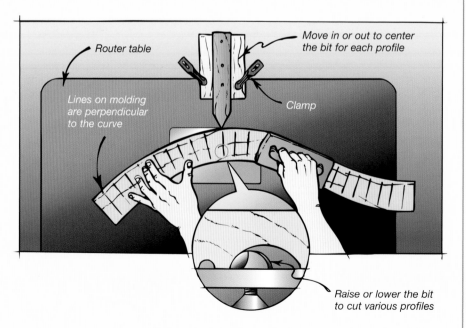

Router table

Lines on molding are perpendicular to the curve

Move in or out to center the bit for each profile

Clamp

Raise or lower the bit to cut various profiles

When selecting wood for your part laminations, choose carefully. Each piece should have the straightest edge grain possible. Some woods are easier to bend than others (see "Straight Talk About Bendable Wood"). Cut and mill your laminations so they're not more than about ⅛" thick for easier bending.

For gluing curved laminations, epoxy is an ideal adhesive. Epoxies have an advantage in this application because they don't creep under tension, as yellow glues are prone to do. Before you apply the epoxy, it's a good idea to lightly sand the gluing faces. Epoxy creates a mechanical bond, so it will benefit from a little extra tooth.

Now apply glue to both faces of all the inner laminations, put them in the mold and clamp it tight. Make sure your laminations are pushed snugly down against the bottom of the mold—you may have to press or tap them down once or twice while applying clamping pressure.

Any stout clamps will work for dry bending, including hand screws, bar or pipe clamps. The best types are those that crank or twist tight; you'll lose your mechanical advantage if you use quick-grip style clamps that require squeezing force—this sort of clamping simply requires too much force to overcome with grip strength.

After the epoxy has cured, remove the blank from the mold—but be sure to transfer the end points to the ends of the blank so you'll know just where to cut it to final length.

Dry bending can create an almost unlimited variety of shapes. It is a practical and creative woodworking trick to add to your repertoire.

Straight Talk About Bendable Wood

White Glue

Yellow Glue

Polyurethane Glue

Epoxy

In general, most species of wood will bend if you select straight grained stock and slice it thin. The denser a piece of wood, the thinner you need to slice it. Thus, a ³⁄₁₆" x ¾" x 60" piece of straight-grained sugar pine will bend to a much tighter radius than an identical piece of oak. Further, some species just seem more flexible. Cedar, ash and even hickory, though they have wide ranging specific densities, all have reputations as woods that bend well.

Selecting the proper glue for dry bending can also have a big impact. Glues differ as to how elastic they remain after they have cured. White glue is the most elastic, epoxy is the hardest and least flexible. Yellow glue, polyurethane and plastic resin glues fall in between. rigid glue is best. Open time is also critical to successful bending. The more time you leave yourself to work with your laminations before the glue sets, the better. For that reason, long-set epoxies and plastic resin glues are your best bet for success.

Steam Bending Basics

Steam bending wood is easier than you think. You'll need to make a plywood steam box, and a bending form. And you'll need to experiment a little bit.

by Peter Korn

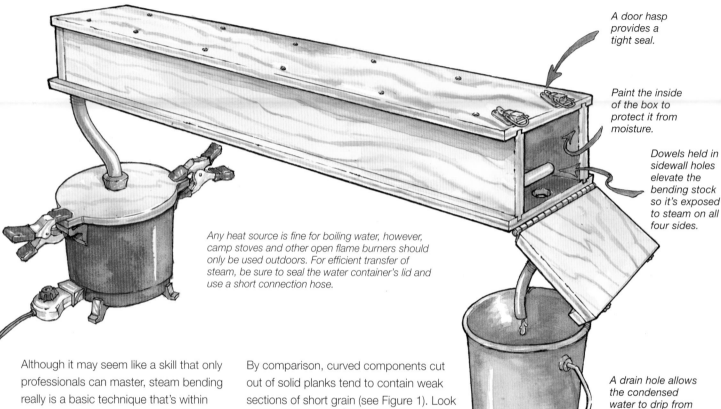

A door hasp provides a tight seal.

Paint the inside of the box to protect it from moisture.

Dowels held in sidewall holes elevate the bending stock so it's exposed to steam on all four sides.

Any heat source is fine for boiling water, however, camp stoves and other open flame burners should only be used outdoors. For efficient transfer of steam, be sure to seal the water container's lid and use a short connection hose.

A drain hole allows the condensed water to drip from the steam box into a bucket below.

Although it may seem like a skill that only professionals can master, steam bending really is a basic technique that's within reach of any woodworking enthusiast. With an adventurous spirit and a few pieces of equipment, most of which you probably have lying around already, you can get started.

Wood bent after using steam to make it pliable is generally strong since its grain follows the length of the curve.

Figure 1: *A curve bandsawn from solid wood (left) usually has significant grain runout, which weakens the piece. The grain lines on a steam bent piece (right), on the other hand, are continuous, making it the stronger alternative.*

By comparison, curved components cut out of solid planks tend to contain weak sections of short grain (see Figure 1). Look out for lumber with severe grain runout, however, for even with steaming methods this wood is likely to crack.

Some Basic Wood Technology

Wood consists of cellulose fibers bound together by a natural adhesive called lignin. The first time a piece of wood is heated and cooled, the lignin permanently loses elasticity. For this reason kiln-dried wood, which has already lost much of its pliability in the kiln, is not your best choice for steam bending. Air-dried wood is the ticket: when it's steamed and bent, the lignin helps lock the new curve in place. Green wood is also bendable, but it has two disadvantages. First, it can take months to dry and second, the wood cells

are often so full of water that hydraulic pressure bursts them open as they compress.

Wood subjected to steam in an enclosed container heats up and absorbs moisture, dramatically increasing the flexibility of its fibers. When it reaches sufficient pliability, the wood should be rapidly bent onto a form. After cooling and drying the wood will retain its new shape, although varying degrees of springback can occur, depending on the character of the wood, the amount of steaming, and the rapidity with which the hot wood was bent to the form.

Some species of wood lend themselves to bending more readily than others. For example, white oak, red oak and hackberry are particularly good, while mahogany and hard maple are unsuitable. Whichever wood you choose, select straight-grained pieces to reduce the likelihood of fracturing.

Building a Steam Box

Making your own steam box is easy, as shown in the illustration on the facing page. An efficient box shouldn't be too big, yet it must allow enough room for steam to circulate freely. For most bending needs, an exterior dimension of about 7" x 7" x 60" will be more than sufficient. If you decide to give it a try, be sure to incorporate the following guidelines:

- Use exterior-grade plywood for the box since its waterproof glue won't degrade from the steam.
- Paint the box's interior to protect it.
- Space a line of dowels across the box's width to elevate the wood above the condensation runoff and to promote the flow of steam.
- Seal one end of the box, and hinge the other end for easy access.
- Drill a small hole through the bottom at one end to drain condensed steam.
- Drill a second hole, at the other end, for the steam hose entrance.

The heat source for your steamer can be an electric burner, a wood fire, a camp stove, or whatever you have that will boil water. For safety's sake, remember to use your equipment outside if it generates a flame or has exposed hot coils.

The water container should hold several gallons and have an access hole small enough to be plugged with a large cork or rubber stopper. If the container is made of iron, make sure it's galvanized or enameled, otherwise the steam will probably stain your wood. By drilling a hole through the stopper you can hold the connecting hose in place. The hose should be made of rubber, plastic, or copper of

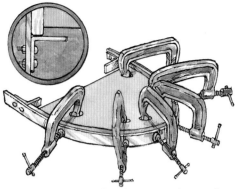

Figure 2: *Make a banding strap using metal between ¹⁄₁₆" and ³⁄₃₂" thick, and bolt angle irons to its ends so the steamed wood fits tightly between them.*

at least ½" in interior diameter. Thin walled plastic tubing is not recommended as it collapses when the steam runs through. In use, be sure to set the steam box at a slight incline so that condensation flows out the drip hole.

Steaming Your Wood

The first step in steaming your wood is to fire up the burner and boil the water. Once steam begins filling the chamber, put the wood in the box and close the lid. Steam the wood until it's pliable, then, wearing gloves for protection, remove the hot wood and rapidly bend it to the form.

How long should wood be steamed? There is no precise answer, so it's a good idea to include a couple of test pieces in the box for experimentation. Species, moisture content, and the intensity of the steam environment are all factors. Here are three rules of thumb for steaming air-dried lumber:

- Keep wood with a moisture content below 20% in the steam box for about an hour and a quarter per inch of thickness.

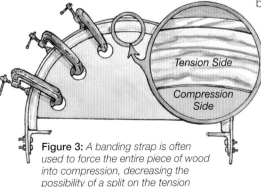

Figure 3: *A banding strap is often used to force the entire piece of wood into compression, decreasing the possibility of a split on the tension side of the bend.*

- Steam wood with 20-30% moisture content for 45 minutes per inch of thickness.
- Wood with a moisture content in excess of 30% needs only about 30 minutes of steaming per inch of thickness.

When pulling hot wood from the box, work rapidly to place it in the bending form. The wood begins to cool instantly, and it's amazing how quickly flexibility diminishes. If possible, leave the wood clamped in the form for several days.

There are a variety of designs for bending forms. The most common is a one piece form, usually built with layers of plywood, to which the steamed wood is clamped (see Figure 2). Another type of form consists of two mating parts between which the work is sandwiched. Since steamed wood almost always has some springback, cut the form to a slightly more severe bend than you want to end up with. However, springback is unpredictable, so until actual test bends are made, the exact amount of over-bend required is anyone's guess.

When you bend a piece of wood, an imaginary line up the center stays constant in length (see Figure 3), while the outside of the curve gets longer (tension) and the inside becomes shorter (compression). Wood is fairly good at compressing, but splits apart readily under tension. It's the tension factor that limits the degree of curvature in a simple bend. Many woodworkers reduce the chance of splitting on the tension side of the wood by using a bending strap —a flexible steel strap about ¹⁄₁₆" thick and as wide as the bending stock, with end stops spaced to enclose the exact length of the workpiece. As soon as the wood is pulled from the steam box, the strap is fitted to the tension side of the stock. With the outside curve unable to expand, the entire piece of wood is forced into compression, minimizing the chance of splitting.

Arts and Crafts Finishing

Achieving a classic Arts & Crafts finish isn't difficult if you know what to use and how to apply it. Our finishing expert, provides two options here. One is a simple stain finish; the other, a more traditional chemical fuming. Whichever route you take, you'll end up with beautiful results without lots of fuss.

by Michael Dresdner

The Arts and Crafts movement signaled a return to simplicity and elegance in furniture design. Here in the United States, proponents of the movement embraced strong, local woods, like oak, coupled with simple, durable lines. Some cabinetmakers felt that the large pores and grain patterns of this noble wood should stand out, so they used finishes that added contrast. Others, like Gustav Stickley, felt the design of

the piece should not have to compete with the wood's patterns. To that end, he chose finishes to mitigate rather than enhance the grain patterns in oak.

In this article, we'll show you the steps to follow for achieving either of these finishing options. First, we'll review a simple, one-step stain approach. It has a rugged appearance that many feel shows off oak to its best. After that, we'll introduce you to traditional

ammonia fuming, which lends a darker, more monochromatic look to white oak. You will have to handle ammonia safely, but if that is still a bit too risky for your tastes, we'll tell you about a safe chemical alternative that attempts to mimic fuming while eliminating the mess and danger.

First, Proper Preparation

In order for stain to color wood evenly, you must sand the wood uniformly. Follow the same sanding procedure whether you plan to stain the oak or fume it. Start with 80-grit open-coat aluminum oxide paper. This is rough enough to take out any machine marks and will let you get your surfaces flat and smooth. Sand by hand, with a block, or with an electric or air sander. If you sand with a power sander, remember that it works best when moved slowly—about one inch per second. Let the weight of the sander provide the only applied pressure on the wood. Pressing down on a sander just slows it down.

Now move on to 120 grit of the same aluminum oxide paper. Since you have already flattened your surfaces, the only goal of this sanding step is to remove the 80-grit scratches. If you have one, set up a strong work light and look at the wood from a low angle with the light on the far side. This will help you see the scratch pattern you are leaving and will make it easier to tell when the larger grit scratches are removed. Follow the 120-grit sanding with 180 — again, merely to remove the 120-grit scratches.

Do your final sanding with 180-grit paper, but this time switch to garnet instead of aluminum oxide. Sand with the grain, and only by hand—no sanding machines. Hand sanding with the grain will eliminate cross-grain scratches and leave the wood ready for staining or fuming.

The Beauty of Gilsonite

One of our favorite oak stains is a mixture called "asphaltum." It is a thickish tar made from a natural mineral, called gilsonite, ground into a drying oil, such as linseed oil or modified soya oil. In addition to being used in many dark stain formulas, asphaltum shows up in roofing tar and tree pruning paint.

Finishers prize this dark brownish black paste for the richness of color

it offers. Like an oil slick on water, it shows highlights of both green and red. It makes an excellent glaze between coats of finish as well as a deep rich stain for raw wood. If you are a purist, you can buy asphaltum in one-gallon containers from Sherwin Williams' commercial stores (Sherwood Wiping Stain Concentrate, stock #S64N44). Cut it 50/50 with mineral spirits.

For those who prefer their stains ready to use, Minwax offers a very close alternative. Minwax Jacobean Wood Finish, used right out of the familiar bright yellow can, will give you a color almost identical to asphaltum stain.

Flood it On; Wipe it Off

Stains tend to settle, so start by stirring or shaking the container to mix the solvent and color. With a rag, brush or sponge, flood the stain onto the raw sanded wood and wipe it all off before it dries. Paper shop towels work well for wiping the extra stain off when you don't have enough rags available. When it is applied this way, the stain will come out even and uniform. Let it dry overnight before you proceed with the first top coat.

Once the stain is dry, go on to your favorite top coat. For a table, sideboard or desk, three or four coats of an oil-based satin polyurethane will serve nicely. The poly will look great and give you the durability and heat resistance you'd want for a heavily used piece. It will take the wear of everyday use and even hold up if an occasional carafe of hot coffee is set on it.

A traditional-looking Arts & Crafts finish is easily attained through a variety of modern products. The tried and true techniques of yesteryear are a great option as well.

Mix asphaltum in a fifty percent mixture with mineral spirits to create a beautiful Arts & Crafts-style stain.

Flood the surface of your properly sanded project with the mixture. A generous application helps to ensure uniform coverage.

Wipe the stain off before it dries. Move quickly, but thoroughly rub the entire piece, working toward uniform coverage.

The stool is nicely stained with a minimum of muss and fuss. This "secret" formula now is known by thousands.

Fuming with Ammonia

At some point, someone discovered that ammonia fumes make high tannin woods, like oak, turn dark. Rather than apply stain to the wood, we can darken oak substantially by causing it to react chemically with ammonia fumes. Because ammonia is harmful to us, the way to fume oak furniture is to seal it in an airtight chamber along with some open bowls or troughs of ammonium hydroxide, which will release ammonia gas and water vapor.

When oak is fumed it turns a dark, blackish brown, often with slightly green overtones. The longer it stays in the fuming chamber, the darker it gets. Heat increases the speed of the fuming process and alters the color as well. The warmer the fuming chamber is, the faster the color change will occur and the redder the color will be. Cooler temperatures mean slower color change and greener colors.

As a rule, white oak fumes better than red oak, and dense wood works better than lighter wood. Heartwood changes color, but sapwood does not. If you plan to fume, build your furniture from dense white oak heartwood. Since the ammonia reacts with tannin, you can intensify the effect by washing the wood first with a solution of strong tea. Tea contains tannin, which will then be deposited in the wood. However, dense white oak usually has enough tannin on its own so that a tea wash is not necessary.

Setting Up Safely

The ammonia used to create fumes is the same 28% solution of ammonium hydroxide used in blueprint machines. You can buy it from any chemical supply house or a reprographics (blueprint) company. By contrast, household ammonia used for cleaning is typically only a 5% solution or weaker. It won't be of sufficient concentration to work properly.

Unfortunately, the fumes created by highly concentrated ammonium hydroxide are quite irritating and harmful to our eyes, nose and lungs. Any time you expose yourself to them, such as when you pour the ammonia or empty the fuming chamber, you should suit up to protect yourself. Wear good, tight-fitting chemical goggles to protect your eyes and an organic vapor mask to protect your nose and lungs. Ideally, use a full-face organic vapor mask that protects everything at once. It is also a good idea to wear long sleeves and gloves, but any type, even the cheap vinyl disposable gloves, will work to protect your hands. Long story short: It's imperative to protect yourself when using such a strong chemical, so be diligent for safety's sake.

Creating a Fuming Chamber

To keep the wood in contact with ammonia fumes for a long period of time, you need to create a fuming chamber that is airtight and large enough to hold the pieces you are fuming. The chamber can be anything from a small Rubbermaid® container that will hold small items, like wood handles, up to an entire room-sized enclosure. (See "John Brock's Fuming Shed" for an ingenious mid-sized fuming chamber option.)

You can make a simple chamber of any size by building a wood frame large enough to enclose whatever you need to fume. Leave the bottom open, but cover the four sides and the top with clear polyethylene film. Leave some extra film rolled up at the bottom to help make the seal airtight, and cover any seams with duct tape. Remove all the hardware and place the furniture on a piece of black plastic (garbage bags will do) that is at least as large as the footprint of the chamber. Place the plastic-clad

Plain Sawn

Rift Sawn

Quarter Sawn

Heartwood

Sapwood

When fuming white oak or other woods with a significant tannin content, the heartwood will change color but the sapwood will not.

Contributing editor Rick White uses a simple polyethylene chamber to fume his projects. Note that Rick left the hardware on this lamp during fuming…a big mistake! Strong ammonia will discolor metals like brass.

Ammonia fumes require time to affect the tannin within the cells of the wood. The test pieces of white oak at left were exposed to ammonia fumes in twelve-hour increments, from zero to 72 hours (bottom to top). We then sealed the pieces with dark shellac. Notice how the sapwood did not react to the fumes.

frame over it and slip some saucers of 28% ammonium hydroxide inside. Make sure there is a good seal where the clear plastic meets the black plastic. Now shine a heat lamp on the entire unit from the outside of the chamber. The heat lamp shining through the clear plastic and onto the black plastic will help raise the temperature inside the chamber to 80 degrees F—an ideal temperature for quick, uniform fuming. There is no need for fans or special air movement inside the chamber, since the ammonia fumes will quickly disperse throughout the enclosure. When it is time to remove the furniture, suit up with goggles, gloves and vapor mask, pour the ammonia back into an empty sealable jug, remove the heat lamp and the enclosure, and put some strong fans on to air out the room while you go somewhere else. The used ammonia can go down the sink or toilet. Though it smells bad, it is not harmful to the environment.

Fuming Times

Since wood is a natural material, some pieces will have more tannin than others and, consequently, may darken at different rates of speed. Before you tackle your finished project, do a set of samples in a small test chamber. Seal some of the

John Brock's Fuming Shed

John Brock, a Seattle woodworker specializing in Arts & Crafts pieces, fumes large items in this cleverly modified plastic tool shed. Note the vinyl gutter along the back wall of the shed. After loading the furniture and sealing all seams with duct tape, he lifts the jug of ammonia and hangs it on a hook. The ammonia runs down through the hose, past the shutoff valve, and into the vinyl gutter. After a few days of fuming, he lowers the jug and the ammonia runs back down into it, since the vinyl gutter is slightly angled. After shutting the valve, he opens the doors and lets the shed air out before removing the furniture.

small cutoffs from the wood you used into a clear food storage container along with a saucer of ammonia. Check the samples at regular intervals (6, 12, 24, 36 hours) to see how dark they get. Follow all the safety precautions, and don't forget the heat lamp. You'll want this test chamber to mimic the same conditions as the real thing.

It is also a good idea to finish some of the samples once they come out of the chamber. You will notice that the color of the fumed wood changes dramatically once finish is applied. Short of finishing, you can get a fair idea of how the wood will look under a finish by wetting it with mineral spirits. If it is not dark enough, wipe it off, let the mineral spirits evaporate, and pop the wood back into the fuming chamber.

After the furniture has been removed from the chamber and aired out so that the smell is gone, you are ready for finishing. At times, the grain

may be slightly raised. If it is, sand the wood very lightly with 320- or 400-grit stearated paper, but sand only enough to smooth the raised grain. If there was any sapwood included in the board, you will notice that it did not change color. You can blend the sapwood areas by selectively staining them with the proper color of dye stain, or leave them as is for contrast.

Fuming without the Fumes

Recently, a new product arrived on the market that seeks to offer the look of fuming without the danger. "Old Growth" is a line of safe, water-based compounds that attempt to mimic many different chemical stains, including fuming (see "Where to Get It"). The fumed oak treatment, like all the others, consists of two clear liquids that are applied separately.

---

*Quick*Tip

PVC Transition Fitting

If the 2" dust ports on your benchtop machines don't fit your shop vac hose nozzle, a short piece of schedule 40 PVC can become a useful transition fitting. Cut a series of 2" saw kerfs around one end to allow the PVC to adapt to the machine's dust port size — either to enlarge or reduce the circumference. If the pipe doesn't quite fit your vacuum hose nozzle, you can cut slits in the other end, too. Then, use one or two hose clamps to connect the parts.

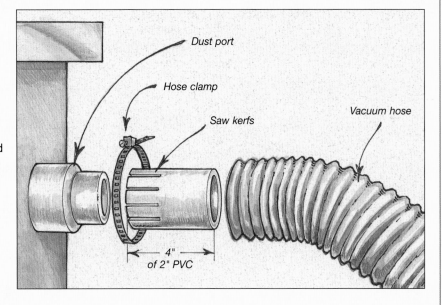

Dust port

Hose clamp

Saw kerfs

Vacuum hose

4" of 2" PVC

Old Growth is a water-based system designed to mimic different chemical stains. It's safe and effective. Apply it in a two-step procedure.

Where to Get It!

If you are planning on trying some of the techniques taught in this article, you'll need to find the various chemicals and finishes described. Ammonia of the strength needed for fuming is found at most any chemical supply house or reprographics (blueprint) company. The Sherwood Gilsonite stain concentrate (asphaltum) is found at Sherwin Williams commercial supply stores. Old Growth treatment is available from Woodworkers Supply. Several sources for dyes to adjust sapwood color inconsistencies are: Homestead Finishing Products, Garrett Wade and Rockler Woodworking and Hardware. Rockler also has Behlen products (stains, tints and dyes) and shellac flakes.

Using a clean brush for each solution, you first apply the #1 portion evenly. After it dries, follow with the #2 solution. As the second solution goes on, the wood immediately changes color, and it continues to get darker until the wood dries.

Because it is water-based, the treatment raises the grain of the oak significantly. You can make it less problematic by raising the grain first with water, letting the wood dry, and cutting it back with 320-grit sandpaper before you apply the chemical stain. Old Growth has an interesting look and comes close to the real thing. However, placed side by side with fumed oak, you can still see the differences if you're experienced with fumed finishes.

Topcoat with Shellac

My favorite finish for fumed oak is a thin coat of dewaxed garnet shellac followed by several coats of dewaxed blond shellac. The garnet adds a nice warm tone to the rather cool color of fumed oak, and the blond allows you to build up a finish without worrying about getting the color even. Although shellac is certainly historically authentic, it is not a good choice for tabletops, bars or areas of heavy use, but it's perfect for chairs, occasional tables and other light-duty pieces. Shellac can be damaged by alcohol, heat or alkalines (such as ammonia-based cleaners and detergents), but it has good stain resistance and is impervious to acids. It has moderately good scratch resistance and is quite easy to repair, even after years of use. If a repair is necessary, sand the damaged area lightly but not enough to damage the wood's patina, and wipe on a thin cut of shellac. It may take several coats to blend in the repair area, but it isn't necessary to sand each time. New shellac fuses into old shellac.

QuickTip

Switching Router Bases in a Hurry

One of the keys to unlocking more versatility from your router is using it in tandem with different shop-made bases. Trouble is, if you only need another base for a quick operation, it can be a hassle removing and reinstalling the base plate screws. Here's an option that won't have you reaching for a screwdriver: Just drill a hole in your temporary base that exactly matches the outside diameter of the bushing on a guide collar. Install the guide collar on your router's regular base, then drop the guide collar into the hole on the temporary base. You're all set to go. When you use this setup, be sure to keep the router pressed firmly down against the temporary base so the guide collar stays put.

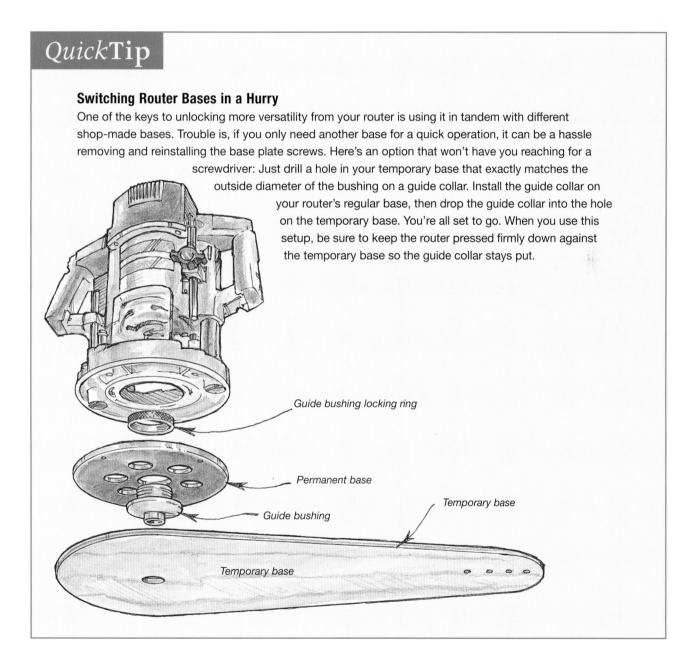

Guide bushing locking ring

Permanent base

Temporary base

Guide bushing

Temporary base

Polyurethane: Oil-Based or Waterborne

Wildly popular among hobbyist woodworkers, polyurethane is durable, easy to apply, and comes in both waterbased and oil-based versions. Some accept it grudgingly, calling it "plastic-looking," while others embrace it as the greatest thing since sliced bread.

by Michael Dresdner

Like many finishes, polyurethane is named for its primary resin, though some cans labeled "polyurethane" also contain other resins. Resin is what remains behind to form a film once the solvent has evaporated. The resin defines the nature of the coating. In general, polyurethane or urethane resins (the terms may be used interchangeably) provide finishes with good durability, including resistance to heat, abrasion, chemicals, stains and solvents. Polyurethane is tough enough for kitchen tables and cabinets, bathroom vanities, walls, doors, floors, all types of furniture and virtually any woodworking project. Woodworkers mainly use either oil-based or waterborne polyurethanes. Both have good qualities, but they are very different in many ways, giving rise to a hotly debated disagreement over which is superior.

Oil-based and waterborne polyurethanes differ in durability, odor, flammability, safety and appearance—it's easy to see why there's a debate over which one is superior.

42

Oil-based Versus Waterborne

The primary differences between the two types of polyurethane relate to how they are made. Oil-based, whose proper name is "oil-modified urethane," is produced by reacting common finishing oils, like linseed oil, with a chemical that causes the oil to form larger molecules. A good rule of thumb is that larger molecules mean more durable finishes. The result is something that looks and acts like oil-based varnish, but is tougher. Polyurethane gel is simply a thicker version of the same thing.

Waterborne polyurethane is an emulsion of resins in water and solvent. It dries fast and behaves more like lacquer than varnish. As a result, it benefits from a different application technique than oil-based, but there are also differences in durability, odor, flammability, safety, and even appearance. Let's compare the two in each major performance category.

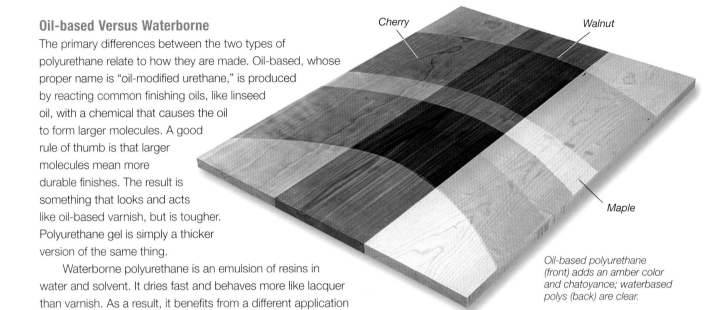

Cherry *Walnut* *Maple*

Oil-based polyurethane (front) adds an amber color and chatoyance; waterbased polys (back) are clear.

Durability

Oil-based polyurethane wins this one hands down. It has better heat, abrasion, chemical and solvent resistance than its waterbased cousin, and for a very good reason. Most waterbased polyurethanes are actually a mixture of two or more resins, usually acrylic and polyurethane. Acrylic resin has properties similar to lacquer, including its susceptibility to some strong solvents, chemicals and heat. It is added to the finish for two reasons: acrylic is less expensive than polyurethane resin, and it brings better brushing and spraying properties to the mixture.

The combination of the two resins puts waterbased polyurethane somewhere in between lacquer and oil-based polyurethane on the durability scale. Exactly where depends on how much of the mixture is acrylic resin and how much is polyurethane. Some brands are largely polyurethane, while others are mostly acrylic, so there can be significant differences from brand to brand. The question is, how much polyurethane is in your polyurethane? The answer to the question can be tough to determine for the layperson.

Drying Time

This one goes to the waterbased side of the scoreboard. One coat of oil-based polyurethane will take several hours before it is dry to the touch, but most waterbased versions will get there in 10 minutes. The faster setup time means it is easier to get a dust-free finish with waterbased polyurethane.

Appearance

Beauty is in the eye of the beholder, so this category has no definite winner, but there are obvious differences in how the two types look. Oil-based polyurethane is amber and will add subtle color to wood, while waterbased is clear and adds no color at all. This is especially noticeable on light woods, like maple, which stay white under waterbased polyurethane but get a yellow/orange cast with oils. The flip side is that oils penetrate into wood better, resulting in greater chatoyance, or shimmer and depth, than you'll get with waterbased. Oil-based polyurethane looks richer and more vibrant, especially on dark and highly colored woods, where waterbased coatings can look pale or washed out.

There are two other characteristics unique to waterbased coatings that exacerbate appearance problems. Waterbased polyurethane can bridge over 180-grit or coarser sanding scratches, leaving minute air spaces below the finish in the scratches. These can make the finish look pale and cloudy unless the raw wood has been sanded to 220 grit or finer. On some woods, such as poplar and oak, certain waterbased coatings can draw extractives from the wood that react with the polyurethane, turning it slightly gray. You can get around both these problems by sealing the raw wood first with Zinsser SealCoat. It's a thinned, dewaxed shellac mixture that provides an excellent sealer coat under waterbased polyurethane and makes the wood look better to boot.

Odor, Cleanup and Safety

Once again, waterbased comes out ahead. It emits less offensive odor and cleans up with soap and water. Oil-based polyurethane smells more, and it requires mineral spirits for cleanup.

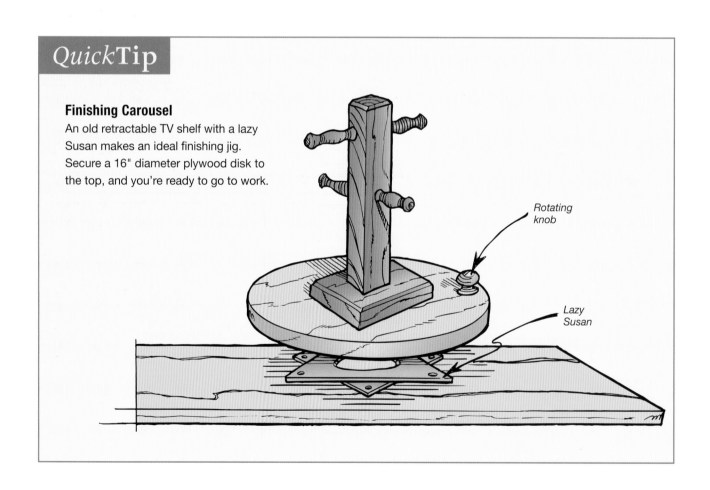

QuickTip

Finishing Carousel
An old retractable TV shelf with a lazy Susan makes an ideal finishing jig. Secure a 16" diameter plywood disk to the top, and you're ready to go to work.

Rotating knob

Lazy Susan

Polyurethane at a Glance

Characteristics	Oil-based	Waterbased
Durability	Excellent	Good to very good
Dry to the touch	Several hours	10 to 20 minutes
Odor	Substantial	Low
Flammable	Yes	No
Cleanup / safety	Mineral spirits rags may be spontaneously combustible	Soap and water rags are safely disposable
Appearance	Amber, good chatoyance	Clear, sometimes cloudy, gray, or pale
Best applicators	Natural bristle brush, nylon abrasive pad, spray gun	Synthetic bristle brush, paint pad, spray gun

The primary differences between oil-based and waterbased polyurethanes relate to how they are made. Oil-based, whose proper name is "oil-modified urethane," is produced by reacting common finishing oils, like linseed oil, with a chemical that causes the oil to form larger molecules. A good rule of thumb is that larger molecules mean more durable finishes.

Most oil-based polyurethanes are flammable while the solvents are flashing off (they become non-flammable once cured), whereas none of the waterbased ones are. Perhaps worse is that oily rags can be spontaneously combustible if you crumple them up while the varnish is still wet, so just in case, lay them out flat to dry prior to disposing of them.

Application
Wiping on oil-based polyurethane will give you a thin, woody finish with no brush or spray marks, but waterbased does not work well as a wipe-on. You can brush or spray both types of polyurethanes, but each works best with a different applicator, method, and spray technique. Here are some guidelines to get you started.

Wipe-on: Use either gel or liquid oil-based polyurethane straight from the can without thinning it. Dip a fine nylon abrasive pad into the polyurethane and scrub it onto the surface of the wood. Wipe off all the excess before it dries. Apply one coat per day. Three coats will afford adequate protection, but you can add more for a deeper looking finish.

Brush/paint pad: Use a natural bristle brush with oil-based polyurethane, and thin each coat about

10 or 15 percent with mineral spirits. Thinning will help you get a smooth, bubble-free finish. Waterbased coatings require synthetic bristle brushes, since natural bristles will splay and go limp in water. On flat surfaces, however, a paint pad works better. It coats faster, creates fewer air bubbles in the finish, and allows you to apply thinner coats, which makes waterbased coatings level better. Apply a minimum three thin coats of either type of polyurethane.

Spraying: Thin oil-based polyurethane 50 percent with acetone, not mineral spirits. Spray an extremely light mist coat onto the wood, let it dry for about 10 minutes, then spray a very light wet coat. The fast-drying acetone will cause the mist coat to get tacky. This tacky coat will help the thin wet coat hang without running or dripping.

Spray unreduced waterbased polyurethane through a small fluid tip (.040" to .050"), applying very light coats. The surface will look as if it is not wet enough and has a slight orange peel texture, but resist the impulse to spray heavier. Leave it overnight and it will level out. Spraying too heavily will result in a rough texture as well as drips and runs on vertical surfaces. Spray at least three or four thin coats of either type.

Final Thoughts About Poly
Is polyurethane varnish the wonder finish for woodworking? In some ways, probably yes. If a glossy, plastic sheen isn't what you're after, there's always satin to try for a duller "closer to the wood" look. As far as durability goes, poly is tough to beat. However, don't be afraid to experiment with other finishing options like shellac or lacquer, too. Each finish has its pros and cons, including polyurethane.

How to Apply Brush-On Lacquer

Lacquer finishes aren't just for the pros. Even without special spray equipment, you can still achieve a great lacquer finish with a brush-on formulation. It doesn't apply the same as ordinary varnish, but the technique is easy to master—and no finish dries faster.

by Bob Flexner

If you've ever used polyurethane, you know what a problem dust can be. Because polyurethane takes so long to cure, some dust settles and sticks to the finish even though you think your room is clean. The embedded dust detracts from your work.

You can overcome most of the dust problem and still get a durable finish by using a brushing lacquer instead of polyurethane. You may not have thought of lacquer as a brushable finish. In fact, it's usually sprayed because it cures too fast to be brushed. To make lacquer brushable, manufacturers slow the curing time by dissolving the lacquer in slower-evaporating solvents.

Using lacquer instead of polyurethane has some advantages, as well as some disadvantages. The principal advantage is that lacquer, even brushing lacquer, cures very fast. This reduces dust problems and allows you to apply two or three coats a day. Another advantage is that, unlike polyurethane, to get a good bond with brushing lacquer you don't have to sand between coats. Each new coat of lacquer partially dissolves and fuses with the previous coat to make a perfect bond. You only have to sand to remove dust nibs or to level other flaws in the finish.

The principal disadvantage of lacquer is that it isn't as durable as polyurethane. Coarse objects will scratch it. Hot objects, such as coffee cups, will leave an imprint. Solvents, such as finger-nail-polish remover, and strong alkalies, such as ammonia, will dissolve it. Therefore, on heavily used surfaces such as table tops, you still may prefer polyurethane.

Preparing for the Finish

You can use any oil-based or water-based stain before applying brushing lacquer as long as you wipe off all the excess stain and allow it to dry overnight. You also can use water-soluble and non-grain-raising (NGR) dyes. But you can't use lacquer-based stains, or dyes dissolved in alcohol or lacquer thinner. The solvent in the lacquer will dissolve these stains and dyes, and your brush will smear them.

The best applicator is a natural bristle brush with flagged bristles. Flagged bristles are split on their ends so they feel soft and apply the finish smoothly. Don't use a sponge brush as it will dissolve in the lacquer.

The most widely available brushing lacquer is Deft Clear Wood Finish. It's available at most paint stores and larger home centers, or you can order it on-line from woodworking suppliers. Deft Clear Wood Finish comes in two sheens—gloss and semi-gloss. The semi-gloss is best for most situations. It produces an attractive sheen without rubbing.

Applying Brushing Lacquer

There are three tricks to applying a fast-drying finish like brushing lacquer: first, apply the finish liberally in wet coats; second, move fast; and third, avoid brushing over areas that have begun to set up, even if you've missed a small spot. This differs from the way you brush polyurethane. With polyurethane you spread the finish over a large surface and then smooth it with long straight strokes running with the grain. With brushing lacquer you need to get each stroke pretty close to right the first time.

For this reason it's important to practice applying brushing lacquer to scrap wood, just as you would practice with a new woodworking tool before using it on a real project. Once you've practiced, get started by brushing on your first coat of lacquer. There's no need to thin the lacquer unless the manufacturer recommends it, and with Deft, you don't need to apply a separate sanding sealer first. Deft sands easily enough itself.

Let the lacquer cure for at least two hours. You'll notice that the surface feels rough because, as with any finish, the first coat locks raised wood fibers in place. Sand the surface lightly with 280-grit or finer sandpaper—just enough to make it feel smooth.

Remove the sanding dust using a brush, vacuum, or tack cloth, then brush on at least two full-strength coats, allowing a minimum of two hours drying time between each coat. If you miss a place and the finish has begun to set up, don't go back and fill it in. You'll just cause more damage. Wait until the finish cures, sand the area smooth, then apply another coat. No matter what problems occur, you can always sand out the damage and apply another coat.

Clean your brush thoroughly in a well ventilated area with lacquer thinner, then wash the brush with soap and water. Wrap the brush in heavy paper so the bristles dry straight, and store the brush in a drawer or hanging from a hook. If lacquer hardens on the brush, a soaking in lacquer thinner will reclaim it.

QuickTip

Spraying Lacquer the Easy Way

Aerosol spray lacquer is another option for adding lacquer to your list of finishing options. Deft makes aerosol lacquer, and it's easy to find at a home center. When applying spray lacquer, it's characteristics are the same as brushing lacquer: fast drying and easy to sand out. Be sure to spray in a well-ventilated area, and wear a charcoal canister respirator approved for vapors. It's also important to spray in a low-humidity environment. Lacquer will trap water vapor in the finish and blush, leaving your finish with a milky haze.

Bleaching Wood: Staining in Reverse

We may never be able to turn two pieces of wood back into one after making a wrong cut, but we can undo some other maladies that occasionally happen. Bleaching gives you the ability to lighten or restore wood's natural color, remove black iron stains, or undo an ugly dye stain choice. Call it woodworking's answer to an eraser.

by Michael Dresdner

Staining means adding color to wood. Bleaching, its logical opposite, is the process of chemically removing color from wood. You can remove accidental stains, intentional (but ill-advised) wood dyes, or the original colors that nature placed in wood, using one of three basic bleaches. Here's a description of each, a guide on how to mix and use them, and an explanation of what they will do.

Safety and Use Guidelines

All these bleaches are waterbased, and all finishes repel water. Hence, all bleaching must be done on raw (unsealed) wood. If you're trying to remove a stain from a finished piece of

Editor Rob Johnstone is dressed for success—which means safety when using bleaching products. These chemicals can clean up your wood, but they're also caustic and need to be used with caution.

furniture, you must strip the finish first. It's also a good idea to lightly sand the wood, to make sure the bleach can easily penetrate it.

More important, these bleaches are either acids or bases and consequently are reactive. That means they can harm us, so use gloves and goggles, and work in a well-ventilated room. Any gloves will do, but don't get these bleaches on your skin. You might also want to wear a vinyl apron, or choose clothes you are ready to abandon.

Bleaches eat cloth and natural bristles, so apply them with synthetic bristle brushes or nylon abrasive pads (such as Scotchbrite®). Always apply bleach to the entire surface of the wood, not just the area with the stain. Spot bleaching can cause permanent watermarks, or hard-to-blend light spots, in the wood. Typically, you allow the bleach to work until it dries, but you can stop the

When To Use Each Stain

	Chlorine Bleach	Oxalic Acid	A/B Bleach
Lighten wood	no	no	yes
Iron stains	no	yes	no
Grayed wood	no	yes	no
Dye stains	yes	no	no
Pigment stains	no	no	some
Food stains	most	no	some
Ink, felt markers	some	no	some

Chlorine bleach, applied top and bottom, will remove a variety of accidental stains but won't remove pigmented stains. Here, the swimming pool version...basically laundry bleach on steroids—is shown on maple, walnut and mahogany.

bleaching action at any time by diluting the surface with plenty of clean water. Because it contains water, bleach raises the grain of wood, so plan on sanding with 320- or 400-grit paper once the wood dries.

Laundry Bleach

Old-fashioned chlorine laundry bleach, or sodium hypochlorite, will remove many accidental stains as well as most wood dyes. However, it will not substantially change the color of wood itself. For that reason, it is a great tool for erasing dye stain, either on new wood or old dyes on stripped pieces. Think of it as the "undo" button. It won't remove pigment stains, but it will remove a wide variety of common food and drink stains, some dye-based inks and felt-tip markers.

Laundry bleach is sold in a 5% or 6% solution, so use it straight from the container. Opened containers of bleach get weaker with time, so buy a new bottle for stain removal. If you need a stronger solution, you can mix your own using swimming pool chlorine (typically calcium hypochlorite) mixed in water. These dry granules are sold at all different active bleach concentrations, so you'll have to read the label and do the math.

Don gloves, flood the bleach on evenly and liberally, and let it dry. Remove any salt residue the next day by washing the surface with plenty of clean water, then wipe off the excess water and let the wood dry overnight.

Oxalic Acid

Sold as a dry crystalline powder, oxalic acid will remove blue-black iron stains that show up on oak and other high-tannin woods as well as some iron-based inks. Iron stains can come from hardware, cans or bits of steel wool that show up as tiny black dots in the oak pores. Widely sold as deck brightener, oxalic acid reverses the silver-gray of oxidized wood, but it won't change its original color, nor will it affect most wood stains or dyes.

Oxalic acid is toxic and irritating to skin and mucous membranes in its dry form. Wear a dust mask and goggles while mixing it into water as well as when you sand the wood after the bleach has dried. Make a 6% solution by mixing about a tablespoon of it into one cup of warm water. Once it is mixed, it is fairly benign and won't smell much. Flood it onto the wood, let it dry, and wash off the salt residue the next day with clean water.

Two-part Wood Bleach

This is the one bleach that actually lightens the color of wood. Wood bleach will also knock out some, but not all, pigment stains but curiously won't affect most dyes. It is the most dangerous of the lot. Each component will burn your skin on contact, so handle with care.

Wood bleach is sold in two containers, usually labeled A and B—respectively, sodium hydroxide (lye) and hydrogen peroxide (not the 3% peroxide sold in pharmacies, but a wicked 35% concentration). Wet the wood thoroughly with the lye solution, followed quickly by the peroxide. When the two wet solutions come in contact with one another, they create a strong oxidizer that bleaches the color out of wood. It is important that the wood is still wet from solution A when the B is applied, so speed is of the essence.

Pour each component into a glass, plastic or porcelain container for

Oxalic acid can remove iron stains from wood. Use proper precautions while mixing; flood it onto the wood; let it dry; then use clean water to remove the residue.

application. Wear gloves and goggles, and use synthetic brushes to apply the bleach. Some brands suggest mixing the two components together, then applying the solution. Again, speed is important, because the strongest action comes just after the two chemicals meet. Don't let the bleach contact metal, particularly steel wool, or it will quickly erupt into a Vesuvius of caustic foam.

Let the wood dry overnight, and repeat the process if the wood isn't white enough. Once you're happy with the results, wash the surface with plenty of clean water to neutralize and remove the alkaline residue. Be careful when sanding: the bleaching doesn't penetrate deeply, and it's easy to sand through to the original wood color on the edges.

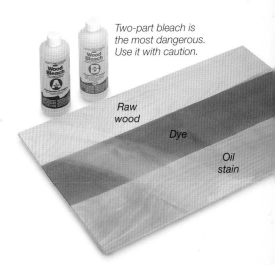

Two-part bleach is the most dangerous. Use it with caution.

Raw wood

Dye

Oil stain

Repairing Damaged Veneer

Even though an old piece of furniture may seem beyond hope, veneer blisters, chipping and peeling are surprisingly easy to repair if you know a few important tips.

by Tom Caspar

Don't toss that old veneered piece of furniture before carefully evaluating it for repair. You might be able to give it a veneer facelift more easily than you think.

Studying the techniques of the masters and working on hundreds of antiques are great ways to learn veneer repair, but you don't have to become an expert to fix veneer successfully. Here are a few tips to help get you started.

If you've found a piece you think can be restored, get started by temporarily taping back any loose veneer. Regular tape is too sticky and might pull off some finish if left on too long. Use wallpaper hanger's tape instead. Next, search for hidden loose spots by tapping the veneer with your fingernail. A dull sound indicates the veneer is well attached to its ground (the wood that veneer covers), whereas a hollow ticking sound means the veneer is loose. Pay special attention to edges, where airborne moisture could easily have entered and loosened the bond of the hide glue.

Once you've identified the damaged areas and marked them with tape, remove the glue from the veneer and ground with an old chisel. Sharpen the chisel first by pointing it right into a fine grinding wheel to get a thick, sturdy edge. Before scraping the glue off, be sure to soften it with hot tap water.

Once the old glue is removed, start the regluing process by working on the hollow-sounding pieces you discovered earlier. The trick here is to slip glue between the ground and the veneer. Usually you can work glue in from an edge if you have a long thin flexible blade, such as those in a set of automotive feeler gauges.

As far as the right type of glue is concerned, liquid hide glue is preferable, although white and yellow glue also works fine. Be sure to put paper between the veneer and some softwood

blocks to absorb any glue squeeze out (paper backed tape is ideal), then clamp the pieces overnight. The next day, remember to wet the paper before removing it so the dried glue won't pull off any of the finish or veneer.

Blisters can be glued down in the same way, although you need to cut a slit with a razor blade to work in the glue. Before you do this, however, check that the blister will lay flat without cracking or overlapping by slowly pressing it down with a piece of plexiglass (so you can see how it goes). If the bubble is stiff from age and won't lay down properly, scrape off the finish and wet the veneer with hot water, then put layers of paper under a softwood block and apply clamping pressure. After a few days the veneer will dry and you can slip in the glue.

Five Basic Steps for a Tight Fitting Veneer Patch

Step 1: *Begin cleaning up the hole where the piece is missing from the rail by straightening one of its edges with a sharp chisel.*

Step 2: *Cut the matching patch from your veneer with a veneer saw. The saw's curved edge allows you to start your cut anywhere in the veneer.*

Step 3: *While holding your block plane in a vise, pass the veneer patch over the blade to straighten one edge for matching the edge of the hole.*

Adding New Veneer

Making an invisible repair with new veneer isn't difficult once you've learned a few tricks. The hardest part is matching the old veneer with new stock (see "Veneer Matching Tips"). Matching the color isn't that difficult since there are lots of ways to stain or dye veneer. The greater concern is getting a good figure match. Concentrate your efforts on choosing a patch with a figure pattern that resembles the area around the missing veneer.

If you're using new veneer to make your patch, it will probably have to be shimmed to the thickness of the old veneer. Try not to make your veneer too thick, however, or you might scrape off the finish and lose the patina in the old veneer when leveling off the patch with the surrounding area. One trick is to go with slightly thinner veneer and build it up with plenty of glue.

Fitting in a Patch

Fitting a veneer patch requires some finesse. Always use sharp tools and make wedge-shaped patches—they are far easier to snug into a hole than other shapes. The example below demonstrates the steps in the patching process. It's common to be missing small pieces of veneer on dresser rails, especially if the grain is running vertically. To replace a missing piece, start by straightening one edge of the hole (Step 1). Next, cut an oversized patch with a veneer saw (Step 2) and joint one edge of the patch with a block plane (Step 3). Be sure to adjust the throat to a very narrow setting and watch your fingers. Now snug the patch into the hole (against its straight edge) and mark a cutting line on the other side of the patch (Step 4). Be sure the patch covers the hole generously and lay out this line at a slight angle to get the wedge shape. Once the line is laid out, use a chisel to chop the veneer (or a plane iron in the case of a longer patch).

Next, lay the tapered piece on the hole with its ends overhanging an equal amount and scribe a line on the rail with a knife, following the taper of the patch. This line is then chopped with the chisel (take several cuts to remove more than $1/16$" of veneer).

Wrap up by test fitting the patch, refining its edges on the plane as needed. Most of the excess length can be removed with a chisel prior to gluing the patch in place. After it dries, file the ends flush to the rail.

Step 4: *After chopping the second edge of the patch at a small angle, push the patch in the hole and transfer this angle to the rail with a knife.*

Step 5: *For a three sided repair, press white tape over the end of the hole, draw the cutting angle and mark the angle on the patch.*

Veneer Matching Tips

The veneers most commonly found on old furniture include curly and bird's-eye maple, walnut, rosewood and mahogany. Many of these woods are still harvested and used to make veneer today, but the exact species are difficult to find and the quality isn't what it was a century ago. There are, for instance, a number of mahogany species available, but Cuban mahogany, a favorite of 18th century cabinetmakers, is unavailable. This makes it more difficult to match new veneer to an old piece of furniture, but don't lose heart. Here are three ideas to help you get the look you're after.

First, remember that modern veneers are sliced very thin and uniform, whereas old veneer was cut thick and unevenly, due to the tools of the day. Try shimming new veneer to match the old by using a second piece of veneer, a thick plane shaving or colored paper. Just be sure to glue the shim to the veneer before fitting the patch.

Second, try pulling off a piece of veneer from one part of a dresser to use for patching elsewhere. A large solid area of new veneer with a slightly different grain pattern, especially if it's somewhat isolated, works better than using many small patches that don't match.

And third…veneer hunting is a good reason to hit auctions and estate sales. These are great places to scout out old veneered pieces that are beyond repair. If they're cheap, it pays to remove the veneer and save it as patch material for more worthwhile projects.

Repairing a Damaged Finish with Burn-In Sticks

Scratched finishes are an inevitable part of the ordinary wear and tear our furniture must endure as it ages. For scratches that are too deep or large to cover up with a color-matched marker pen, your next recourse is to try shellac burn-in sticks. Here's how.

by Jerry TerHark

The most frustrating thing about finishing a project is knowing that sometime, some way, it will eventually be damaged. When it comes to repairing damaged finishes, one approach we recommend is using shellac burn-in sticks. While this technique takes many hours to master, it's an invaluable skill to learn.

The type of finish on the piece will make a difference as to whether or not you can repair it. Damage to varnish, shellac, and lacquer finishes can be burned-in; polyurethane and other plastic finishes tend to blister and are almost impossible to fix.

The materials you need on hand to do a burn-in repair include burn-in knives, knife heater, patch lube, shellac sticks, sandpaper and paper towels. Here's how the process works.

Step 1: *The first step, and the most important one, is to clean up the burn or scratch. All foreign material must be removed and the area should be feathered. This can be done by sanding, but some burns will require a little scraping with a knife first.*

QuickTip

Shotgun Approach

One seldom has enough clamps around the shop for a major glue-up. If the surfaces are wide, it's difficult to get the clamping pressure where you need it most. If you have a friend that reloads shotgun shells, buy a 25-pound bag of pellets and keep it around the shop to use as auxiliary clamps. You can also use other weighted options like pea gravel or even sand. Having loose-weight, pliable bulk material in these forms is particularly useful when gluing curved laminations or other situations where conventional clamps can't reach or provide an even force against your workpieces.

Step 2: *The second step consists of filling the defect with shellac stick to blend with the surrounding finish color and fill the recess formed by the scratch. The knives must be heated up at this stage using a knife heater. The easiest way to tell if the knives are ready to use is to touch the shellac stick to one of them. If the material turns molten without smoking, it's ready to use. If the shellac starts to smoke when touched to the knives, your knife is too hot and will turn the stick a reddish color. Give the knife blade a few minutes to cool down and try again on a fresh area of the burn-in stick.*

Step 3: *While you're waiting for the knives to warm up you should be determining what color shellac stick to use. This is done by matching the lightest color in the immediate area of the scratch. When the knives are ready and you've chosen the proper color shellac, put a dab of stick shellac on the tip of the burn-in knife and apply it to the scratch. Keep working the repair until the spot is slightly over-filled. During the application process, always wet your finger and press down hard on the stick in the repair area while it's still warm. This will eliminate any air pockets and prevent a "cave in" when your repair job is coated with spray materials or when French-polished.*

Step 4: *The fourth step is to clean up your repair. The product to use is called patch lube or burn-in balm. This material has the feel of vaseline, and it aids in removing any excess shellac stick, while preventing the hot knife from damaging the surrounding finished surface. This is important because at this stage you'll want to slow down your knife so that any excess shellac has a chance to solidify on it for removal. After every pass with your knife, and especially before you put it back into the oven, you must wipe your knife on a paper towel to remove the excess. The one drawback to using patch lube or burn-in balm on a repair is that you cannot reapply shellac stick over these products. The shellac won't adhere properly and will start to flake after a short time.*

Step 5: *The fifth step is to scuff-sand the area to remove any rough spots or shellac residue that remains on the surface. Ideally, this all you need to do, however, it might be necessary to grain-in or French-patch the area so the repair blends in better.*

Burning-in is a technique that requires many hours of practice but we hope this article helps you get started. Just be sure to do all your practicing on sample boards before you decide to take on that old scratch in the middle of an heirloom dining room table!